DELIVERANCE

HOOCH AND MATT'S STORY

MARQUESATE & TA BROWN

CAMOUFLAGE PRESS

Visit Marquesate's website *Gay Military Fiction* at www.marquesate.org

DEDICATION

To all our wonderful friends on the forum. Thank you for everything, and most of all for your friendship.

Particular thanks go to Sequelguerrier, The Reader and best friend, and BAM, our consultant on the South.

By Marquesate

Novels

Basic Training

Her Majesty's Men

Beyond Her Majesty's Men

Deliverance
  Co-Authored with TA Brown

Short stories

Code of Honour

For Queen and Country

Friendly Fire

Special Forces epic

  Co-authored with Vashtan

SF Soldiers

SF Mercenaries

SF Veterans

INTRODUCTION

Deliverance is a spin-off from the epic Special Forces, which is available for free online, as ebook and for print-cost only as paperback (www.marquesate.org/special-forces.html).

Deliverance is the story of Hooch and Matt, secondary characters in Special Forces, who first appear in 1991 and several times after that.

It is not necessary to have read the epic, but there are certain chapters in Special Forces which are pivotal to Hooch and Matt's lives before the events of Deliverance.

The following links point readers to crucial moments for Hooch and Matt.

MATT'S FIRST APPEARANCE

1991 Chapter XXII—War Junkie: January 1991, Saudi Arabia
→ www.marquesate.org/special-forces/special-forces-mercenaries22.html

HOOCH'S FIRST APPEARANCE

1991 Chapter XXVII—Deliverance: August 1991, the Persian Gulf
→ www.marquesate.org/special-forces/special-forces-mercenaries27.html

IMPORTANT REVELATIONS ABOUT HOOCH

Chapter XLI—Blank Slate: May 1992, Berlin, Germany
→ www.marquesate.org/special-forces/special-forces-mercenaries41.html

Chapter XLII—Wind of Change: May 1992, Berlin, Germany
→ www.marquesate.org/special-forces/special-forces-mercenaries42.html

Chapter XLIII—Fadenkreuz: May 1992, Berlin, Germany
→ www.marquesate.org/special-forces/special-forces-mercenaries43.html

BEGINNINGS

MAY 1993, UNITED STATES OF AMERICA

"I know you're an opportunist, but that's not me." Leaning against the doorframe, Matt watched the other man, who was silent, as ever. Hooch was chewing gum, shades tucked onto his forehead and one strap of the backpack over his shoulder. Dead cool, as always. Matt didn't expect him to say a word.

"I'm not a romantic, Hooch." Matt shrugged, half-expected a smirk from the other man, never received it. "Been there, done that, didn't work out." He paused. "I'm sorry, man, but this here isn't what I want either." Matt glanced down, shook his head. "I don't want to be one of many stations you pass through, I want to be the central station." He fell silent.

Hooch opened his mouth and drawled, "I understand."

Matt nodded. Nothing left to say.

Flicking his shades back on, Hooch tapped a couple of fingers against his temple in a mock salute, turned and opened the door. No hesitation when he stepped through and left, closing the door behind him.

Matt stood. Stared at the door. Less than sixty seconds and it was all over. What had he expected? Fuck.

He stood for several more minutes, heard nothing, finally turned and walked into the kitchen to grab a cold beer. He threw himself onto the couch but forgot the TV. Just staring at the ceiling for hours, not thinking about anything, just floating in grey space.

What now? Whatever. Work. Marines. Military. Closet and all that shit. Don't ask don't tell. The usual.

Matt's beer had turned lukewarm in his hand when he was jerked out of his musings by the door bell.

"Fuck," he frowned, got up despite himself. Hoping it wasn't anyone from the nearby base. "Leave me the fuck alone, dickheads." Putting the unopened beer on the table in the miniature hallway, he pushed the buzzer and counted the customary time it took to make it up the stairs, unless whoever it was had taken the elevator. Opening the door, he nearly did a double take into the mirror behind him.

Hooch.

Hooch, pushing his shades back up onto his head, and re-shouldering the bergan.

"Been thinking." Two words, more than usual. "Been around a bit." Six, speech worthy of a national holiday. "Looking for a station now." Eleven, whole fucking fireworks. "Central station." Thirteen, and the heavens came down for Matt.

"You still offering?" Sixteen, and the world stopped spinning.

Matt stood thinking for a while, not a muscle in his face twitched. He finally stepped aside, gestured the other man to follow him, then closed the door.

"One condition."

Hooch's brows rose for a split second.

Matt broke into a grin, which threatened to split his face. "Promise not to talk too much."

PROLOGUE

NOVEMBER 1997, REBEL STRONGHOLD

The pain was like nothing ever before, as if his legs had been ripped off on impact, but worse, much worse, and Hooch knew that he was fucked. He tried to get out of the tangle of parachute and lines, but the pain from his hip and pelvis was so bad, he blackened out for a second.

Scrabbling against the ground, trying to pull away the moment he came to, he pushed himself up to look at his legs, expecting a mass of bones and gore, but nothing. Yet he couldn't use them to get up and when he tried again, he screamed in agony. He knew, then, that he'd got it this time.

Hooch heard voices and the sound of engines, rapidly getting closer. He frantically cut the entangled parachute ropes, managing to wriggle out of the harness, trying to get out of there. He pulled himself forward on his belly, using his hands, determined to never give up, when they broke through the thicket and a boot stamped onto his hand, amidst angry shouting. Others started to kick, again and again, his head, shoulders, legs, arms and finally his hips.

Then it went black, and the pain didn't matter anymore.

* * *

"Bozic, Hubert, Sergeant First Class, 546798362." Hooch forced out, for the tenth or twelfth time. He'd lost count. Lost count, too, of the number of times he'd lost consciousness out when they dropped him, the excruciating pain in his pelvis too much to bear. Or the number of times he'd fought for his life, struggling for air, when his head had been pulled back out of the water butt. Or the number of blows and kicks that had pounded onto his defenseless body, rendering his face a bloodied and swollen mess. Worse than any session, anything he'd ever had done to him. This was real, and more destructive than anything else in his life had ever been before.

A voice shouted once more in broken English: "why did you come here, what are your plans, who else is here, who has given the orders, what are your orders, who are you," and why and what and wherefore. All he could find in himself was the groaned, whimpered, cried out, screamed and whispered answer:

"Bozic, Hubert, Sergeant First Class, 546798362."

They couldn't get any of the information out of him that they were looking for. No matter how much they beat him, how many cigarettes they extinguished on his body, and how often he passed out from the unspeakable pain of being dropped onto a broken pelvis.

He didn't know most of those answers, could only hope that he wouldn't have told. he had known. Nothing to say, nothing to admit to, except for:

"Bozic, Hubert, Sergeant First Class, 546798362."

Barely audible at times, and hardly human.

He had no idea how close he was to getting killed, didn't realize that the faction that had captured him was warring with another that wanted to see a better use of the captured resource: him. The resource that would humiliate the US further. Once they'd understood that he wouldn't talk—couldn't talk, he could still be useful. As long as he was alive.

They pulled him out of his stupor once more, and he didn't resist, knew it was useless anyway. He couldn't move his legs, didn't dare to twitch lest he fell unconscious again from the pain, and being unconscious meant another barrage of mindless beating. He hardly recognized the camera that was pointed at his face, but when he did, he defiantly raised his head, angry, snarling, but all that came out was a pathetic whimper before a boot impacted in his middle, once the camera was switched off, and he let out a hoarse scream, passing out, cold, on the ground.

* * *

Hundreds of bodies, a small room. One single source of air and light from a tiny, iron-clad window high above. Hundreds and hundreds of bodies, so crowded none of them could do anything but stand.

No space, and he couldn't sit, couldn't lie, forced to stand, and the pain was unbearable. So was the stench, the filth, the heat and the smell of death and decay. Excrement, piss from the guards, shit and blood and fear from the prisoners. He couldn't move, unable to get to the little water that was given out, brackish and teeming with parasites.

One option was death.

Death to stand and die of pain, death to lose the fight and be trampled underfoot, death to ingest the contaminated food and water, death not to gain any sustenance, and death to go insane.

The other was pain.

Pain was better. Pain didn't kill. If Hooch knew anything, he knew that. He'd learned it scripted into his flesh and blood, and knew, too, that pain always brought relief in the end. Even if it was only the relief of its absence. Eventually.

He refused to be one of the corpses that were shuffled towards the front every morning. The prisoners who had died in the night and whose bodies were handed from one to another, to be thrown outside. Somewhere. Anywhere. Didn't matter, just corpses.

He mattered, though. Mattered to the memories of a young man who laughed and joked, who shared his bed and his thoughts, who touched him and kissed him, who sometimes fucked him and always offered his body. That perfect, sculpted, smooth body without a single scar. That man who'd told him he'd always be there, always be waiting and would always want him. That man to whose image Hooch clung, every time he blackened out from the pain, pissed and shat into his torn uniform, and threw up from the stench and the little he managed to get into his stomach.

NOVEMBER 1997, UNITED STATES OF AMERICA

6 AM and Matt sat bleary eyed at the breakfast counter in his kitchenette, shoveling corn flakes down his throat while watching CNN. Half-heartedly listening to whatever was going on on the screen, while reaching for the carton of milk to pour into his cereal before it got soggy. The milk never hit the bowl.

US soldier. Special Forces. Captured. Video. Demands.

Matt put the carton back down onto the table, reached for the remote to up the volume, but stalled in mid-motion, when the badly done video flickered onto the screen, showing a soldier, soiled US uniform, no name tag, no rank nor affiliation insignia. Face bruised, bloodied, hardly resembling a man anymore. The broken body was held up into the camera while the man's head threatened to roll back, but then he lifted it, opened his eyes and…

"No!" Matt jumped up, the remote clattered across the table and onto the floor, followed by the bowl of cornflakes.

Hooch. Bloodied. Beaten. Injured. Tortured.

Hooch.

NOVEMBER 1997, REBEL STRONGHOLD

When Hooch was thrown back into the cell, he didn't have the strength to scream anymore. The pain had worn him down, out and gone, a shell that hardly managed to cling to those images that had kept him sane. He could see nothing in his memories but flashes of a smile, and a joke he could not remember either. Yet this time, before he hit the bulk of bodies, he was caught by arms that held him up, and dark eyes that searched his own.

"American?" A voice asked, rough and worn, like his own. If only he hadn't screamed that much and still had the strength to speak.

He nodded.

Another hand pushed something against his lips. He wanted to turn his head away, but more hands held him steady and the first ones poured liquid down his throat. Liquid. Water. Or at least something akin to it, and he swallowed greedily. Taste didn't matter anymore. Life. Death, he had almost lost the zest for either. Existing, barely.

"We help."

He didn't question why they helped the foreigner. He only knew that a pair of arms was holding him up, then three, four, and more, keeping his body off the ground, away from the feet that might trample him to death underneath, should he fall and give up from the pain of standing wedged in between hundreds of bodies; standing with a broken pelvis.

It was the first time he fell asleep for several minutes at a time, the first time in days and nights he kept the little strength he still had.

NOVEMBER 1997, UNITED STATES OF AMERICA

It was well after 7 AM, but Matt didn't care that he'd get the bitching-out of his career, for not turning up to work in time. Couldn't go in, couldn't explain. Hooch was not just a 'best buddy', but he could never admit to it. Matt's hands were shaking and he felt sick, barely keeping himself from throwing up.

It had hit him with a sledgehammer. All the way to the core, and the image of Hooch's broken body and disfigured face, barely alive, had imprinted itself on his mind, until he was unable to see nor smell nor feel anything else.

Yet had to keep himself together somehow and head into work. It was the not-knowing, the keeping up appearance and pretending to wear the mask, that was the worst. But he kept going, stuck in the US.

All he could do was wait.

NOVEMBER 1997, REBEL STRONGHOLD

Hooch's screams reverberated through the compound. The last man had found his worst weakness, and was manipulating his hips with both hands.

He couldn't breathe, think, couldn't faint either, because every time the darkness swallowed him, he was beaten awake, and it was impossible to say which pain was worse. Until it started all over again, those hands, his hips, and the movements that brought him out in cold, stinking sweat; made him foam and splutter and his eyes roll back as he forgot everything about himself and anything that had ever mattered. Screaming, as if the sounds from his hoarse throat could alleviate the pain.

Cut it open, tear it out and scatter it to the winds.

It never worked. Each scream returned to his body, this finite entity that was fragile, weak, and could hardly breathe, let alone force out those words, again and again: "Bozic, Hubert, Sergeant First Class, 546798362."

They broke his arm when he tried to protect himself, and he finally passed out. Nothing could wake him, he didn't hear the angry voices, nor witnessed the arguments, didn't feel the kicks to his kidneys, and didn't know when he was thrown back into the crowded cell that contained those inexplicable acts of human kindness.

He didn't fall—couldn't fall. Too many bodies, those of the dead, the dying and those who were still living against all odds. He didn't care anymore, except for those thoughts that still remained. The number. The name. The face, the body, the smile, even though he couldn't remember the voice anymore.

* * *

He could no longer protect his head or face with his arm, and perhaps he should have simply let them kill him by smashing his face and grinding his brain into the ground, but he couldn't. Just couldn't allow it, not without trying…for what? Returning to that hellhole that didn't allow breathing, that had the guards above use the prisoners' bodies as latrines. Filled with the unbelievable stench for which he had no words, no thoughts, except for 'everything'. It was all and everything and everywhere around him, like a thick molasses that made it impossible to draw in air.

This time, he let himself fall back into the bodies, not trying to find leverage nor hold himself up. Not fighting the pain nor the ultimate relief that would come once he'd slipped low enough, with enough bodies and weight on top of him, to stop breathing forever…but those arms were back and pulled him up. He protested, didn't want them to, how dared they, how…then something pushed against his lips. He opened them, no strength left to find out what it was, and simply swallowed. Whatever. Food. Water. Poison. Excrement, it didn't matter. Liquid followed, and again he swallowed, head rolling from side to side, until he managed to focus, his eyes no more than swollen slits, met by another pair, so dark, before he lost his sight and slipped out of pain, fear, stench and filth, and whatever was crawling across his body, and living inside himself. Slack in the many arms that held him up, until the morning, when—against all odds—he once again was not amongst those who got shuffled towards the front, out of the door and onto the pile.

* * *

Hooch almost passed out again when he was pushed through the bodies, towards the front. Clinging to consciousness with the thought that he would not be another corpse to be discarded. No. He wouldn't. He would survive another bout of torture. But instead of being pulled out and taken to be interrogated again, nothing happened. Partly being held up, partly leaning against the solid mass of bodies, he looked up, blinking against the sudden light. It hurt. Hurt his eyes, and a thought wormed its way into his broken mind: astonishment that anything could hurt in a new way.

"Sergeant First Class Hubert Bozic, US Delta Force?" A female voice asked.

She was pretty, he thought, once his eyes had adjusted to the light, and he wondered why the hell the last shreds of his memories of the young man had been replaced with a woman. Blond. Face illuminated by something. Flashlight. Not sunlight. Hurting his eyes. Still.

"Do you understand me?"

He nodded, the question didn't require him to speak. The name and number were the only answers left in his mind anyway, everything else had been burnt away. Beaten and kicked, punched, drowned and smashed away. Or just died away, amongst the stench of decay and the agony that only those arms could alleviate.

"You have to tell me your name." The voice insisted, the English...foreign, and Hooch, unable to find one single clear thought, couldn't understand why he noticed the accent.

"Bozic, Hubert, Sergeant First Class, 546798362." Name. Rank. Number. Hardly audible. That was it. Another round of interrogation, all a trick, but at least it didn't hurt right now. Not yet.

But no pain followed, instead he felt himself moved, carefully, oh so carefully, and yet he cried out hoarsely. Hardly a sound came out, even though his screams reverberated in his head, and then he was placed onto something. Lying down. Flat. On his back. The moment he was horizontal on the stretcher and the pressure was taken off the broken pelvis, he passed out. Again.

When he came to, he was in a different place. A room. Lying on the ground. Space. No stench. After a moment he made out the woman's face again, crouched beside him. Someone else, a man, touching him, and the touch felt strange. It took him a moment to realize the man was wearing rubber gloves.

"Can you understand me, Sgt Bozic?"

"Hooch," he whispered.

She smiled and nodded. "Hooch, of course. Did you understand what I said earlier? I am a delegate from the International Committee of the Red Cross, and I brought a medical doctor with me, Dr Mirabeau. We are here to ensure that you are being taken care of, Sgt..." she stopped herself, "Hooch."

"I...don't..." so hard to form words beyond name and number, "have to...go back?"

"No, not if we can help it, and trust me, we *can* help it. The rebel force has contacted us to negotiate on their behalf and your country has agreed."

Hooch nodded.

"Tell me what happened, while Dr Mirabeau is working on making you more comfortable."

Hooch looked at her, hardly noticing how the soiled uniform was cut off him, and how he was cleaned down. Telling her, best he could, what had happened and what he knew; what had been done to him and how he'd survived. He was put on a drip, cleaned up and sponged down, fed water—clean, clear water—and given bites of food. Shot full with antibiotics, his arm was set and fixed with plaster, his wounds treated and bandaged, and powder and potions administered, to kill the parasites that had taken residence in his weakened body. His pelvis stabilized with a brace, after some clean and simple clothes were put onto him, Hooch was allowed to write an open letter. He hardly managed, his hand shook too badly, too weak to hold the pen, but she helped and they gave him time, precious time. A letter to his family, but how much he wanted to write to his lover instead. His family had to do, hoping that somehow, against all odds, it would reach the one to whom it actually mattered if he lived or died.

She folded the sheet of paper, to show it to Hooch's captors for censor, before it was sent off to the American Red Cross. She briefly smiled down at him. "Hooch," it was comforting to hear his name, he thought, no longer a faceless number, "your friends are thinking of you."

Matt. *Matt.*

A ghost of a smile crossed his face as painkillers were shot into his body. By that time he was drifting, barely taking in how she explained they would make sure he was treated right while they were going to work as neutral intermediaries. When they finally left, he lay on his back, unmoving, a blanket over his body, and a bottle of water and edible food beside him. Clean. Lying down. No arms to hold him up, no fingers to feed him rotting scraps. No one. Just silence. Sleep. Exhaustion. The memory of someone so dear…the only memory that had survived. He slept, undisturbed, without those who had saved his life by holding him up and who continued to fight on every day and night to stay on their feet and stay alive, with no one to save them.

He didn't know that she was throwing up outside. Didn't hear her retch and didn't see the doctor wordlessly handing her a packet of tissues.

He was asleep, for the first time in an eternity in hell, and he knew that from now on he would not simply vanish. He had a name, a face, and a number that was known to the world, not just to his captors. No corpse to be shuffled out in the morning. No nameless body, burnt or ditched, and no faceless being, contorted in pain, dying alone, to be missing in action.

He had a name. He had become part of the machinery. The old lady in Geneva, as she had called it, would take care of him. He trusted that old lady.

Because she was all he had.

* * *

Hooch was not aware of the negotiations that happened outside. With the ICRC as neutral intermediary, the rebels had already gained what they wanted: the humiliation of the US, via its military, and that humiliation was broadcasted across the world on the news channels that had been greedy enough to ignore the rules of ethical behavior.

It was push and pull for a while, until the rebels agreed his release, under conditions and demands that never saw the light of day outside of some US headquarters.

DECEMBER 1997, MILITARY HOSPITAL
UNITED STATES OF AMERICA

Matt sat on the plastic chair beside the bed. Legs braced, knees open, his cap on the small side table. Hands trembling so hard, he'd been gripping his own thighs since he sat down, to keep himself from touching.

Hooch. Pale, thin and haggard, with buzz-cut head and badly shaved face. Lying on a water bed to keep the pressure off the pelvic area, supine and still, the lower left arm in plaster, and all Matt could think of was how much Hooch hated to sleep on his back.

The pelvic brace was just about visible under the sheet that had been draped over Hooch, and a drainage tube vanished beneath the cloth. Matt could see glimpses of small burn wounds on the chest, looking closed but angry, and he wanted to hurt whoever had done that.

Hooch. Alive against all odds, and all he could do was sit there, push a small portable DVD player into the other man's good hand and pretend he was just a buddy, paying a visit. He tried to come up with some stupid bullshit a buddy would utter—and failed. miserably. He couldn't get a single word past that fucking lump in his throat that he couldn't swallow down, no matter how hard he tried, and it hurt like a motherfucker. Couldn't even look at Hooch, who was checking out the pack of DVDs by lifting each one to eye level. Looking at him caused the sting in Matt's eyes to get worse and he stared at his white-knuckled hands instead.

"Thanks." Hooch's husky drawl tore Matt out of his catatonic state. The voice sounded disused and hoarse.

Matt wanted to touch, kiss, hold, reassure himself that Hooch really was there, alive, but all he did was press out a desperate: "shit!" He couldn't keep it up anymore. Fuck the charade, he wanted to curse or cry, or maybe even laugh. Insanely.

Matt's trembling hand raised to his face, his head dropped, elbows on his thighs, and he covered his face with his hands when he couldn't stop the silent sobs that were heaving his chest and shaking his shoulders. He made no sound, except for one strangled choke. He couldn't get his goddamned act together, despite being all too aware of having nothing but a thin cloth partition between Hooch's bed and the next. In a ward full of nurses, soldiers, and their visitors.

Hooch remained silent, left hand in his lap, the right on his chest. Silent, as long as it took Matt before he finally drew in a shaky breath, fighting out of the breakdown with all the strength he could muster. Too much truth, too raw, too open. He rubbed his face vigorously, realizing that he couldn't go back to pretending he was nothing but a goddamned buddy. Eyes red rimmed, Matt studied Hooch's impassive face, the dark eyes, and the whole—silent—man. Don't ask don't tell had never been that much of an issue before, until now. He'd gone insane with the not-knowing and the fear of loss. Not just a buddy, not even a fuck-buddy, but the man he loved. He couldn't deal with the lie any more, but he was tied to its confines.

Matt shook his head, unable to say what he thought, let alone what he felt.

Hooch didn't say anything either, looking up at Matt, without a twitch.

Not that Matt had expected anything, and he shrugged, once again shaking his head. Suddenly feeling misplaced, as if this whole shit had happened to someone else and he had stumbled into a crazy soap opera. He was about to get up and get away, when Hooch opened his mouth, and Matt stayed put, leaning down, to hear the quiet murmur.

"When it got really bad, when nothing else got me through, I was thinking of you. How you tilt your head when you laugh; the way you eat your cereal really fast so that it doesn't go soggy; how you squint your eyes and scrunch up your face into a grimace, every time anyone mentions eggs." Hooch dropped his voice even more, until Matt had to lean closer to hear the whisper. "Your shit-eating grin when you wave your ass into my face, telling me to fuck you. The sound you make when you come, going straight to my cock and blowing my mind. The smell of your sweat right after sex..." Hooch paused, pulling in a careful breath. "When I wasn't sure if I could make it through another hour, I thought of your face that looks so damned young when you're asleep, and I remembered how you sometimes say my name, and how the sound of your voice makes me ache inside."

Hooch fell silent and Matt stared at him. Wide-eyed, frozen in shock. Insides churning, a pain he hadn't known before, travelling from his heart throughout his body, and it felt so fucking good. Understanding with every fiber of his being what Hooch had said in too many words. More than he'd ever used before, and without those three simple ones that would have sufficed.

Matt felt his eyes sting again but a smile grew on his face. Too much emotion again, but of an entirely different kind. "I don't..." his voice trembled, "scrunch up my face." Couldn't trust his voice, as shaky as his hands.

Hooch grinned, he looked as if he had shrugged had that not hurt too badly.

"Alright, I do." Matt whispered, "but it's better than throwing your underwear onto the wet bathroom floor."

Hooch let out a dry huff of laughter, grimacing at the slight jostling of his body.

Matt fell quiet again. Companionable now in the silence, looking at Hooch while vigorously wiping his eyes, then settling into a wobbly grin. They sat like that for a long while. Hooch checking out the small DVD player, Matt helping him, a damn fine excuse to touch now and then, while every movement could be overlooked by the nurses.

"Five more minutes." One of them announced as she walked past. Just a few more minutes before he had to leave and fly back to his own camp.

Hooch suddenly murmured, "I want to hear that sound again."

Words and voice twisting Matt's guts in the most delicious way. "You will," he whispered.

Hooch nodded, lips quirking up in the customary half-grin, before he reached out and took Matt's hand for a moment. Holding longer than a buddy should.

"Till then."

FEBRUARY 1998, UNITED STATES OF AMERICA

Several weeks later, Hooch was let out of hospital and into subsequent aftercare. Refusing to go back to Fort Bragg, where he wouldn't have anyone take care of him and would have to get hospitalized again, and equally refusing to be taken to his family's ranch in Texas, he demanded to be sent to a friend instead. In his special circumstances, the request had been granted. That friend had a small apartment and time to take care of him—which he lied about—and who was willing to take over the task—which was nothing but the truth. He had been flown to the nearest town, then taken in an ambulance to the local hospital.

After having been checked over, signed in as an outpatient for physiotherapy and set up with crutches, walker, and been put into a wheelchair, he was given transport, which took him to Matt's apartment. Matt was still on base, working, and would arrive in an hour. Hooch somehow managed to get into the elevator, and with the help of walker and crutches back out again, and into the wheelchair. Being able to get about, no matter how laborious and painful it was, gave him a sense of freedom that was unparalleled to anything he'd experienced since the mission.

When Matt returned home, Hooch was lying flat on the bed, fully dressed, but with the remote in his hand and channel surfing. He was glad that Matt had no idea how he'd cried out when he'd got himself out of the wheelchair and onto the bed, for the first time on his own and without any supportive aids. He'd succeeded, though, and the independence had made up for all the pain. Ignoring that he'd left the drugs in the living room and really couldn't face getting up, not even for a piss.

"Hooch?" Matt called out from the hallway.

"In the bedroom." Even shouting caused pain and Hooch rolled his eyes at the annoyance of it all.

A couple of seconds later Matt stood in the doorway. Still in uniform, running a hand over his scalp. The smile on his face grew bigger and bigger until it lit up his whole face, grinning from ear to ear. "Shit, never thought I'd be so glad to see you in my bed, even though you're dressed."

"Yeah, you try taking the fucking socks off with that." Hooch pointed at the pelvic brace over his jeans. When his shirt sleeve moved up, Matt saw that the plaster was gone.

"Can I?" If possible, Matt's grin grew.

"Take my socks off?" Hooch groused.

"No, dickhead, the brace. I promise to put it back on."

"You could start with the socks." Hooch grinned, peering up, head raised with the two pillows on Matt's bed. "Or with yourself."

"Guess I could do that, or I could kiss you."

"Not much I can do about that." Hooch's grin almost matched Matt's by the time Matt was beside the bed, kneeling on the floor, and proceeded to kiss Hooch until either of them gave up or gave in, but neither did, and so they kissed until they were both breathless.

"Shit," Hooch groaned.

"What, did I hurt you?" Matt's alarm was almost comical.

"No, just too horny."

Matt's grin was part relief and part wickedness. "I can do something about that..." His hands were on the brace and then Hooch's trousers, but when Matt pulled on the jeans, Hooch got jostled and had to clench his teeth not to groan. Matt slowed down, and together they managed to get them off, same with the briefs, until Matt could take off the socks while Hooch was getting out of the shirt himself. When Matt came back up to look down at Hooch's naked body, for the first time in months, he was shocked at what he saw. Trying valiantly to hide it, but too late.

"I know." Hooch drawled.

"Yeah." Nothing Matt could say, and so he ran his hand over the far too thin body that had lost muscle mass and definition, but none of its allure. Not all of the tan was gone, and the surgery scar, still fairly fresh, stood in stark relief. No better than the burn wounds, those small round dots that were scattered across Hooch's upper body with no sense nor pattern.

"You'll get back into shape. I'll make you a recovery PT program when you can use the gym." Matt looked up, smiling.

"Eventually," Hooch commented drily.

"Well, at least we have proof you're alive." Matt cocked his head, flashed a grin and pointed at Hooch's erection. "Been a while, right, buddy?"

"Yeah, lifetime."

"Best I remind you, then." Matt moved down, his lips touched Hooch's cock, tongue drawing out and lapping, eliciting the deep groan that Hooch had suppressed earlier. His lips closed around the cut head, intent on sucking down, when Hooch awkwardly batted at him.

"No."

"What?" Matt came up, surprised and confused, "why not?"

"I'm not tested."

"Huh?"

"HIV. Can't get tested yet."

"I don't understand…" Shock, fear, worry and confusion warred in Matt's face. "But they didn't…I mean…"

"No, they didn't, but in that shithole…I had open wounds. Anything could have gone in. Blood, saliva, shit, piss, anything." Hooch's eyes were intense, haunted, and Matt twitched visibly. The glimpse of the horror was almost worse than knowing the full extent.

"The risk must be almost none."

"I had every other crap, though."

"But not that, come on, it's not possible."

"I don't care." Hooch reached for Matt's shoulder, managed to pull him closer. "I'm not going to risk you. You understand?"

Looking at Hooch for a moment, Matt nodded slowly, acknowledging the ache that was gripping his insides. Heart or guts, he wasn't sure, just this ache that intensified the longer he looked at Hooch. "Okay."

"Handjob?" Hooch asked.

"I'd suck you with a condom."

"No, no more goddamned rubber." Too many gloves that had touched him in the hospital.

Matt nodded, got up and onto the bed to very carefully stretch out beside Hooch, still in his full uniform, boots and all. Managing not to jostle the mattress too much, he propped himself up on his elbow, grinning down at Hooch while his free hand began to lightly stroke the cock that had lost its erection. "Let's see how still you can lie…"

He moved down to kiss Hooch again, whose hand found its way to Matt's neck. Holding close, smelling, tasting, touching, and needing so goddamned much to feel alive, Hooch ignored the pain. Matt stroked faster, adding twists and using everything he'd ever known about Hooch's preferences.

Eventually, Hooch felt his balls draw up and the pain of his orgasm almost blackened him out. He cried out, nearly a scream, which Matt swallowed in a deep kiss, not realizing that part of Hooch's desperate attempts to remain still—and his complete abandon—was the blinding pain in his pelvis, fuelling the orgasm itself.

Matt drew back, hand still on Hooch's cock, as he grinned down on him, watching him pant for breath, face sweaty, and something in Hooch's expression that he'd never seen before. Something above and beyond mere lust. Being alive, maybe that was it.

"You alright?" Matt murmured.

"Yeah, shit. Couldn't be better." Hooch grinned, started to laugh and stopped himself immediately. Laughing was torture. "You?"

"I'm alright." Matt smiled, wiping his hand on the bed linen.

"Bullshit." Hooch looked at him.

"Okay...got me." Matt laughed, "but how?"

"I want to watch. Stroke yourself."

Matt nodded, eyes alight. "Guess I can do that." He was soon kneeling on the bed, in full view, opening his BDUs and pushing down his briefs. Cock in hand, he began to stroke, all the time looking at Hooch, who didn't take his eyes off him.

"Want to see you." Hooch murmured, and Matt obliged. Ripping the tunic off, the t-shirt flew to the ground straight after, then returned to stroking himself. Muscles rolling and bunching beneath smooth skin. Perfectly chiseled and still as unblemished as the first time they'd had sex, in a safe house in the Gulf. Matt craned his head back, being watched intensified every sensation, and he slowed down for Hooch's benefit, while tensing his abs and working with his body until each and every muscle stood out, as hard as his cock. When he sped up once more, his movements turned harsh, punishing, and his breath came fast and noisy.

He went over the edge with a strangled sound, cum splattering onto Hooch, catching himself in the last moment before he let himself fall down onto the bed. On his knees instead, struggling for breath and grinning down at Hooch, who was still watching him with burning intensity in his dark eyes.

"I was right." Hooch murmured.

"What?"

"The sound you make when you come."

Matt stared at Hooch, remembering every word in the hospital.

"I..."

But Hooch waved him down, pulling him into a kiss instead, only letting go of Matt's neck when he broke the kiss and murmured, "you, you are quite something."

Matt was confused, but Hooch said nothing else, too exhausted. He let Matt take care of both of them, wiping them both down.

"Want to go onto the couch?" Matt smiled, his hand splayed out on Hooch's chest, fingers covering two of the burns.

"Give me an hour? Pretty damn wiped."

"Sure." Matt looked for the blanket, "mind if I stay?"

Hooch just snorted softly and Matt quickly got rid of the rest of his clothes, then lay down beside Hooch, pulling the blanket over both of them. Lying close, he breathed in the scent that was Hooch and yet was different. He'd be back to the old Hooch, though, he'd make sure. He'd lose the clinical scent, the otherness.

Matt lifted his head when he heard Hooch's regular breaths, watching the face, relaxed in sleep. Forging this image over all of the ones of the past.

Hooch. Alive. Nothing else mattered.

✱ ✱ ✱

Over two hours later, Matt had helped settle Hooch on the couch in the living room, in a pair of shorts underneath the brace, to watch a Dallas Mavericks game on TV. The remains of a chicken dinner stood on the table beside him, and a couple of empty Buds right next to it.

Hooch looked up and grunted a nonsensical question as Matt came back from the kitchen, dropping a letter into his lap.

Matt shrugged, gestured at the letter before wandering back into the kitchen to grab a couple of fresh beers. He stalled midway, fridge door open, breathing deeply. Had he done the right thing? Fuck knew, but he'd gone with his gut instinct and his gut had twisted into a knot at the thought of staying any longer in the 'don't ask - don't tell' pit of lies. He shook himself out of his musings, pushed the fridge door shut with his elbow and opened the bottles. Leaving enough time for Hooch to read.

When he stepped back into the main room of his small apartment, Hooch was holding the letter in his hand. "Why?"

Matt set the beer down onto the table and slouched on the chair which he'd pushed right next to the sofa. Feeling strangely reluctant to touch Hooch right now. 'Why', a good question. It had been perfectly clear in his mind at the time of making the decision. Putting it into words was suddenly a challenge and he took a good swig from his bottle, stalling for time, before looking at Hooch.

"I had enough." It was that simple, when it came down to it.

"You loved it."

"Yeah…" Matt shrugged. He had, being a Marine was what he'd always wanted. As a kid, playing soldier, as a teenager, and finally as a man. Before he realized how very much his sexuality was himself. Lying about that part of himself? He'd managed, until Hooch's capture. Love was a strange and powerful thing, and entirely unplanned. "Had enough of the fucking lies," he finally offered.

"Suddenly?"

"Yeah." Wrong, and Matt drew in another breath, expelling it noisily. "No, but I thought I'd gotten used to it."

"Had something to do with me." Hooch made it a statement not a question, and Matt grimaced. At least Hooch didn't ask him if he knew what he was doing, accepting Matt's decision as what it was: final.

Matt suddenly raised his head in anger. Aggression born out of frustration, but damn, Hooch had changed the rules of this game entirely. "Fucking yes! It has to do with you. Not knowing, not being able to ask, just lies. Lies and more lies. No grieving allowed, not a fucking thing. Couldn't contact your family, haven't got a fucking clue where they are, and Texas is damned big. Couldn't even pretend I was your buddy, in case anyone wondered why the fuck a Marine was buddies with a Delta. No messages, not a fucking thing and I was going insane!" Matt was getting more agitated, and he stood up. "I was so fucking desperate, I would have tried anything. But who the fuck was I? Just some stupid fucking Marine who was going off the edge, not knowing if he's lost the fucking man he fucking loves!"

Matt was fuming, but Hooch didn't show a reaction, except for a quiet, "do you?"

"What?" Matt snapped.

"Do you?" Hooch calmly repeated.

Matt felt as if all air had been driven out of his lungs. Deflated, he sat back down on the sofa. "Yeah."

Hooch nodded, folded the letter and placed it back on the table. "Okay."

Matt looked at him in confusion, then shook his head with a frustrated grunt. Hooch was still as exasperating as he'd always been, and Matt really didn't appreciate feeling like an idiot right now. "What the fuck does 'Okay' mean?"

"Got a job offer."

"Huh?" Matt leaned closer, "what?"

"Promotion. They want me to train Delta. Stationed in Fort Bragg." Hooch shrugged, "no more battlefields."

Frowning, Matt tried to make sense and get an indication what Hooch thought about this, but no chance. "You're not that old yet, you got some years left on active duty." Pointing at Hooch's pelvis, "and the injury's not cause for retirement from active duty, is it?"

"Probably not. They'll know in a few months. Recovery can be up to a year."

"Then what are you going to do? They can't force you, can they?"

Hoch shrugged, "no, not yet."

"Well," Matt drew in a breath, "that's alright then. Back to normal once you've regained your health and strength."

"No."

"No?" Exasperation was creeping into Matt's voice.

"I take it."

"You...what?" Matt leaned forward that abruptly, he almost slid off the chair.

"It's time."

"Why?" Painfully aware of how he echoed Hooch, whose lips quirked into the customary half-grin. Taking hold of the waistband of Matt's shorts, Hooch twisted his fist into the fabric and pulled him up and close, while Matt could do nothing but follow the motion, letting himself drop onto his knees on the rug in front of the sofa.

"What now?" Matt raised both brows.

Hooch's fist twisted tighter, pulling Matt even closer, until there was no further to go without jostling him. "You tell me. You'll be out of a job."

Matt rolled his eyes, "I'm going to open a fitness club with the money I've saved. It'll be based on military fitness training."

Hooch grinned. "You'll be fucking rich."

"Question is, where do I settle down? I have no fucking clue."

"Fayetteville."

"You're not fucking serious!" Matt's eyes widened, "that's right next to Fort Bragg."

"Precisely. Camp beds are shit."

"How the fuck are you going to explain living with a gay guy? Because I'm fucking sick of lying."

Hoch shrugged. "Spare room."

"Bullshit! Nobody's going to believe that."

"I'm too high profile now. Don't ask don't tell? This shit works both ways. You think they're going to prove I'm not staying in my own room?"

Matt grinned. "It might just work if we're careful, but you're fucking crazy."

"No, just alive."

That sobered Matt, but before the dark shadow could touch him, Hooch reached up to draw him closer, and Matt forgot all about it during the kiss.

APRIL 1998, UNITED STATES OF AMERICA

A few weeks later, when Matt came home from work on a Friday, the strong scent of freshly brewed coffee greeted him. "Hey, Hooch!"

No answer, and Matt strained to listen. Improbable that Hooch was out and about, but not impossible. He'd been moving further and further lately, and had been coming on in leaps and bounds, thanks to the physiotherapy he meticulously followed, doing his exercises religiously.

Matt eventually noticed the sound of the shower and, as expected, the bathroom door was ajar. "Fair enough," he muttered to himself, whistling under his breath as he took his tunic off, hung it onto a hook in the hallway, and marched into the kitchenette. The coffee was steaming in the pot and he poured himself a mug before he sat down at the breakfast bar.

He noticed a sheet on the table, unfolded, the letter pointing the other direction. Curious, he turned it round and skimmed over the letter while taking a sip of the strong, black coffee. He almost burnt his lips when he stared at the writing. Putting the mug down, he pulled the letter closer and re-checked the heading. Medical Lab. Test results. Then read it once more, and then again, for good measure, where it said in bold letters: 'Bozic, Hubert. Negative.'

Negative.

The grin that spread across Matt's face threatened to split it side-to-side and he jumped off the chair. "Hooch!" Hollering across the apartment, but Hooch, hair still wet, towel around his hips, and leaning on his walker, was already standing in the doorframe.

"Why the ear-splitting noise?"

"You damn well know, buddy."

Hooch raised his brows in the most infuriating manner he managed. "And?"

"*And?* What does *and* mean, you dickhead?"

"You tell me."

But Matt didn't. Wordlessly pulling the t-shirt over his head, he flung it into a corner. Flexing the impressive muscles of his smooth chest. He wasn't a PT instructor for nothing. "Does that remind you of anything?"

"Waxing?" Hooch deadpanned.

Matt rolled his eyes while unbuttoning the BDUs. He pushed them down, together with his briefs underneath. The trousers slipped and got caught around his ankles at the top of the boots. His groin was just as smooth—except for a neat patch. "And what does *that* remind you of?"

"Shaving?"

Matt laughed with exasperation. "You're insufferable."

"And horny."

"Now we are getting somewhere." Matt stepped closer, pulled the towel off Hooch and steadied Hooch's hips with his hands, holding him carefully, just enough to push his groin against Hooch's. He grinned at the immediate reaction. "If I fucked myself on you, very carefully, would your pelvis manage?"

"If it doesn't I don't give a shit." The sudden, husky quality to Hooch's voice caused Matt to take in a sharp breath.

"In that case..." Matt murmured, giving his hips a slight twist, "fuck me, Hooch."

He hadn't realized how much he'd missed Hooch's rare, shit-eating grin.

* * *

A couple of weeks later, Hooch was moving round on crutches, the walker discarded. He was getting better, but the pain had only eased minimally. Still, he could piss and shit without major distress, and if that wasn't a victory to be proud of, then he didn't know what was. Getting back into the living room, he watched Matt from the hallway. He could see his profile, the handsome face and that perfect body. Young, unspoiled, and if he could help it, Matt would remain like that.

Watching him for a while, until Matt lifted his head, cottoned on that he was being watched, and cast a smile at Hooch. Another one of those motherfucking dazzling smiles, the sort that made Hooch's knees go weak and his mind step onto a merry-go-round. He didn't quite understand why this particular man, this 'kid' had managed to crawl beneath his skin and settle down inside his heart.

"See anything you like, buddy?" Matt grinned.

"If I didn't I wouldn't be here." Hooch made his way towards the couch.

Matt moved over, making space for him to sit down. "Smartass." A lazy fist connected gently with Hooch's shoulder once he had maneuvered himself to sit.

"You alright?"

"Couldn't be better." Hooch glanced to the side. "I just managed to take a shit without screaming in pain, I call that a glorious day."

Matt laughed, "thanks for the gory details."

"Thought you would appreciate it."

Sitting comfortably in silence, each with a beer in their hand. Hooch had his legs up on the stool, and Matt slouched with his feet on the couch table, watching a baseball game. Hooch realized quite some time into the game that he had no idea who was playing.

"Matt?"

"Huh?" Drawn to the game, Matt took a moment before he turned his head, looking at Hooch. "What's up?"

"I got to tell you something." And wasn't attack better than defense.

"You've turned into a right chatterbox lately." Matt grinned, taking a mouthful of his beer.

Ignoring the quip, Hooch went straight on. "I never told you that I'm a masochist."

"What are you talking about?" Matt laughed. "Was there something in your lunch today?"

"No." Hooch twisted to look at Matt, "but I think it's time to tell you about the rest of me. Sometimes, I need to be beaten and fucked up until I crack."

"You're fucking kidding me."

"No."

"Then why the hell do you tell me? Now? What's the point?" Matt slammed the half empty bottle onto the table.

"I need you to know."

"After what, five years? I don't fucking believe it, you bastard!"

"Bastard, because I didn't tell you, thinking that this part of me had nothing to do with you?"

"Bastard, because you fucking lied."

"How?"

"By not telling me!" Matt's eyes were ablaze.

Hooch had never seen him that angry and hurt before. "If I had told you, what good would it have done?"

"I would have tried to be for you what you needed."

"No, Matt," Hooch's voice turned softer, "you don't have it in you."

"What the fuck are you telling me? You say I'm a pussy? I don't fucking have it in me?"

"It's not you, Matt."

"That's not what you said."

Hooch shook his head. "It's what I meant."

Getting up from the sofa, Matt was fuming. "What you *said* is that I am not what you want."

"That's bullshit and you know it."

"How would you see it then, if you were me? You tell me, after five fucking years, that you need to…what the fuck should I call it, get punished. And that is *not* telling me that I'm not alright? That I'm not missing something?"

Hooch quietly interjected. "You're not missing anything."

"Don't you fucking kid me." Matt's hands were in fists and he started to pace the small living room. "I thought we had a relationship."

"We do now. The question is if we had."

"You always came back."

"Yeah, because you were convenient. And pretty."

"Fucking *what*? Convenient? You asshole."

"You were, not saying that's what you still are."

"You have the guts to tell me that?" Matt shook his head. "Convenient? Like a fucking door mat?"

"No," Hooch said quietly, looking at Matt with a serious expression, "but I am telling you the truth right now. Back when it all started you were convenient. Great fun, fantastic source for sex, and…pretty."

"Pretty? Fuck you, Hooch."

"Yeah, but you are."

"Girls are pretty, I'm a man. I'm not pretty."

"What would you rather be? Handsome? Adorable? Perfect? Stunning? Gorgeous? Breathtaking? Beautiful?"

"Am I?"

"All of it and more."

"Shit." Matt groused. He deflated, had some of the anger taken out of him, but the sting was still there. "You're fighting dirty."

"Delta." Hooch beckoned Matt closer.

"Yeah, and I'm outgunned. As usual." Matt reached for the beer again, but a hand on his arm stopped him.

"You've never been outgunned."

"You're fucking kidding me again."

"I told you before, Matthew Donahue, you are quite something. Outwitted, perhaps, but never outgunned."

"Charmer."

Hooch didn't reply immediately, just looked at Matt, fingers twisting into the fabric of his t-shirt. Looking at him for a long time, before he pulled him across and close. "If I told you that I wanted to spend my days and nights with you, live with you, as my partner, because out there, in Hell, I realized that you mean the world to me? If I told you that you are my sanity, my laughter, my lust, my love, my comfort, my day and my night, my heat and cold and everything? If I told you all that, would you think that translates to 'convenient'?"

Matt swallowed, staring at Hooch wide-eyed. "N…no."

"Damn right. Now shut up, Donahue, and tell me that you'll spend the rest of your life with me."

Matt pronounced his next words very carefully:

"I do."

1998

LATE SUMMER 1998, FAYETTEVILLE, NORTH CAROLINA
UNITED STATES OF AMERICA

It smelt of wet carpet and of tile grot. Of crumbling plaster and fresh paint the realtor had hastily slapped on in a spirit of forlorn hope to make it look slightly less depressing. A large building that had once been a furniture workshop and showroom, most of it double-height, though there was office space on the second floor that had been used by the managers and could be easily converted into a small apartment—well, small to civilians. For a former Marine, it was going to be positively palatial compared to some of the places he'd lived in. Even with the addition of a roommate, his Delta-instructor best bud who happened to be moving into the spare room.

Despite its run-down state, the building itself was solid. It was cheap, well located in a decent part of Fayetteville, it had a large parking lot and it was *his*.

Matt dumped his rucksack down onto the ground and walked around, kicking up swirls of dust. He picked his way around the space, the morning sunshine flooding down from the windows set in the clerestory-style roof. There were smaller offices and storerooms on the first floor, the pipes already in a good position for the wet areas, and the wide expanse of space, dividable in so many ways, which filled in his mind's eye with fitness equipment, a sound system, and the long shopping list of gym gear living in his head. Or, more reliably, on the new laptop computer in his bag.

The other man in the room had been silent as Matt moved around. He was so still and unmoving, he seemed to barely disturb the air. Specks of dust settling in his dark hair, Hooch stood, slightly leaning on a cane, dark eyes tracking Matt's movements.

Matt took a deep breath and turned around. Despite the times he had visited here to inspect the building, the long hours spent on the phone with the realtor, the bank, the insurers, the builders, the architect and what appeared to be every single remotely responsible local government body in Fayetteville possible, the realization that he had only taken the first steps towards his new dream had set in. His name on the title deed. A frighteningly large amount owed to the bank. Pages and pages of sketches and plans and specifications and a team of guys ready to start work the following day. "Well? What do you think?"

"It's big," Hooch commented. "How much did you pay?"

Money. The question of money again. The only time they had fights over the last months at Matt's apartment was over money and the fact that Hooch tried to pay his way in a manner that infuriated Matt, and Hooch just wouldn't get it.

Matt hoped his sigh was inaudible. While overflowing enthusiasm was probably out of the question, it would have been nice to have some sort of appreciative comment. "It was a bargain, actually," he said, voice level.

"How much?" Hooch repeated, dark eyes in line of Matt's sight, like a sniper rifle.

There was that feeling again, the one he'd had far too often in the recent months as Hooch recovered. The feeling that he was being inched into a corner. Matt said the figure. It wasn't something he needed to keep a secret, but the fact that Hooch had pushed for it, that was the bit that stung.

They never told you about this part of living with someone. Or else nobody else had a someone quite like Hooch.

Hooch nodded once. "I'll pay my way. If I'm going to live here, I'll pay you rent."

Could he not wait more than ten minutes after getting here before taking *that* up again?

"Does your…" Matt stopped. Hooch's parents were completely off-limits as far as conversation went, so he was stumped as an example. "No." There, one word. Not hard, was it?

"Why not?" Hooch put the full force of his pig-headedness into those two words. He'd had months of boredom to perfect it, cooped up in one place, unable to do most things on his own, let alone go out and do his job. He'd never again go on a mission, and it drove him insane, far worse than he'd expected—and he'd expected a lot. But he'd pushed it all down; down and away. The constant pain had been the least of his troubles.

"You're my…" Matt started. What were they, actually? It wasn't 'boyfriend', that was trite and laughable, certainly not 'husband', and he ran through the various unsatisfactory options—lover (too icky), mate (eww), partner (too…no). Stumped, he tried again. "It's not as though we're just roommates. You just…can't…" Matt trailed off again. Hooch had been increasingly insufferable as he regained his strength, as though all the energy that he wasn't using for his physical recovery was channeled into being an unbearable prick.

"Okay. We're not roommates, we're not even fuckbuddies. Does that mean you get to keep me and I don't get to pay my share?" The laser-beam stare was back in Hooch's eyes. His whole body strummed with energy; an energy he couldn't expend, no matter how much physical therapy he did, and that goddammed, infuriating, fucking cane was a symbol of how he was most definitely not himself.

"We'll share. We'll work something out as we go along. Like everyone else does when they move in together. But. You. Are. Not. Paying. Me. Rent."

"Then what am I paying?" Hooch's fingers drummed onto the cane's grip, in an ever faster beat.

Matt threw up his arms. "Whatever one part of a couple does when they move in together! The bills when they come in and you're there! Flatware with bent prongs and where none of the teaspoons match! A couch that doesn't match anything I have! A movie collection that doesn't fit on the shelves! A bed that doesn't fit up the stairs or in the door! Stuff! We. Will. Fucking. Work. It. Out." He was vaguely aware that he was shouting at the top of his lungs.

Hooch opened his mouth as if to retort, but merely drew in a sharp breath. He stared at Matt, while the tension in his body shifted perceptively from fight to something entirely else.

The distinct downside of having a shouting match with someone who didn't talk was that it tended to end in a most unsatisfactory way, and Matt finished with: "we don't have to work it out today, or tomorrow, or to anyone's fucking schedule. It's home, and nobody can fucking say what we fucking can or can't do here. Just…I don't know…just look at it. This, this is the fucking beginning and…it's the beginning…"

"…of what?" Hooch voice was quiet. "Of what is this the beginning?" Up close, Hooch's pupils were blown wide, and he had stilled completely except for his breathing.

"…of…us…" How was he supposed to be coherent when Hooch did that? It felt disturbingly like being stared down by a cobra. A horny one.

"How is that 'us' going to be?" Hooch's voice had dropped another octave, until it hit a low rumble.

Matt swallowed, then stared straight back.

"Whatever we want it to be." He had no idea how he kept his voice steady while being bored into by those eyes, "and whatever we call it, but we're a couple, and couples don't pay each other rent."

"Matt…" Hooch drawled, his low voice leaving no doubt about his intentions. "I give you my word, no more talk about rent if you give me your word: stop treating me with those goddamned motherfucking kid gloves you've been wearing for the past months. Stop it," he drew in a slow, shaky breath, "right now."

Matt's eyes flicked downwards, then back up to Hooch's face. "Okay…" His eyes drifted back down. "You can *not* be serious." This directed at Hooch's crotch.

"Have I ever been not serious?" Hooch raised his eyebrows, cast a quick glance across the dusty and empty space, then stopped at one of the steel girders. "Fuck me, right there." He nodded towards it, "and I'll never mention rent again. I'm going batshit crazy, here. I need...damn, Matt, I'm going fucking insane when you treat me like I could fucking break. I don't give a shit about rent, or rooms, or money or however the fuck I'm supposed to behave as part of a couple. I. Just. Want. You."

The very first thought, whether Hooch's pelvis would be up to it, faded. Matt closed his dropped jaw, looking for a suitable place. "Fuck, if this is all it took to stop you acting like a spoilt brat, I should have done this weeks ago."

"Yeah, you should have," Hooch murmured. He dropped the cane to the floor, kicked it aside as if discarding the past months, and started to move towards the steel girder. "Fuck the pelvis, fuck no lube, fuck everything, but fuck me. Now."

Matt glanced towards the girder. "Not there, it'll leave marks you don't want to explain to the medic." He scanned about for an alternative, "the reception desk." Already there, only a few feet away, and made of smooth carved wood. Bolted into the floor, it hadn't been removed when the previous tenants had left, and was the perfect height.

Hooch nodded, and steered them towards the desk instead. Only letting go of Matt when they reached it. He opened his fly and pushed down his black denims and briefs underneath. Impatient, when he turned around and bent over, bracing himself on the desk. Elbows on the hard surface, as far down as he could go.

With fumbling fingers, Matt pushed Hooch's jeans and briefs down further, before unzipping and shoving down his own. He cursed his suddenly dry mouth as he tried to get enough spit.

Hooch craned his neck briefly, saw Matt floundering, and reached out to catch Matt's hand. He couldn't twist that far, but Matt got the picture and leaned forward, to have Hooch spit on his hand.

Hooch spread his legs as far as he could, then braced himself for the onslaught that would be dry and painful. Deliciously, goddamned painful; tearing into him and casting away all the boredom, the pent-up energy, the badly ignored hatred of his body that had let him down and that wouldn't allow him to be again who he'd always been. Reckless. Dangerous. Demanding, and...

"Fuck!" Hooch groaned out, arms trembling on the desk, his shoulders so taut, he could feel the tension ripple down his spine, only to concentrate in the one point of his body, that was forced to open up.

Matt's breathing was harsh, sweat beaded his forehead, as he concentrated on forcing his entry. Discomfort for him, too, and how he relished Hooch's surrender that was everything but. The way Hooch's breath came whistling through clenched teeth, small, suppressed sounds that urged Matt on, that showed how much he wanted the pain, wanted every single ounce of strength Matt could give him, as he buried himself in Hooch's ass.

With the ever increasing thrusts, Hooch gasped out Matt's name, forced him on, harder, no holding back. To make him forget the last months, and it was good, so goddamned good, that he pushed Matt's hand away, as he tried to stroke his cock. He wanted to feel the pounding, the strength, the craved-for ache of Matt's cock deep within his body.

Hooch lost himself, forgot everything but the lust that kept spiraling higher the harder and faster Matt let loose. When Hooch came suddenly, bucking and crying out with relief, with pain, with everything that he'd needed for so long, he took Matt by surprise.

Matt's own release, no matter how much he was lost himself, suddenly made sense of one word, one confession, months ago: masochist. And he came with the intensity of knowing that he had given Hooch what he'd needed. He'd made him come apart underneath his hands and body, and he was so much in love with that motherfucking bastard right now, that he pulled Hooch up against himself, kissing the sweaty neck, and just holding as he shuddered through the come-down.

Hooch calmed in Matt's arms, his heartbeat slowing down, until it beat steadily.

"You are quite something, Matt Donahue." Hooch rumbled hoarsely.

"Am I?" Matt murmured into Hooch's ear, feeling, rather than hearing their heartbeats merge. "Something good, I hope?" he teased as he carefully eased his way out.

"Yeah, all good." Hooch took in a deep breath, and reveled in the soreness and the knowledge he'd be a sticky mess, hidden beneath respectable clothing.

Matt quickly righted himself before pulling up Hooch's briefs and jeans—carefully, but not quite as slowly or gently as he had been when helping Hooch dress in the last few months.

Hooch turned around with a grin on his face. Relaxed and sated, all tension gone for now. "So, about that rent..." he let out a sharp gust of laughter at Matt's immediate eye rolling. "Calm down, you fucked some sense into me. I get it now. The gym's your new life and you want to pay for it, and couples don't pay rent to each other. I need you to understand that it's a new life for me, too. I want to pay for the apartment."

Matt nodded slowly. Hooch's stubbornness over the money thing finally made sense. "Deal." He paused, then rephrased what he was going to say, "do you wanna look at the upstairs?"

"Yeah, if you get me my motherfucking cane?" Hooch quirked a rueful grin. Stairs were still a bastard.

The cane had somehow ended up halfway across the room and Matt went to pick it up. The cane, that last remaining aid, and Hooch actually asking for it was enough of a concession in itself.

The stairs were behind one of the doors near the reception, which Matt thought would have been damned inconvenient when the space above was being used as an office, but gave a measure of privacy to an apartment.

It had cheap synthetic carpet and paper-thin walls, the memory of office furniture and the smell, like the rest of the building, of dust and abandonment. On opening the door at the top of the stairs, there was a reception area, meeting room and boardroom with a less-than-inspiring view of the parking lot, which would be their living area and kitchen. The remainder of the space was divided into a number of rather depressing offices, where the status of the previous inhabitant was painfully obvious by size and windows. Matt and the architect had decided to reconfigure these into two good-sized bedrooms, a compact study, and a bathroom.

Climbing the stairs reminded Hooch once more of what they'd just done. He relished the soreness, following Matt and looking around the place. Calm, with the tension and anger literally fucked out of him, he gave a shrug.

"I don't have a fucking clue how it's going to look like, I have the imagination of a gnat. You do what you think is right, and let me pay for this place." He hesitated, turned his head to look at Matt, as he tried out a new word for the very first time. "*Our* place."

The word made Matt smile. "Deal. But you gotta tell me if you hate something."

Hooch gave a rare, bright grin. "I veto pink."

Matt laughed. "Done."

A new life, for both of them, as Hooch had said. And wasn't that fucking amazing.

Once the builders got started, work was underway remarkably quickly. Carpet ripped up, floorboards polished, walls put up, mirrors installed, wet areas tiled and plumbed, a truly amazing amount of wiring and cable, and the all-penetrating smell of fresh paint. Matt thought that the place looked like the aftermath of an earthquake, but it was *his*.

It seemed that every waking moment was spent talking to the builders, meeting with the architect, and setting up the rest of the business: arranging for the equipment to be delivered, interviewing new staff, finding himself flooded with enquiries from freelance trainers who wanted to use the gym as a base, while getting used to the strange feeling of being without Hooch all day, every day, unlike the past months.

Hooch had returned to Fort Bragg a couple of weeks ago, when he'd been signed fit for desk duties, just when the builders started in earnest. He had moved temporarily into a room on camp, where he should have felt at home in the impersonal four off-white walls. Yet he didn't, because nothing was as it had been before his capture.

Besides, the desk job was driving him insane, cooped up day and night within offices, while his old team was getting ready for another mission.

They caught up mainly on weekends—still feeling their way around their new life.

✳ ✳ ✳

Friday lunchtime, and Hooch was ready to leave camp, but the prospect of spending the weekend in a building site didn't appeal at all. He almost called Matt with an excuse to stay in Fort Bragg, but he wouldn't lie to Matt and there was no real point in staying with a team that was no longer his. He grabbed his daypack and made his way back to the gym, forced to drive a rented car, because he couldn't easily climb into his truck yet. With that extra annoyance, his mood had deteriorated further by the time he reached the gym.

The place was almost finished, though the smell of the polish on the hardwood floors and the various solvents and sealants were enough to singe the hair. When Hooch stepped through the entrance door, he recoiled from the stink, then looked around. The equipment had started to arrive, it was stacked in big boxes and shrouded in protective plastic wrap.

Matt was sitting in a paint-splattered office chair in the office he had claimed as 'his'—the makeshift desk full of the various brochures, files and paperwork he had accumulated.

Facing him across the table was a perky looking blonde of about eighteen, who was earnestly pointing out items in a furniture catalogue.

"Who are you?" Hooch demanded from the girl.

"Hi!" she stood up quickly and held out her hand, seemingly unfazed by the pissed-off man in uniform. "You must be Captain Bozic! I'm Mandy!"

Hooch's brows shot up, then steepled in a pained expression. At least he found the decency in himself to shake her hand. "Mandy. You work here now?"

She nodded enthusiastically. She was cheerfulness and bounciness and sunshine. Behind her, Matt hid a smile behind his hand.

"Oh! Do you guys want anything for lunch? I'm just going to be headin' off down for a couple of catalogues for the apartment. This is so cool!"

"Right." Hooch tried to sort his thoughts, but he had a headache forming behind his eyes, and the last thing he wanted to do was to deal with an over-excited terrier in female form. "I don't know." He looked at Matt over her shoulder, with an expression that quickly became one of helplessness. "Do we?" before he realized what he'd said. 'We'. Shit.

Matt didn't seem to notice as he handed over some bills. "Just a some sandwiches and a couple of bottles of soda on your way back."

She put the money into her purse and headed out the door, stopping on the way to admonish a painter roughly three times her size for leaving open cans of paint at the very edge of the dropsheet.

They watched her go, waiting until she was well into the parking lot before Matt asked. "Well? Any particular reason you want to maim my new receptionist?"

Hooch was still staring at Mandy's retreating back, when Matt's words filtered through. "Huh?" He turned round, felt barely suppressed frustration well up, when he caught the look on Matt's face. Open, accepting, with the hint of a fond smile coupled with fatigue. The last he could do, Hooch realized, was to not add to Matt's stress. This relationship stuff was hard, he'd never before had to take really someone else's feelings into consideration.

Hooch scrubbed the heels of his hands over his face. "You don't need my shit mood. Got enough on your plate." He made an abortive movement across the building site.

"No," Matt agreed, "so what's pissed you off so much this time? Other than, of course, the complete and utter buttfuck here. Any other girl would probably have freaked and if you're going to be in the habit of sending them into hysterics, I'd like to know."

Hooch let out a breath he hadn't been aware he was holding, and set the daypack down. "Just the job." At Matt's expectant gaze he understood he was supposed to elaborate. If this was what people in relationships did, damn, it was tricky. "My old team's getting ready to head out."

Things made sense to Matt, then. "Ah," trying, damnit, for the right words, "the missing it or the sinking in?" He kept his distance, not touching Hooch like he wanted. Too many people just outside the door, painters, plumbers and electricians, who could come in at any time.

"I don't know." Hooch shook his head, rubbed his eyes again. He was damned tired and wasn't that ridiculous, since all he'd done was paperwork and his physical therapy. "Not being part of it, I guess." He shrugged again as if it all meant nothing, while it was anything but. He didn't feel like dealing with it right now, and so he changed the subject. "How's the upstairs going?"

Matt snorted, "even further from finished than here, but the painters haven't got there yet, so it doesn't reek as much. Come and see."

Upstairs, the walls of the apartment had been rearranged into the new plan, but were still bare plasterboard. The tiling had been done for the open kitchen area and the bathroom at the same time as the wet area of the gym, so while the bathroom was fully functional, if unpainted, the kitchenette was still nothing but some taps with a bucket underneath, a fridge, and a microwave precariously balanced on a cheap table.

Matt had been living amongst the mess while most of the work was carried out downstairs, the workmen venturing to the apartment only when they needed to wait before continuing the job downstairs. An air mattress on the floor of one of the bedrooms indicated which one Matt had claimed.

Hooch did a 360 degree. "Holy shit, you live in this? I didn't expect it to be that bad." Suddenly a hell of a lot less pissed off than before. "Guess my own shit takes on perspective." He reached out for Matt to pull him close. The place was a building site of the worst proportions, but at least they were alone. Touching Matt, holding the strong and firm body close, had never lost its appeal, and it still gave him a sense of grounding. "And that," he jerked his chin towards the air mattress, "is your bedroom?"

Matt's chuckle was only partly muffled by Hooch's neck. "Officially, I guess." He stopped. "How much space do you think you'll need for your stuff? Though there'll be space in the other room of course, and your study down the hall."

"I'll need about the size of my CFP." It was good not have to explain to Matt. They both knew which backpack he meant. "I don't have 'stuff'. Table top for my laptop, space for my kit, spot for my toothbrush and razor, and a place to sleep, that's all I need." He mock-headbutted Matt. "The latter preferably not on my own."

"Not while I'm here, and not while you're here. Though probably with a better bed." Matt wanted to pull Hooch down onto the mattress but that was going to be an all-or-nothing effort. Hooch would get pissed off again if he suggested trying to go down slowly, but at the same time Matt didn't fancy explaining things to Hooch's medical team. He settled for tightening the embrace, hoping Hooch didn't notice his quick calculating look down to the mattress. "We need the spare for guests anyway."

Hooch had noticed the glance, hardly anything went unnoticed with him. "What guests are you expecting?"

Matt snorted, "Short list, I know…" he trailed off. Not a lot of people who knew; fewer who could carry the burden even if they were trusted.

"What about your, you know…" Hooch hesitated, then forged on, "…your family?" This was unknown territory and he had no idea how to tread, but they'd been skirting around the subject of families for ages. With Hooch's an absolute no, he was unsure about the subject of Matt's.

Matt shrugged a shoulder. "They know that I'm gay, yeah, since before I joined the Marines. They're used to DADT, but with them, it's all or nothing. One invite and you're likely to get all of them—Mom, Pop, brothers, sisters, nieces, nephews, hell, even the cat and dog—in here. So, no, for reasons of space." A pause, not quite knowing how to bring up the subject. "Mom's been talking about Thanksgiving. What do you think?"

"They know about me?" The sudden note of panic in Hooch's voice all too obvious.

"They know there's someone, and that he's still in," Matt replied. "They're not stupid. They know I didn't quit, move halfway across the country to a place I've never been to which has an enormous Army base, and tell them that I'm still in the closet, just because I woke up one morning and felt like it."

"Okay." Hooch's face and sudden tension was anything but okay. "I'm shit at families. Shit at relationships. Shit at all that normal stuff. Hey, fuck, shit at ninety-eight percent of life." He ran a hand through his short hair, "and the two percent I'm good at is fighting and fucking!" He tried to reach for Matt to pull him onto the mattress.

Matt's first instinct was to grab Hooch and do just that, but stopped. The gym was still full of workmen, and Mandy was due back any moment. Though he'd locked the door behind them, someone banging on it seeking his attention would be almost as bad as them coming in. More importantly, sex really wasn't what Hooch needed, even if it was what he said he wanted.

Matt stepped forward and took hold of Hooch's forearms, feeling the tension strumming through him. "Much as I'd like to screw you, or better yet let you screw me, through that goddamned uncomfortable mattress, that's not what this is about. You are quite extraordinary, Hubert Bozic, so don't give me that bullshit, and of course stuff's going to be different with us than with regular joe shmoes."

"Are you telling me you want me to visit your family?" Hooch had faced unspeakable dangers, went alone and on foot into the Mog, but this, this was above and beyond anything he'd ever handled. "Goddammit, they'd hate me!"

Matt recoiled, the blustering defense coupled with the obvious 'why?' both dying before they made it out. "Course I do—we're partners." He tested the word, so new and he could count the number of times he'd said it out loud on one hand, "and why wouldn't they trust my taste in men?"

"Because I'm not what they'd want for you. I have the social skills of an amoeba, and know fuck-all about living a normal life. I can't stand too many people around me, and don't like talking." Hooch shook his head, "and because of me you still have to live a lie."

Matt blinked. "They trusted me to know what I was doing when I enlisted," he stepped forward again, "do you think they'd do any different now?" He kept his voice low, oddly reminded of a summer camp, many years ago, trying to coax some wild creature towards him. "I know it's soon. But…just think about it." No lies, no false promises, it wasn't as though he could say 'and we can leave at any time if you're uncomfortable' because frankly, the sheer logistics of getting from Flint back to Fayetteville was a nightmare at the best of times, let alone Thanksgiving.

"Okay." Slowly and hesitantly, unlike the Hooch everyone—except Matt—knew. "I'll think about it." Hooch moistened his lips. Damn, when had he become such a pussy? He was determined to cope, no matter what, and he forced himself to let some of the tension out of his body. "Tell me, how much would it mean to you?"

"Honestly?" Matt thought, "I can't say I wouldn't really want you to meet them. They'll like you. My Mom's a great cook and she'd want to feed you up." Keeping his voice low, "but seriously? What matters to me is *you*, and if you don't want to come, then we won't." The words hovered between them.

That was it, the crux. Hooch wanted the same, 'what matters is *you*', and wasn't that another first in his life. "Alright." He nodded once, his decision was made. If he could walk into hostile enemy territory, he could dam well go to a family Thanksgiving, especially if it was the family of the one person that truly mattered: Matt. He'd paid a high price to learn that lesson.

He was going to treat this like any other mission, and to hell with everything else.

Matt let out a breath he hadn't thought he'd been holding, and one of his motherfucking big smiles spread over his face. "Good."

When they came back downstairs, Mandy had already been and gone. The table had been cleared of most of the clutter, and two bulging bags containing sandwiches (labeled with fillings) were in its place. A couple of bags of chips, two large bottles of coke with condensation dripping down their necks, and a couple of large paper cups, one filled full with ice, completed the arrangement. On one end of the table was a high stack of catalogues with pages helpfully marked with slips of paper.

Mandy wasn't far, though. She was audible from the main area, doing an inventory of the deliveries and talking on the phone to suppliers. Clearly, Hooch's life wasn't the only one that was being ruthlessly, efficiently and cheerfully ordered into place.

They sat down to eat at the desk. Hooch in his customary silence, more thoughtful than usual, while Matt rifled through the catalogues and checked out Mandy's notes.

"How old is she again?" Hooch asked eventually.

"Eighteen," Matt grinned, "you can just tell she's an Army brat, can't you? Needs the job to pay her way through college, sounds like she doesn't get along with dad's new wife or mom's new boyfriend. Most importantly, she's a good deal smarter than Cheerleader Barbie she pretends to be." He looked down at the empty bottle he was holding in his hands. "It'll all be okay."

"Good," Hooch nodded, "and you should get her to enlist, she'd whip any platoon into shape." He finished his coke and pushed the almost empty bag of chips away. Setting the bottle down with a thud, he turned and looked at Matt, fixing him with the intense stare that meant nothing else was on his mind, and nothing else mattered right now.

Hooch waited until Matt looked up at him, and then offered a half-smile. "Yeah, it will okay."

THANKSGIVING WEEKEND, 1998, FLINT, MICHIGAN

Civilian air travel was awful at the best of times, let alone Thanksgiving, where it seemed that the entire country was on the move. Complete with screaming children, excessive luggage, and the inability to do anything so simple as read a schedule.

It didn't help that Matt's stomach was turning into knots. What had seemed like a fantastic idea only a few weeks ago now loomed far too close, as they headed to the taxi stand. It wasn't helped by a usually quiet Hooch being positively silent and focused, as if preparing for a covert ops.

The streets flew by, at once familiar and alien, before stopping in the suburbs in front of a plain brick house with a high white picket fence. Matt let himself in through the gate but before they had climbed the stairs to the front door, it opened to a friendly looking woman with a huge smile of welcome.

"You're here at last!" Matt's mom pulled her son into a warm hug while nodding at Hooch, "and you must be Hooch. Welcome and thank you for coming all this way and bringing Matt with you."

Hooch shook the woman's hand. He'd done his intel, his recce, and brushed up on the lingo. He knew at least theoretically how he was supposed to behave. This included not packing any weapons—not that he'd been able to smuggle them through civilian air travel anyway. "Pleased to meet you. Thank you for having me here."

Matt knew Hooch's tone and the polite facial expression. It was the one that screamed 'professional' at him.

She led the way up the front steps, through the door into the house, and up the stairs. The two men followed in her wake, until she stopped in front of a door near the back of the house. "Just put your things in Matt's room, we're down in the kitchen when you're ready."

Behind the door was a small, tidy bedroom, spotlessly clean. There were little plastic figurines lined up on the windowsill, football trophies holding pride of place on the bookshelves, and Marines posters covering the walls, some looking rather tattered around the edges. The space was dominated by a large wooden bed that didn't quite match the rest of the furniture: newer, and made up with crisp linens with the tell-tale sign of being freshly out of the packet and the first time through the washing machine.

"I've put the extra blankets and pillows on top of the wardrobe, if you boys are cold. Come down when you're ready, everyone's nearly here." With that, Matt's mother disappeared out the door and down the stairs.

Matt looked at his silent partner, who'd made a choking noise at the last sentence.

"This…" Hooch finally said, pointing at the bed, "isn't your bed. Is it?"

"Um, no." Matt shook his head as he dropped his bag on the ground. "This is new from last time. I used to have a single."

"Your. Parents. Bought. A. Double. Bed. For. Our. Visit." Hooch pronounced every word very carefully, staring at the offending piece of furniture as if he was looking through the crosshairs of a sniper rifle. "Oh fuck." He dropped his backpack and scrubbed the heel of his hand over his face. He hadn't expected that; hadn't even expected to stay in the same room as Matt. And now, not only in Matt's old room, looking like it probably had before he'd joined the USMC, but a bed that had been specifically bought for two men to sleep in. Two men. Matt and himself. Fuck. That was too much too soon. No closets to hide in here.

"I told you that they know," Matt felt slightly defensive, "and considering how many people have got to be here this weekend, it's a damn sight better than the floor or the couch in the den." He sat down experimentally on the bed, the mattress was firm, and there was a thick goose feather pad on top. "Everyone's used to not asking." He wasn't sure whether this was to reassure Hooch, or himself.

"Yeah, I know they know. Confronted with the practicality it throws me for a loop." Hooch sat down next to Matt. "I've never been part of a family like yours. The ranch is big, maids, gardeners, the lot, and my parents played the socialite hosts. I haven't got a fucking clue how to fit into a real family, least of all as part of a gay couple."

Matt smiled, trying to be encouraging. As much as he'd pushed for this, the reality was something else. He'd always thought that he'd be able to come out as soon as he'd left the Marines, that his family could stop having to tiptoe around certain things. But now, since he was with Hooch, all those years of family conspiracy would have to continue for a while yet. "You ready to face the horde?"

"Give me five minutes and that patented smooch of yours and I'll be as ready as I'll ever be." Being on a mission was one thing, but having to show more than just a blank game face was entirely another.

Matt chuckled and obliged with the kiss, which, though it didn't last quite the five minutes, was still entirely satisfactory.

He stood up, waiting for Hooch to collect himself, and then exchanged one last look before heading out the door and down the stairs, where a small, fast-running object attached itself to Matt's leg.

"Uncle Matt!" The little boy got everybody else's attention, and they were immediately swamped by what seemed like a never ending herd of very tall, very loud, and extremely friendly people, all trying to hug Matt, slap his shoulder, introduce themselves to Hooch and drag them both into the dining room simultaneously.

Hooch suffered through the onslaught of boisterous, welcoming, and most of all *tactile* people with what he hoped was a friendly smile plastered across his face, which might or might not have had more in common with rictor mortis. He kept checking Matt's position in the room from the corner of his eyes, keeping him in line of sight at all times. Just like he'd do on a mission.

Eventually, they were separated, and Hooch had to fight on his own in the middle of the family that kept asking him questions, one talking over the other; telling him stories, welcoming him into the family and pushing beer into his hand, while wanting to know how long they'd been together and what he was doing in his job and and and and…until Hooch was ready to jump up and run. Holding the beer bottle in a white knuckled death grip, his dark eyes wildly searching for the exit. He couldn't answer those questions; couldn't bear the close proximity of all those strangers. He knew they meant well, but he couldn't cope with.

"Hooch, dear," came a voice, "I wonder if I could trouble you to give me a hand with something?" Matt's mother, who'd appeared out of the midst of people around Hooch.

"Ma'am?" Hooch looked up, disoriented for a split second, and wasn't that a shit reaction time for an elite soldier. "Yes, of course, Ma'am." He stood up immediately, relief barely disguised on his features, and followed her less like an obedient puppy and more like an eager IED sniffer.

She led him into a small room off the kitchen, where a couple of trestle tables was laid out. They sat down at one which had plates with cute rabbits on them. Since not everybody was going to fit onto the table in the dining room, clearly these ones had been set aside for the children.

A tumbler with something stronger than beer materialized in front of Hooch. "It's Anne," Matt's mother smiled, "Ma'am makes me feel old, much as I adore hearing it in that Texan drawl." She paused. "Forgive me, but you looked a little overwhelmed with my brood."

"Anne. Got it." Hooch nodded, then allowed himself to take in a deep breath, slowly expelling it as he accepted the tumbler with a thanks. "I'm not used to…" hesitating, "family. I'm sorry." He took a mouthful of the brandy, relishing the burn down his throat. "I've never been to a Thanksgiving dinner." He couldn't call the formal affairs at the ranch Thanksgiving dinner, and he'd been avoiding them for ages.

There was compassion in her eyes. "Then we'll just have to make sure you have a good one this year," a pause, "and you're family to us now, too, even if you're far away in Fayetteville." She didn't reach out to touch him, as though she knew he wasn't tactile the way Matt was, that he'd be uncomfortable with the contact. "Matt sounds like he's very happy there." There was a way that she'd said it, both an inquiry if he chose to answer, or an observation if he didn't.

Hooch drained the brandy to give himself some time. If he was ever going to be successful on this mission, he had to continue the recce to know where he stood. "Matt…" Hooch trailed off, then made a decision and looked at her. "What has he told you?" The 'about us' implied.

If anything, her smile broadened.

"Oh, Matty. You wouldn't think it, but he's always been very careful with what he says, what he does. He's never made a decision lightly, and most certainly not in who he loves."

How it had broken her heart for all those years her Matty had been caught between the man and the job that he loved. At first, she'd thought that it was a civilian, and it had been the strain of a dual life on and off base. She'd had her suspicions for the last couple of years, but when Matty had called her to say that he'd quit the Marines and was moving to Fayetteville, she'd realized that she was way off the mark.

Hooch nodded. "He's the one who's always known what he wanted."

She inclined her head, "and no matter what he's said in the past, it was obvious what you are to each other the moment you walked up that drive."

That hit Hooch like a sideways punch. "It is? What is it that gives it away?"

She almost said, 'because mothers just know,' but held back, given what Hooch had said earlier, and how his own mother likely did not know. "A feeling, I suppose. It's hard to put into words. The way you look out for each other, how you don't take your eyes off him for very long, how you two need to almost remind yourselves to stand a little further apart."

"You think strangers would notice, too, or is it a family thing?" Hooch asked.

She chuckled, warm and motherly, refilling his glass. "Neither. It's knowing Matty, and knowing what I was going to see. I wouldn't worry too much—people see what they expect to see, after all. Even Matty's pop was shocked, when he told us he was gay, just before he enlisted. To this day, I don't know what took more courage. Besides," the very slightest pause, "if Matty was old enough to go to war, he was old enough to decide who to love."

Hooch nodded, and with the brandy refilled, he kept drinking. He'd barely known this woman for more than an hour and he felt more comfortable with her than he had with anyone other than Matt for a long time. Or perhaps it was the brandy talking on an almost empty stomach.

"Welcome to the family," Anne raised her own glass, "we're all so glad that Matty's found someone who appreciates him."

"What's not to appreciate about Matt? He's remarkable." Hooch smiled his half-smile, took a last mouthful, and felt his tongue loosened. As far as missions went, he was well and truly outclassed by this woman. "I was worried," he spun the empty glass in his fingers, "cradle snatcher, not house-trained nor socialized." He paused, "one could think that of the two of us I was the tougher one, what with my job, but it's *Matty* who always knew what he wanted. Took me torture to figure it out."

Her eyes had widened at the mention of torture, but she didn't say a word. It was not the time, nor the place, not here, not how. Instead, a rueful chuckle. "Ah, 'Matty', yes. It's so easy to forget, with him being the youngest. He'll always be my baby, even when he's long outgrows the old names."

"Yeah, and he'll always be the kid to me, because I'll always be ten years older." Hooch felt comfortably mellow. He hadn't been able to drink anything stronger than weak lager for so long, thanks to medication, the brandy was having quite an effect on him now.

She poured a last, generous splash into Hooch's glass. "I'm not too sure how much longer pop is going to be able to hold the horde back from their dinner, but I promise they're all much better behaved when they're at the table."

He glanced towards the door and the main room. "Your family has been asking me questions. I understand that, but most of them I can't answer. I don't want to be rude."

She nodded. "I'm sure by now Matt's managed to get a word in sideways and reminded everyone just who happen to be stationed at Fort Bragg, and…" she paused, "as you will notice in time, it is almost entirely impossible to offend any of my brood. Unless, of course, you disparage football, hockey, hunting or fishing."

There was the distinct sound near the door of hungry children wanting their dinner.

"I'm in no danger, then." Hooch's smile came easier now that he wasn't on edge anymore. "Back into the lion's den?" He finished his brandy and stood up. Once more ready to face the family that was so much like Matt, just in a very large dose.

✳ ✳ ✳

They made it seem accidental, but it was probably by design that Hooch found himself sitting between Matt and his mother, and across from Matt's fishing-fanatic brother, who, after establishing that Hooch was from Texas and lived in Fayetteville, immediately spouted a bewildering lecture of fish species and river systems of the South. Anne had been right—clearly Matt had spread a quiet reminder to the rest of the family about topics of conversation best avoided, though to a casual observer the impact seemed negligible. Everyone still had lots to say, much centered on Matt's antics as a child, stories that made him alternatively blush and cringe.

Far more at ease now, Hooch relaxed even further throughout the meal. Zoning out of the lecture on fish species and rivers, with the occasional nod and inquisitive grunt, he relished the food that was truly divine. He hadn't had a home cooked meal like this in…not ever. His parents' cook had been too professional to create anything but sleek perfection. As it was, he realized after a while that he was enjoying himself more than he'd ever believed possible.

He even laughed out loud when Matt's mom heaved more turkey meat, mashed potatoes, dressing and gravy onto his plate, because evidently he "wasn't eating enough, was too wiry, and she had to fatten him up," which made Matt smirk and elbow him with a 'told you so' expression.

Though everyone felt stuffed to the gills by the time the older children came in to help clear the table, they all suddenly found the elusive extra dessert stomach when the table was re-laid and filled with pumpkin, apple and pecan pies, and cookies for the kids. By the time dinner was finished, Hooch's polite offer of help was adamantly refused (much to his relief) and they settled in for an after-dinner drink.

When it was eventually time for bed, Hooch was quite relaxed.

Matt shut the door behind them and gave Hooch another of his legendary smooches, tasting of pumpkin pie and nutmeg. There was a mischievous expression on his face as he pulled away from the kiss. "In the interests of full disclosure, my parents are just on the other side of that wall," he nodded towards the far side of the bed, "how quiet do you think you can be?"

"Are you fucking kidding me?" Hooch shot a glance at the wall towards Matt's parents' bedroom.

The grin got wider. "I think you deserve a reward for being so well behaved," there was a wicked gleam in Matt's eyes, as he quickly undid Hooch's jeans and pushed them down, together with his briefs. He got down on his knees and nudged Hooch against the closed door. "Making small talk and not scaring the kiddies, that deserves something very nice." His breath was warm against Hooch's groin.

"Shit." Hooch let himself get pushed against the door. "You get turned on by making out in your teenage bedroom?" Despite the teasing, he was already showing the stirrings of interest. Not that Matt had ever failed to arouse him. Whenever and wherever.

Matt kept looking up at Hooch while he gave a few playful, quick laps, barely flickering over the skin and leaving only the faintest hint of coolness. "Not the first time this room's seen a bit of making out," his eyes glanced over a few feet to Hooch's left, "and more—I lost my cherry just over there, you know."

Without giving Hooch a chance to respond he swallowed him down with practiced ease, barely pausing as Hooch's cock met the back of his throat.

Whatever mockery Hooch was about to come out with, it was swallowed, literally, by Matt. All thoughts of teenage Matt were gone, as the adult one gave pleasure to Hooch.

Which he did with his usual meticulous skill and the occasional glance upwards at Hooch, eyes gleaming, as if daring him to make more than a few muffled sounds.

Hooch clenched his fists at his side, no contact, except for the heat of Matt's throat, his tongue that knew all the sensitive places, and his hand. Hooch's face contorted with the effort of control, but no sound came out from between his gritted teeth, not even as he came.

Matt took much longer than was really necessary to swallow every drop, ensuring that Hooch was clean with long, lazy swipes of his tongue, before standing up and doing Hooch's fly up again. The kiss this time was softer, almost languid, just letting Hooch taste himself as well as the faint ghost of nutmeg.

Once he got his heartbeat and breathing back under control, Hooch took hold of Matt's shoulders and pushed him back at arm's length, studying him with an ever growing smirk.

"You, Matt Donahue," he finally said, "are going to pay for that. Undress and onto the bed. It will be christened tonight, and in absolute silence!" He reached to grope Matt's hard-on through his trousers.

With a raised eyebrow, and pretending a nonchalance that his strangled gasp and increased breathing betrayed, Matt stepped back out of Hooch's grasp. He pulled his sweater up over his head, before kicking off his shoes and pulling down his trousers. The room was small enough that it was only a few steps backwards to the bed, and he landed on it with the faint puff of feathers in the duvet as it was hastily pushed to one side.

Hooch remained standing at the side of the bed for a while longer, feasting on the sight of the perfect body, laid out before his eyes. Not touching, not talking, just looking while taking his fill, until he moved onto the bed at long last, still fully clothed.

For the next hour, he took his time to explore the body he knew so well, attempting to re-learn it all over again, with only his lips, teeth and tongue. He almost had to gag Matt, to keep him from making noises he couldn't hold back, until he finally, mercifully, allowed him to come.

"You bastard," Matt's grin was weary and his voice hoarse, as though the effort of keeping quiet had put strain on his vocal cords. He looked up at the ceiling, where a few glow-in-the-dark stickers remained, then returned his gaze to Hooch. "I thought you said a proper christening," the pointedly looked at Hooch's crotch as he spread his legs further, lying back on the pillows.

"You trying to tell me you never got fucked in here? I thought you'd lost your cherry in this room." Hooch let his finger run all the way down from Matt's smooth throat, along the chest, down to his spent cock.

"Hmmm…" Matt's purr was noncommittal, "not for more than ten years, not in this bed, and not by you." He pushed up lazily into Hooch's hand.

"In that case, one more day won't matter." Hooch flashed a downright mean grin, then stretched out beside Matt. Still fully clothed, hands beneath is head, he looked up at the glow-in-the-dark stickers on the ceiling. To all intents and purposes ignoring his more than half-hard cock. "Go to sleep, kid. I'm a middle aged man who needs his rest."

Matt made a muffled sound of outrage but there was no budging Hooch when he was in one of his moods. Grumbling about sneaky, unreasonable, sadistic Deltas, he turned onto his side, careful to present a tempting sight of muscled back and butt, and then, to all appearances, obeyed and went immediately to sleep.

Hooch chuckled quietly, eventually got up, but not without running his hand all the way along the smooth, bare flank. Soon after, the sound of the shower running came out of the bathroom, and a few minutes later the mattress dipped when a slightly damp, fully naked Hooch climbed into bed behind Matt. He pulled Matt against his body, holding him. Something he'd never done before the capture.

The house was silent, and it didn't take long for Hooch to fall asleep, lulled by Matt's steady breaths and the warmth of his body.

✱ ✱ ✱

Arms, bodies, pain and stench, death, filth and ever more bodies. Fear, all-encompassing; fear he'd never admitted. Fear to give up, just give into the pain and the stink and let himself fall down, far down, down into the darkness.

Hooch woke with a start. He was drenched in sweat, on his back, while the sleeping body beside him lay curled up, making a soft snuffling sound. Hooch lay still, trying to force his wildly hammering heart to calm, while ruthlessly pushing back down the sound of terror that tried to rip out of his throat. The cover was off his body, sweat cooling in the air. The last thing he wanted was to wake Matt. He couldn't bear for him to know, not Matt, not having to explain to him that there was more of a legacy from his captivity than the scars from cigarette burns and pelvic surgery.

When he had himself under control, with the same recklessness he applied to anything in his life, he slipped out of bed and searched for shorts and t-shirt. He couldn't stay in the bed, not with the damp patch of his terror and sweat on the sheets. He padded quietly downstairs and into the kitchen.

He only dared to switch on a small light above the sink, and while he'd love a hot drink, he didn't want to wake anyone, nor felt it appropriate to make himself at home in a home that wasn't his. So he merely filled a glass with cold water from the tap and sat down at the kitchen table, sipping the water while staring into the faint glow of the single lamp.

A movement in the corridor alerted him to someone approaching. Hooch looked up a few seconds before Anne appeared in the door. She gasped and held a hand against her chest at the sight of him, illuminated in the faint glow. "Oh," she said, "sorry, you gave me a bit of a fright. Is everything alright? I was just getting myself a cup of peppermint tea—would you like one too?"

Hooch half stood, but sat back down when she spoke. "Yes, anything, please. Tea is fine. Thanks." Carefully avoiding her question if everything was alright. What was he to say? Things were okay, of course they were. If only he didn't dream of that goddamned stench.

She seemed to sense that he needed silence, as she boiled water and readied the tea. Soon, she had two large pottery mugs full of the brew and placed one in front of Hooch.

"When my dad came back from the war," she said in a conversational tone as she sat down, "he had trouble sleeping nights now and then, particularly if it was in a new place. It made for interesting family holidays, to say the least." She turned the mug in her hands, as though conscious that chatter was the last thing that Hooch needed.

Hooch looked at her without any expression, until a ghost of a smile crossed his face. "None of your kids could ever hide anything from you, right?"

She smiled. "No, but we've been very lucky with our brood. None of them have felt the need to conceal anything. Discretion, sometimes, of course." Letting that hang in the air, and allowing Hooch to pick up on it or not, as he chose.

Hooch nodded. "Fine line between concealing and discretion," a pause, "and protection."

"But a line nonetheless." Anne's fingers tapped on the handle of the mug and Hooch was struck by how similar in shape they were to Matt's. "He never hid from us that there was someone. He simply never said who. And might I say that we are very glad to find out who it is."

The ghost of a smile crossed Hooch's face again. The similarity in speech and manners was striking, and oddly comforting, too. "Thank you, but you don't know who I really am, what I've done, what I've seen."

She tilted her head. "I don't have to. In any case, I am fairly sure you're not allowed to tell me." She reached out a hand and put it on his forearm. "You and Matt found each other, and you let him bring you here. That's all that matters, here and now."

A minute twitch of his arm, an automatic reaction he could not control, before he relaxed into the touch. "I just..." he trailed off, studying the hand on his arm. He finally looked back up. "Tell me, Anne, do you think Matt would ever feel sorry for anyone?"

"Of course," the answer was immediate, "but that's not the question you're really asking, is it?"

Those steady, penetrating eyes, just like Matt's, bore into him.

"No, it's not. Of course not." A rueful smile flitted across his face. "I should have asked if he'd ever pity anyone." Again this almost-there smile, and then a shake of his head. "No, wrong again." He met her gaze straight on, with a fearless one of his own. "Do you believe he would ever pity me if he knew I am perhaps not as tough as thinks?"

Her eyebrows went up. "First, I think your particular starting point of toughness is rather off the far end of any normal scale. Second..." she hesitated, "forgive me if I pry, but Matt's already nursed you through a very bad illness or injury?"

"Yes," Hooch nodded once, no more than a curt jerk of his chin. "Almost a year ago now. I came out of my last mission with a broken pelvis." The art of understatement one he'd learned too well.

She didn't pry further into the injury. "I thought so. I think if he was going to pity you, it would have been then. But no, I don't believe he did, because that's simply not how the two of you work, is it?"

"No, but there's something he doesn't know. Something that isn't physical." Unspoken that for Hooch physical injuries were acceptable. Others…not.

Clarity, then, and understanding in her eyes. "Matt is very perceptive, you know," another pause, "and a much lighter sleeper than you might suppose."

A deep furrow appeared between Hooch's eyes, as he pondered her words. "But if he knows, why does he pretend he doesn't?"

"Ah, well," Anne's fingers curled around her mug, "probably for the same reason we never said anything to my dad about his sleepless nights." She took a sip, "pride is a touchy thing, isn't it?"

"Yes." Hooch took a sip, then studied the green tinged contents of his mug. "Matt…" he finally looked up, "I don't want to…" he shrugged and his face contorted for a moment in an expression of helplessness and frustration. "I don't know."

"We always do want to keep them from knowing the horrible things in the world, as though if they didn't know about it, somehow it would mean that the world wasn't all that bad." After a pause, that seemed to stretch out forever, "true enough that even most Marines won't have seen or gone through the things you have—but that doesn't mean he doesn't know very well." She sipped her tea. "Dad never really did do anything about his sleepless nights. There wasn't much that could be done, back then, even if he had sought help. They all wanted to simply forget, but that's not possible for anyone, even if they wish it."

"Yeah," Hooch's voice was soft, "that's it. If I pretend he doesn't know then it didn't really happen. It's bullshit, though."

The length of his silence matched her earlier one. Time for thoughts and understanding, perhaps even the beginnings of some realizations.

"I respect your opinion, Anne. What would you do?"

"Let him know, from you, and not just guess." She put the mug down gently. "He may or may not be able to make things any better, but I suspect both of you will be the better for it. You both are burdened with too many secrets already, and maybe he can be upfront to you, too. I suspect he's been trying to make sure you're too exhausted at night to dream."

Hooch's eyes flew open at the last bit. One thing to talk about what was innermost with her, another for the mother of his lover to imply them having sex. "I…" he stammered, "yeah, I guess, Matt…" Despite his best efforts, he colored slightly, hiding his discomfort behind the mug as he drained the last of his tea.

"I'll talk to him." He sat the empty mug down. "Thank you."

"You're welcome," Anne tried not to smile at Hooch's fluster and fumbling. "Anytime," she added, as Hooch left the kitchen, and she finally let herself grin widely into her cup. She'd been worried about him, but strangely, though clearly Hooch was a dangerous man to others, she didn't doubt at all how much he loved her baby boy. And that, at least for now, was what she cared about. The rest could wait, a very long time if need be.

When Hooch returned to the room, Matt was awake and sitting up, the covers bunched around his waist. "Hey," he looked anxious, "something wrong?"

"Hey." Hooch sat down on the bed in his shorts and t-shirt, pulling himself up to lean against the headboard. "Everything okay now. Had some tea with your mom." He looked at Matt, studying the handsome face and that goddamned perfect body, and yet all he could see right now was what he knew resided beneath the attractive exterior. "C'mere a sec."

Matt scooted closer, but there was still a wary concern in his eyes. "The last time you went all funny like this you told me you were a masochist," he grumbled, "any new surprises?"

"Not quite." Hooch chuckled low, as he wrapped his arm around Matt's shoulders to hold him close. It felt damn good, and it had only taken him a few years to realize that. "How often have you noticed me waking up in the middle of the night?"

Matt froze momentarily, then relaxed. "Less often than when you first came to my old place," he said, after a few moments' reflection.

Hooch huffed. "And you never said a word." He mock-slapped the top of Matt's head with a couple of fingers, taking his time before he continued. "It's always the same. Always the room we were locked up in."

Matt's frown was hidden in Hooch's shoulder. "Nightmares? Or memories?"

"Memories." Hooch looked down and right into Matt's eyes. "I never told you any details, I didn't want to burden you, but..." he shrugged gently, "I made that decision without giving you the chance to decide for yourself. You're no sensitive flower, you're a tough guy, Matt, I don't always keep that in mind." He took a slow, deep breath. "It's time to ask you now: do you want me to explain what I dream of?"

Matt nodded. "Yes," he moved out of Hooch's grasp and tugged at the covers, "but you should get under here. Central heating's not that good."

Pausing while Hooch pulled off the t-shirt and slipped out of his shorts, then got under the covers, before Matt scooted up close again, a hand ghosting over the scars left by the cigarette burns. "Never wanted you to think I was digging, not when I didn't know when I was going to hit a mine."

Hooch held Matt close, looking up at the ceiling, the night light still on. Not having to look at Matt while talking made it easier, and for once he allowed himself some cowardice. "I fractured my pelvis in the landing, you know that, and you know I was tortured. Cigarette burns were the easiest, much worse to be dropped from a height, landing with my broken pelvis, and then manipulating the broken bones." Hooch's voice was matter-of-fact, nothing else would do. "That's not what I dream of, though. What I didn't tell you was the place I was locked up in. A room with hundreds of men, all prisoners. So many, we stood crammed, pushed against each other. The stench...I can't get rid of it. Piss, shit, sweat, decomposing flesh. Each morning the corpses were shuffled towards the door." Hooch paused a moment. "Eventually, I wanted to let myself fall back and give up. That would have meant death, but I couldn't care anymore. That's the worst, knowing I gave up then." He paused again, forcibly relaxing his hand and his fingers, which had gripped Matt tightly. "I was saved by kindness. Fellow prisoners held me up, made me swallow food and liquid, took the weight off my pelvis. It's their arms I literally owe my life to."

A movement in his arms as Matt shuddered, and then stilled. "Yes." Because what else could be said that wouldn't add to Hooch's burdens? Matt's hands soothing Hooch, his chin on Hooch's shoulder. "Often?" he asked. "You don't toss and turn or anything...you just...stop...so it's hard to tell when it happens."

"Not that often." Hooch threaded his fingers into Matt's hair. It felt good, for more reasons than he'd ever cared to examine. "Had a lifetime of having to be silent in any situation, guess that's helping now." He let out a soft sound of brittle amusement. "It mostly happens when I'm in a new place, a new situation. Never figured I'd need stability and routine in my life. I've turned into a boring old fart."

"You? Never." Matt wriggled closer. "Plenty of new stuff this weekend, too." He stopped. "You said you talked to Mom...she tell you about grandpops?"

"Yeah, she did. That why you enlisted?" Hooch let his fingers run down to the back of Matt's neck, rubbing circles over the short hair there. "She also told me you made sure you tired me out every night so I'd sleep dreamless. Now that was fucking embarrassing."

Hooch wasn't the only one who evidently found that embarrassing, as Matt burrowed into Hooch's shoulder. "Oh, she *would* do that," he groused, "not that you seemed to object." He added, then sighed. "When I was a kid, I wanted to be just like grandpops. He was at D-Day, the works. I used to think of him, what he'd have thought, what he would have done, when I was in the Gulf." A pause. "He died when I was ten."

"Did you ever feel you were doing what he did?" Hooch increased the pressure of his fingertips. "I wanted to believe that what happened to me was for the good of our country, but it didn't work. The country knew jack shit about the reason why I was out there."

"Not quite the same thing, now, is it?" Matt sighed, "or at least it didn't...doesn't feel like it."

"Not the same thing at all, no matter what bullshit they feed us." And yet he still did his job. "The newscast...you mentioned it once, in the hospital. You saw me." Hooch didn't quite make it a question.

"Worst moment of my life," Matt's voice was muffled, "I think that was when I knew you meant more to me than anything. All the more so that..." He trailed off. No point re-iterating the craptastic situation after Hooch's capture: Matt unable to get any information or even seek any out, without raising some very awkward questions. Just getting to see Hooch at hospital had involved new heights of ingenuity and outright lying to achieve. Not to mention having to skulk around the corridors to avoid Hooch's family.

"Hey," Hooch murmured, "I'm here now, in your goddamned teenage bedroom, and I'm only sometimes back there in my dreams." He craned his head so he could look down at Matt. "I'll even go see a shrink if you want me to, or have a mug of hot cocoa before bedtime, if you prefer." Hooch smiled, one of his rare ones, which warmed the darkness of his eyes. "I belong hide and hair to one Matt Donahue with a loud family and a very clever mom."

"And you haven't even managed to survive brunch yet," Matt answered the smile, "I swear, I've never been able to work out how she gets Thanksgiving dinner and brunch done every year." He freed a hand from the tangle of duvet and ran a finger down the length of Hooch's nose. "As for the rest of it, we'll just take it as it comes. If I can be of any help..."

Hooch followed the fingers with his gaze until he was cross-eyed. "If I wake up again from that dream, can I wake you? Seems that being talked out of that godforsaken place of my dreams works quickest." He gave Matt's neck a squeeze. "I am making the assumption we'll soon be sleeping in the same bed every night. The apartment's almost finished?" He yawned, the late hour finally catching up with him. "I'm looking forward to informing my superiors of my change of address."

"You know you can wake me anytime" A chuckle from Matt, "I'd like to see the looks on their faces." Then, serious, "you think any of them know?" Unspoken 'about us.'

"I don't think they know, and if they do, they carefully don't want to know." Hooch looked positively amused. "They'll soon have a hard time 'not knowing'."

Matt chuckled quietly, his fingers lightly tracing up Hooch's cheekbone. "Sleep? We've got another few hours yet before the madness starts again and you promised a proper christening of this bed."

Hooch smiled a little. "Not sure I can right now, Matt."

One of Matt's rueful smiles, as he deliberately misunderstood. "I'll let you get away with it, for now, after the heart-to-heart and all. But I'll be gagging for it in the morning, just to warn you," echoing Hooch's words earlier in the night.

"As long as you don't mention your mom along the way, I am sure I'll be ready and waiting." Hooch slid down and onto pillow before reaching for the light. He held Matt close, his arms around him, as they went off to sleep at long last.

* * *

Matt was grateful that his body clock was still on Marines time when he blinked awake in the hazy predawn, still curled around Hooch, who was still asleep, his face relaxed. Unusual in itself, because Hooch tended to drift away during the night.

Unwilling to wake Hooch just yet, Matt slowly inched himself away. Propping himself up on an elbow, he took in the rare sight. Even during his recovery, Hooch was almost always awake before him.

A minimal shift in breathing would alerted Matt to Hooch sliding from asleep to awake. "Still a frog, not a prince yet, no matter how long you stare." Eyes still closed, a smile stole onto Hooch's features, keeping the frown at bay for a while longer.

Now that deserved a proper kiss, and Matt dived in. "Enough of the fishing for compliments," he said as he came up for air, "but I think that's enough to wake Sleeping Beauty?" He wriggled closer suggestively.

Hooch chuckled in the back of his throat. "You could always try to kiss me awake lower down."

A wicked grin spread over Matt's face as he pressed closer, feeling Hooch harden fully. "I think you're quite awake already," he reached over and behind Hooch to the dresser, where he'd left the lube.

Hooch was tracking him with his eyes, lying as still as a stature. His grin, though, began to widen, as Matt pulled the duvet back over them and moved about. Somehow, not being able to see what Matt was doing under the covers, made it all the more erotic. A few moments later Matt had straddled Hooch and was looking down at him.

"It's time for a swap of places." Hooch's voice remained quiet, always aware of the parents asleep in the adjacent room. He flipped them both over, letting the covers slip off, as he loomed over Matt, grinning down. "I bet you my ass that you won't be able to stay silent."

With the wager on, he threw himself into preparing Matt, like he'd throw himself into any mission: with utmost focus and equal skills. He knew just how to speed enough and yet not too much, before he buried himself into Matt's body, unleashing the strength of his own to give ultimate pleasure, his own secondary right now.

Matt's gasp at Hooch's entry was only barely muffled, and the grip on Hooch's arms tightened as Matt fought to keep silent. Usually a vocal lover, the effort to keep quiet showed in the tension in his muscles and his tightly gritted teeth, fighting against Hooch's skill and the urge to cry out. When he came, he bucked and bit his lip, but made no sound.

Once he had his breath back, he smirked up at Hooch. "I do believe that means I get to collect."

Hooch hadn't come yet, holding himself back for Matt's benefit, and he stilled any movement at Matt's smirk, matching it with one of his own.

"Right now?"

Matt's smile grew lazy and replete, like some big cat lazing in the sun as he tilted his hips upwards. "I suppose you can finish what you're doing first."

Hooch immediately began to move again. Long, slow thrust, gentle still.

Matt looked like he was going to purr, but remembered the terms of the bet and raised his arms to grasp the headboard. Watching Hooch from under hooded lids, clearly enjoying himself.

When Hooch let go he didn't do it with absolute abandon, but with a single focus that burnt through Matt. All of Hooch's lust and need, all of his strength, gathered in one point only, in the connection between their bodies.

Hooch made hardly any sound, controlling himself except for his harsh breath, and when he came, his eyes flew open, looking straight at Matt, as he shuddered through his orgasm.

Eventually, when he'd calmed down after collapsing on Matt, sweat and cum between their bodies but neither of them caring, he murmured sleepily, "guess you won."

Matt chuckled and held him tight, enjoying the weight and the sound of their heartbeats thudding together, but not the sound of the radio-alarm turning itself on in the next room, followed by movement. "But not in time to collect," he said softly into the almost-asleep Hooch's ear, before easing himself out from under Hooch, sliding out of the bed and pulling the covers up over Hooch before finding some clothes and padding to the bathroom.

* * *

The next few days were spent with Matt's family, the two of them being constantly overfed both in the house and when Matt took Hooch to all his old haunts. He was introduced as Matt's buddy from back in the Gulf War, in need of some good old-fashioned feeding up at Thanksgiving, which was true for Hooch, who hadn't been back to his normal weight yet. It got easier around Matt's large, loud and loving family, as they realized that Hooch wasn't as tactile as they were, and that they needed to give him space.

By the time they were ready to go, Matt's mother dropped them off at the airport with plenty of encouragement to come again, and boxes of cookies and cakes to take with them because they "could both do with some home cooking." She was surprised to find herself embraced by Hooch, who murmured "thank you" into her ear before letting go.

Matt gave one of his grins as they waved goodbye, just before heading to the boarding gate. "Told you you'd like them," he said to Hooch, as he shouldered his rucksack and balanced the box of cookies.

Hooch answered Matt's grin with one of his own. It was an odd feeling, he thought, but not at all an unpleasant one. A home, a partner—even a proper family unlike his own, things that had been the furthest from his mind the day he had enlisted, two decades ago.

NOVEMBER 1998, FAYETTEVILLE

When they returned to Fayetteville, Hooch stopped at the threshold of the apartment, staring, because the whole place had been finished while they'd been away. When he asked Matt how the fuck he'd managed to get anyone to work over the Thanksgiving weekend, he just grinned and shrugged.

The apartment had clean and simple lines, leather, white and chrome, with comfortable furniture that was just right for two tall and fit men who didn't give a crap about nicnacs and for whom the idea of interior decorating brought them out in hives.

It was the first true home Hooch had ever had since he'd joined up at eighteen, and even the ranch had never truly felt like home, except for the stables and the wide open land. This place, though, did, and it scared the shit out of him, because it was so goddamned good.

The bedroom got christened that night when Matt demanded the payment of Hooch's lost bet, and the next day saw a pleasantly sore and almost mellow Captain Hubert Bozic deal with a piece of admin in his life he'd never expected to deal with: the cancellation of his quarters on base and the change of his address.

A part of him had hoped that it would just slip by in the black hole that was administration on the base, but unlike countless other forms that had disappeared, it was not the case. The polite but firm summons to the office of the Colonel came all too soon.

The seriousness with which this triviality was being taken, was evident straight away. The Colonel was sitting at his desk, frowning, when Hooch came in. "Sit, Captain." It was between a request and an order.

Hooch's face immediately settled into the blank expression he'd mastered no matter the circumstances. This was going to be a pissing contest, he could read the signs as if written in neon capitals above his superior's head. "Good morning, Sir." Hooch greeted despite the lack of courtesy he'd received, and sat down. Two could play this game, and while he wasn't a Colonel he'd had more years of experience in the field than any of the more senior staff could ever dream of gaining. Besides, what did he have to lose? Not Matt, no matter what. Everything else paled in comparison, he'd learned that lesson during captivity.

"I see you're moving off base, Captain," the Colonel stated the obvious. "Quite sudden, isn't it?"

"The apartment hadn't been ready until now."

Hooch leaned back in his chair, legs a little open, staking his claim of the space and of his position in the pecking order. No superior had ever intimidated him, and this one wasn't going to change that.

Eyebrows raised, the Colonel looked down at the forms. "True enough, but you've never done so before. I see it's above a gym. Have you considered the security risks of such a location?"

"Yes." Hooch's gaze went slowly back to the Colonel's face. He wasn't crossing his arms just yet, but the invisible barrier could be felt in the charged atmosphere. A pre-emptive strike suited him better than defense. "I know the owner. He's got security clearance and is aware of the necessity of security measures due to my active status."

"Yes, I see, Mr. Matthew Donahue, recently Gunnery Sergeant, USMC, honorably discharged." The Colonel looked down, "I see that you stayed with him during your recovery. A friendship of long standing, I take it?"

"Since the Gulf, Sir." Hooch wasn't giving his superior even the fraction of an inch.

"I see." A completely unnecessary flipping of some papers in Hooch's file. "Unusual." Equally nonverbal, but a faint undercurrent of disapproval. "You'll be sharing the apartment with him?" The question came sideways, like a switchblade in an alley.

"I have my own room." Hooch's answer came just as quickly and as precisely, without a change in his neutral expression nor a blink of his eyes.

The Colonel made a noise that on anyone else would have been a dissatisfied grunt. "Convenient," a mountain of meaning in the word, "a qualified PTI keeping an eye on your condition."

"It is, isn't it, Sir?" Hooch wasn't going to budge, wasn't going to offer his superior even the tiniest hook to latch on. The man couldn't ask, after all, that was what DADT was all about—and thus he didn't have to tell. "I'm lucky."

A narrowing of eyes, and momentary speculation. The Colonel was an arrogant, unpleasant sod, but far from stupid, and he was rapidly putting together a few loose threads. "I gather so." Lips thinned, moved, as though he was working out what to say next. "A long-term arrangement?"

Bastard. Hooch knew exactly what he meant. He hyper-focused, just like he would during a mission. "That depends on the circumstances."

"I see," another unnecessary shuffling of papers. "I see." The Colonel paused, seemingly deep in thought, "and what are those circumstances?"

"The rent, for example." Hooch deadpanned.

Another not-grunt, as wheels visibly turned behind those disapproving eyes. "I see." A pause, considering, "quite a change for you, since you've lived on base for all of your career." No mention of just how many years that had been. "Remember that you'll need to be careful out there in ways you haven't needed to be on base."

"I am perfectly aware of any additional security measures, Sir." Hooch didn't acknowledge anything else. "Is that all now, Sir?"

The other man looked like he'd sucked on a lemon. "Yes, Captain," he said curtly, "so long as that's understood."

"Perfectly, Sir." Hooch stood up and saluted, then turned sharply to make his way out of the room.

Once outside he couldn't help the ugly grin appear on his face, as he went back to his office. He had men to train and a medical appointment that afternoon, he didn't have time to dwell on a stuck-up officer who'd probably like to see him fall.

Yet something inside of him raised its head, an itch he'd buried deep down for so long, but which he once more pushed away. Not yet. It wasn't time yet.

* * *

When Hooch returned home that evening, later than usual but still with the novelty factor of actually returning to a home, Matt was throwing something together in the kitchenette. Hooch figured it would be some sort of lean meat and some sort of salad. Matt's culinary skills were marginally better than Hooch's nonexistent ones, but his interest in nutrition was a lot more developed.

"Hey," Matt flashed a bright smile, "something wrong?"

"Just a stuck up bastard of a superior." Hooch shrugged and dropped his pack near the door.

Matt made a noise of sympathy, "that sucks." He laid out plates and glasses on the dining table.

"Yeah, especially as he kept going on about my change of address." Hooch went to the fridge and took out a large bottle of carbonated water. He looked at it, put it back into the fridge, then pulled out a beer instead.

Matt visibly tensed. "Do you think he's guessed?" It was a strange feeling: he didn't have to be wary for himself anymore, but he had to be for Hooch, which was a lot more nerve-wracking.

"I'm damned sure. The guy's as subtle as a tank." Hooch cracked open the beer bottle and finished half of it in one long draft, before sitting down at the table. "Of course, he couldn't ask."

Matt visibly relaxed, taking Hooch's words at face value, as he dished out the food and added a bottle of water for himself. "I never thought to ask—but do you think anyone on base is going to be a shithead about us?"

"Apart from that dickhead? No." Hooch poured Matt a glass of water. "None of the guys I worked with ever gave a shit about where I want to stick my dick." He watched Matt help himself to the salad, then got a smaller portion for himself. "That's precisely what's pissed off the Colonel."

Matt made a non-committal sound, "and your guys would just see what they expect to see anyway, even if they did give a shit." He took a piece of meat. "How's it going on the other side?" Leaving it open for Hooch to interpret whether he meant as a trainer, or an officer.

Hooch's fingertips involuntarily fluttered against the beer bottle, before he took control and stilled them. "It's not the same." His gaze slid away from Matt, concentrating on his chicken with a little too much focus to be convincing.

Matt had to remind himself not to hover too obviously, because that would piss Hooch off. He settled for eating in silence for a few minutes. "No, it wouldn't be," that sounded neutral enough, leaving Hooch room. It was a funny thing, this living together, no more passing by and being 'Central Station', but a true, honest to goodness couple.

Hooch finished the chicken and most of the salad, fork and knife still in his hands, unmoving. Eventually he took in an audible breath and looked at Matt. "Part of me hates it. Really fucking hates it. Other part knows I'm too old even without the injury. Still having trouble with the first part. Makes me itch."

Sympathy was generally inappropriate around Hooch, and platitudes an even worse idea. All the more so now, when there really was nothing anyone could do. "Ah," Matt settled for the monosyllable, and for giving Hooch space.

That got a lightning-fast grin from Hooch. There and gone again, but the after effects lingered around the corners of his eyes. "Yeah, 'ah'." He put the cutlery down. "As for good news, phys exam today came back clear. X-rays show the fracture's completely healed and the MD thinks I'm fit for all the duties of my new role."

Matt answered the grin with one of his own, longer lasting. "That's great," it was mixed with relief. "Pity this is as close to anything with bubbles we've got." He looked at the carbonated water. "Or else we should have a toast to new beginnings."

"Don't feel like celebrating. It's a new beginning alright, but except for being here in this place can't find that much to celebrate." Hooch twisted the almost empty beer bottle in his hand. "Give me time, Okay? Need to get my bearings in the new job."

Matt looked like he was going to say something else, but settled for nodding instead. "'kay," he echoed, giving Hooch a long look. Caring, but not intrusive, letting the other man sit with his thoughts.

"Thanks." Hooch smiled before falling silent as well, until Matt finished his own meal. "Have we got any dessert?"

There was a look on Matt's face, slightly chagrined, that Hooch didn't quite understand, until Matt went back into the kitchen area and came out with a plate with red velvet cupcakes, frosted with cream cheese and decorated with little red sugar hearts. "How did you know? Mandy brought them in today." He paused, as though considering whether to confess something, "they're very good." The words were reluctant.

Hooch showed his teeth in a sudden smirk. "Did the saintly Matt break down?" Still grinning, he reached for one of the cupcakes, greedily biting into it. "What's the occasion?"

"Belated housewarming, she said," Matt watched Hooch with amusement. "She was certain that you'd like them because you're a Southerner, too, and she was horrified when I told her that I've never had them before." He took one off the plate. "You can have the rest, if you like," he added rather unnecessarily at Hooch's covetous look.

"Looks more like a Valentine's offering to the attractive boss to me." Hooch swallowed the last bite of the first cake and reached for another. "What with all the hearts."

Matt opened his mouth to counter Hooch's remark with a reminder that it was November, not February, and most importantly that he was a good ten years older than Mandy, until he realized it was exactly the same gap between him and Hooch. Mandy really wasn't all that much younger than he had been the first time in that safe house in Saudi Arabia. "I hope not," he said after a moment, "that would be the last thing that I need, but I doubt it. She's bound to have plenty of boys her own age after her—she's not going to look at her old boss that way. And despite the ditziness, I think she's too sensible to risk it."

Hooch nearly sprayed cake crumbs across the table with his sudden laugh. "Old boss? How old is she? Eighteen, nineteen?" Hooch leaned back and grinned. "Last time I checked, you knew damn well how good you look, and while it would be annoying for different reasons," he gestured between Matt and himself, "I think Mandy fancies you. Cupcakes with hearts? Dead give-away."

Matt was frowning. "No, seriously, I don't think so. Not that either of us can claim to be an expert on women. If you're right, though, at least it'll be good cover, and I'll have an excuse to say 'no' to her if you are right."

"What would that excuse be?" Hooch clearly didn't believe Matt.

Matt gave him a look. "I don't screw staff. Figuratively, literally or in any other sense."

"Do you screw roommates?" Hooch flashed a predatory grin.

Matt returned it, glad at least that this part of Hooch remained unchanged despite the earlier low mood. "Only those who help with the dishes first."

"Bastard." Hooch countered good naturedly, but got up and grabbed their plates. "I'll buy a dishwasher."

Matt snorted under his breath, and said something inaudible about people who couldn't fill up a sink, but got out a tea-towel to dry and put away the dishes, the shared domestic chore somehow soothing in its normality.

When the last dish had been dried, Hooch pushed Matt forward and against the sink. "And now?" He moved his hips against Matt's deliciously perfect ass.

Matt pushed back, "and now we go into the bedroom, like proper, civilized people." He threw a grin over his shoulder as he slipped out and sauntered off towards the bedroom.

"Civilized. As if." Hooch followed Matt in record time and kicked the door shut behind them.

✳ ✳ ✳

Though the early days were difficult, particularly since they were starting in the winter, Matt's gym quickly began to take off. Word-of-mouth spreading and he soon had a core, loyal clientele that was split between the active and ex-military and the gay professionals that seemed to grow by the week. Much to Matt's amazement, the gym broke even months ahead of schedule, and he watched with satisfaction as the mortgage was steadily paid down.

Mandy proved to be an organizational wizard, had the gym running like clockwork, while somehow fitting in her college classes around the operating hours. Save asking for a few days off for exams twice a semester, Matt scarcely noticed a break in the bubbly, ruthless efficiency and the smiles and cheerfulness that permeated the gym.

The red velvet cupcakes had started a tradition, and Mandy often brought in cakes and cookies and pie for Matt and Hooch. 'Love offerings' Hooch continued to tease, but Mandy never gave any indication that she saw them as anything other than her boss and his roommate, two military men who couldn't bake but needed some treats. She had an irregular series of no-hoper boyfriends, none, in Matt's mind, good enough for her, and certainly not deserving of the momentary gloom that each caused at the inevitable breakup.

Hooch settled into his new job best he could, never quite making his peace with not being out in the midst of danger anymore, but very much getting into training 'his boys' and relishing the responsibility of preparing them to the very best of their ability—and beyond—to face the worst possible situations. He rapidly became the most feared, and the most loved and respected training officer in Fort Bragg. Anyone who was good enough to be selected for Delta training was equally looking forward to and being apprehensive of being drilled by him, because Hooch demanded everything and more, while respecting them as they respected him in return.

Domestic life settled into a comfortable routine, as comfortable as living with Hooch could be. His most redeeming trait, that of always and everywhere being up for sex and never waning in his appetite for Matt in whichever and whatever way they wanted, balanced out all the annoying traits of being mostly silent, occasionally obnoxious, and sometimes oddly sociopathic.

All in all, things were settling in nicely in Fayetteville, and life was as good as it could be.

2001

JUNE 2001, FAYETTEVILLE

Hooch came home one evening to a somber, silent Matt sitting at the dining table, toying with a half-full tumbler of the good Scotch that had been a gift.

"Matt?" Hooch knew something was wrong at the sight of the whisky. Matt hardly ever drank anymore, something about the negative effect of alcohol and its calories on the perfectly balanced body. "What's up?" He dropped his pack beside the door and walked over to the couch.

Matt looked up, tight lipped, definitely more than worried. He pushed something that had been lying in front of him towards Hooch. A photograph, and a slip of paper with typed lines.

Hooch sat down and reached for the photograph. He stared at it, frozen. Not saying anything for a long time, just looking at the picture, until he eventually read the few lines. His face remained expressionless when he turned back to Matt, but the storm raging in his dark eyes showed the fury bottled up inside of him. "How?"

"Fuck knows." Matt swallowed, and finished the rest of the drink. "I found it pushed under the door when I came up after the 1800 hours class."

"That," Hooch pointed at the photo print, "was on fucking Sunday. We were downstairs."

Matt twisted the glass. "Mandy was in in the morning." He kept his eyes on the empty glass. "We were doing the new website this week so she was behind on the schedules for next month."

"Mandy? Shit." Hooch looked at the photo again, then the note. "That makes no sense. Does she have money troubles?"

Matt shook his head. "Not that I know of." He gazed off into middle distance. "She hasn't said anything. And she would." He paused. "I'd have thought she would," he corrected, hating himself.

"I can't imagine I could have got her character so fucking wrong!" Hooch clenched his hand in a fist. "What the fuck do we do now? 'Wait to be contacted' isn't my goddamned style."

"It's not hers, either," Matt didn't touch the bit of paper, "at least I thought not." He closed his eyes. "Of all people, she's got to know us and this place inside out, and has for years. Why now?" He opened them again. "And she's off for the next three days."

"Yeah, why now. Makes no fucking sense." Hooch had a hard time holding himself back, the anger raging inside. "We need to talk to her." He slammed his fist on the table, the unspent angry energy too much to contain.

"Fuck! I'm going to fucking kill the bastard who's responsible for this, and I don't give the flying fuck who that is."

Matt looked pale. "I frankly don't know what would be worse, that it's Mandy, who I've trusted with practically everything but this, or that there's someone else out there." He paused, looking at the phone lying on the table. "Should I call her cell now and say it's an emergency and to come in tomorrow morning, or surprise her when she's back in a few days?"

"Call her now. Don't give her time, if it was her. If this photo gets into my CO's hands…"

Matt nodded and made the call, sounding far calmer and measured than he felt. A twinge as Mandy promised to be in first thing in the morning, before the first class, as bright and bubbly as ever.

Hooch kept pacing the room, listening to the one-sided conversation. When Matt switched off, he looked across at him. "And now? What do we do now? Nothing?"

"Not while you're in that state." Matt was deadly calm, as though the anger, the hurt and the fear had already burned through him.

"This isn't anything I was trained for. This is personal."

"And if we're wrong? It doesn't make any sense for it to be her, and you know if we're wrong we'll be outing ourselves to her anyway."

"Shit." Hooch stopped his pacing. "It's almost worse if we're wrong and it isn't her."

Matt nodded. "As I said, I don't know what would be worse." He slumped. "So, since it was all shit anyway, I'm drinking again." He toasted Hooch with the empty glass.

"Right." Hooch took a deep breath, fighting hard to get himself back under control and into mission mode, even though this was everything but a mission. "It's Friday. I suggest we get shitfaced."

"Excellent idea," Matt agreed.

Hooch knew it wasn't an excellent idea, in fact it was most probably the stupidest one they could come up with, but it was also the only one that seemed fitting right now. He went to the fridge and got the six pack of beer, a second glass, and a three quarter bottle of Russian vodka. He brought his haul to the couch area, parked it on the table next to the whisky bottle and Matt's glass, then poured himself a large glass of vodka and Matt one of whisky. "Whatever happens, Matt Donahue, I take dishonorable discharge over anything else. Got it?"

Matt nodded, "got it," and slammed down his drink.

Neither slept well that night, and despite nagging hangovers, they were up and downstairs in the office well before Mandy pulled up in the parking lot and unlocked the front door of the gym. Her habitual perkiness only slightly punctuated by a yawn.

She caught the looks on both men's faces. "What's wrong?" she asked, concern all over her features.

Hooch was about to step right into her personal space to loom over her, when Matt held him back.

"Hooch, maybe you should just wait outside the office," he said firmly, and turned back to a very confused Mandy.

"Okay." Hooch reluctantly let his stare slide off Mandy. Watching their backs as they went into Matt's office, the door kept ajar.

Mandy looked at Matt, the smile fading off her face. "What's happened?" her voice low and, for once, no exclamation mark at the end of the sentence.

"Please sit down." Matt indicated a chair at the small round table in his office, and sat down as well. All too aware at any time of the presence of Hooch outside. "Mandy, this is a delicate question." He rubbed the heel of his hand over his eyes. Damnit, he had a hangover and his head was pounding, but he had to get through with this. "Do you have money troubles?"

She frowned at him. "No, well, no more than usual."

Matt nodded slowly. Okay, that wasn't going all too well, the subtle approach had never worked for him anyway. "So you aren't looking for ways to make more money?" Damn, but that was a stupid thing to say. He blamed his headache, or just the fact he had no clue how to go about a situation like this. "Thing is, I received a photo. And..." this was it. He heard Hooch pace outside, and this was the moment of no return, "...and a blackmail letter."

A gasp, and her jaw dropped. "You...and Captain Bozic? And you think that I..." her bottom lip trembled, and she stared at him with wide, shocked eyes.

"I'm sorry, Mandy, I really am, but..." Matt flustered the moment the trembling bottom lip was joined by large eyes filled to the brim with tears. When she began to cry, he realized he'd just accused her of a major breach of trust. He didn't know what to do with the crying girl, but Hooch rescued him when he stuck his head into the room.

Hooch was unfazed by the tears. "Mandy, did you say 'you and Captain Bozic?'"

She sniffled, "what else would they blackmail you with when you're both here? It's not as though you're cheating your taxes or underpaying anyone or hiring anyone illegally or building code violations or anything."

Hooch stepped inside the room, looking first at Mandy, then at Matt. "You know we are…?"

"Together?" Mandy finished helpfully, sniffing again, "aren't you?"

"Uhm…" Matt stammered, while Hooch reached for the box of tissues on Matt's desk, wordlessly handing it to Mandy, while Matt tried again. "Well, yeah, but how?"

Mandy took a handful of tissues. "It was pretty obvious right from the beginning," she blew her nose, "sending me off to get you both lunch that first day and just paying for the two of you automatically without either of you saying anything because you needed to talk about something personal; when you kept mentioning whether Hooch wouldn't like this or that when we were doing the apartment, how you nearly always go on holidays together, spend most weekends together, go to Matt's family for Thanksgiving together; all your bills go out from the same account and there's never any quibbling; how both your bedrooms are always locked when I send the cleaner in but most times there are only footsteps going in and out of one of them when either one of you is getting changed; neither of you've ever had a woman stay overnight and you're nearly always here every morning; you never have buddies over to watch the game or anything; you never check out any of the women who come here, even though the few who come here are all pretty hot; you don't do your laundry or your grocery shopping separately, and you're always so careful not to touch each other in public." It was a long, disjointed list, which ended with Matt holding his pounding head in his hands and Hooch sitting down with a groan.

"Shit." From both of the men, almost simultaneously. Followed by "we're so busted," from Matt.

She looked at them while wiping her nose. "I mean, there was also that neither of you made a pass at me, but that's quite easily explained by good manners."

"And age," Hooch commented drily. He'd pulled himself together quicker than Matt, and for the first time ever in Mandy's presence, he rested his hand on Matt's shoulder. "I'm sorry we suspected you." Matt nodded and sighed as Hooch continued, "but who the hell took a photo of us in the gym?"

"Here?" She was taken aback, "but I've made sure that nobody's ever on the same routine long enough to see any patterns."

"You did?" Matt gasped out, looking at Hooch who appeared suitably impressed with her foresight. "The photo was…wait." Matt searched in his pocket, producing the photo and the blackmail note. "Here. It must have been taken on Sunday."

She bit her lip and looked out the window into the gym. Almost the same angle. "It's from my office," she said softly, "I see how you thought it was me, but it was just me in there. I told Mike to wait for me outside." Her shoulders slumped.

"Mike?" Hooch immediately latched onto the name and the person like he'd focus on a target at the shooting range. "Who is Mike?"

"My boyfriend," Mandy replied, "we were heading out afterwards for lunch so I told him to pick me up from here."

"Did you ever, at any time, leave your boyfriend on his own? Think, Mandy." Hooch urged, while Matt reached for the photo and gently took it back out of her hands. Hooch and Matt, kissing. Just a simple kiss. One that could destroy Hooch's career and annihilate all his military successes.

She shook her head slowly. "I don't think he came in here this far. I remember when I saw his car pull in I was just about finishing up, so I went to the bathroom and when I came out he was waiting for me just inside the door. It was windy out." She added, "so he stepped in out of the wind."

"That must be it," Matt concluded. "You take a while in the bathroom, Mandy, no offence, and that would have given your boyfriend enough time."

Hooch looked at her, "how long have you known him? Are you aware of any money troubles that he might have?"

Mandy looked miserable, shredding the tissue in her hands. "Sorry," she said in a small voice, "just a few weeks. No money problems as far as I know, but..." She paused, as though realizing something, and shrank even further. "He had a new digital camera on Sunday," her eyes were firmly on the table, "and I remember it was odd, because he wouldn't let me have a go on it, when usually he can't wait to show off his new stuff."

"Where did you meet the guy?" Hooch was like a dog with a bone.

She sniffed, her face blotchy from tears, "it was at a party in the student union. I don't know who brought him with them, he isn't one of the students." She blew her nose noisily. "I thought he was cool."

"Cool." Hooch snorted, but anything else he was about to let rip remained unsaid, when Matt placed a hand on his arm to calm him.

"Can you remember what you might have told him about your job, or anything that might have given the guy the idea to snoop around and take pics?" Matt asked.

"No, I…don't know." Mandy admitted, misery incarnate. "I was so happy, because he came straight to me at that party, and he was flirting with me all night."

Matt looked pointedly at Hooch, before he asked carefully, "do all of your friends know where you work?"

"Sure," she nodded, before blowing her nose once more. "It's a cool job, so I told them all about you and the gym, the guys who come here, how much fun it is."

"Did you also talk about me?" Hooch tried to keep his voice from being razor sharp, but when Mandy cringed nevertheless.

"Uhm…no, not really, just that there's a cool Delta guy who's my boss's roommate." She blushed furiously when she looked down at her hands, sounded wretched and guilty. "I think I was a bit drunk and I might have boasted about how cool you two are."

Hooch groaned, but was quickly silenced by Matt, who had a lot more sympathy with Mandy's faux-pas than Hooch could ever muster. She wasn't exactly enemy and counter-intelligence trained by the military.

"Could it be," Matt carefully asked, "that some of your friends who are friends with this guy, talked to him about what you told them?"

She was still looking at her hands. "I don't know…but it's possible?"

"I'm just thinking that all of this might have been planned by that guy."

"You mean he was never interested in me and just used me to get to you for blackmailing?" She was more upset than ever, tears falling once more.

"I'm sorry, Mandy." Matt said softly while handing her another tissue.

"Can you imagine Mike doing something like that? Blackmailing us?" Hooch chipped in.

"I don't know," she looked like she had to force herself to look at them, eyes puffy and swimming with tears that kept spilling over. "I hope not," she said miserably.

"Well…" Matt tried to comfort her, "you've not been having a whole lot of luck with boyfriends since you came here. I'm sorry, Mandy, but I couldn't help notice.

"I never really have," she agreed. She took a breath, considering, deciding, weighing up, but in the end it was clear to her. "Do you want his address?" she asked, somewhat unnecessarily.

"Yes." Hooch said a little too quickly.

She reached for a pen and paper in its usual place on Matt's desk and wrote it down, handed it over. Dabbing at her eyes before blowing her nose, she visibly pulled herself together and sat up straighter. "Oh, Hooch?" she asked, "it all of this is true and he really plan the blackmail..."

"Yeah?" Hooch raised his eyebrows.

"Could you leave enough of him for me to dump?"

Hooch carefully smoothed his expression back to blank. "I don't know what you mean, Mandy."

Neither Matt nor Mandy commented on that blatant lie, both of them wise enough to realize the less they knew the better.

They sent her off with reassurances and apologies, Matt being particularly concerned that Mandy would take it badly that for a while he hadn't trusted her, but she seemed alright albeit heartbroken at yet another, this time epic, failure of a boyfriend.

When she was gone, the two men went back upstairs before the gym opened.

"You know what I want to do, don't you?" Hooch said the moment the apartment door closed behind them. "Question is, is it wise to do what I want to do right now, or better to wait for the next contact?"

"Not right now," Matt fiddled with the coffee machine, "not when we're both feeling rather..." someone else might have said 'homicidal', but they were people for whom it would be rather easy to put it into practice. "Soon. I don't like waiting any more than you, and given what we suspect, I don't want to give him any more time to do anything stupid."

Hooch nodded. He ruthlessly shoved down the restless energy that wanted him to act right *now*. "Exactly my thinking. Wait till he contacts us again, and I'll be there like that." He snapped his fingers.

Matt nodded, put a large mug of coffee in front of Hooch, sparing a glance at the scrap of paper. A name, an address. "That stupid, stupid child." He shook his head. "So much damage from such a stupid idiot."

"He won't be able to do any further damage." The dangerous glint in Hooch's dark eyes hinted at what exactly he was planning.

"Just nothing that..." Matt thought for a minute for the right word. Not 'regret,' as Hooch didn't tend to do that. "Nothing that's going to make this an even bigger mess." He finished.

Hooch let out a short, sharp, entirely humorless laugh. "I'll just frighten him enough to never again think of blackmailing anyone, least of all us. No major damage, I promise."

Hooch's idea of 'major' was rather different to most peoples', but Matt had a hard time feeling sorry for the imbecilic, hapless Mike.

"Okay."

"Deal." Hooch stepped close, the energy still strumming through his body, running right beneath the surface of his skin. "And now, since it's Saturday, we should go back to bed. I know a fail-safe cure for hangovers."

Matt snorted, but smiled despite the headache and the worry. He collected both their coffee cups and dumped them in the sink before heading back into the bedroom.

Making very sure that the blinds were pulled down.

* * *

The weekend remained tense, and early on Monday morning, in amongst the mail, was a plain typed envelope and another note, naming a nearby park as a location to meet, where the blackmailer would hand over the memory disk for a price.

"It's hard to believe this guy's really that stupid." Hooch read the note before handing it back to Matt. "It'll still be light by the time he wants to meet, I need to stall him."

"I'm not sure whether stupidity in this case is a good or bad thing." Matt folded the note and put it back in the envelope. "It's not as though we don't know where he lives. He could always be delayed at home."

"Good point." Hooch was on his way to the door where is pack was waiting for the day ahead. "I will make sure I get off base on time. I have a change of clothes with me, no need to make myself easily identifiable."

Matt watched as Hooch shouldered his pack and headed down, footsteps somehow louder than usual.

It would all be over soon, he thought, and catching sight of the note and the envelope, he scrunched them up and threw them against the wall in a rare expression of temper. Cursing their own carelessness, the viciousness of a greedy boy, and the stupid rules that hung over his and Hooch's life.

It was going to be a long day, and he felt a twinge of relief that Mandy would not be in. Facing either the guilt of having accused her, or her over-enthusiastic cheerfulness if she had decided to let it all pass, was unthinkable today.

* * *

That late afternoon, an hour before the appointed time in the public park, Hooch stood in front of a door to a small apartment in a run-down apartment building. Dressed inconspicuously in black jeans and white t-shirt, he stepped out of sight of the peephole, as he rang the bell.

"Yeah?" The voice that came through the thin door was young, male, and punctuated with a yawn.

"UPS, got a parcel for ya." Hooch exaggerated the drawl of his accent.

The door opened immediately to reveal a tall, dark-haired man in his early twenties, unshaven and wearing a stained T-shirt and threadbare jeans. "Whatcha got?" he asked, not really looking at Hooch.

"A very special delivery." In one fluid motion Hooch stepped inside, bodily pushing Mike backwards, while kicking the door shut behind him. Before the guy could gather his wits about him, Hooch had him with his back against the wall, the full length of Hooch's body pressed against him, effectively pinning him in place.

Hooch's voice was deadly calm and quiet. "The special delivery is that of a ransom note. The ransom for your life, buddy."

Mike's mouth moved, but it was a few seconds before any sound came out. "Who the fuck are you, man?"

"Don't recognize me from the photo?" Hooch pressed his forearm against Mike's windpipe to emphasize his question.

Mike's eyes widened, taking in the cool, calm man, such a contrast from the pressure on his throat.

"Well?" Hooch smiled an entirely fake smile that never reached his dark eyes. "Do you?"

There was movement against his arm that indicated Mike was trying to swallow or nod, and in the end he did some strange hybrid of both. "Fag," he coughed, not realizing the trouble he was in.

"What did you just say?" Hooch's fake smile widened until all teeth were on display.

More bravado than bravery, Mike looked back. "Fag," he repeated, with all the stupidity of some small rodent facing down a panther.

"I'm not sure I heard right." Hooch said very quietly. Without warning, he spun Mike round, with a hand twisted into the guy's hair, he slammed his forehead into the wall, then followed with his body, pressing all along Mike's back. "Could you repeat that again?" Hooch stood still, as if nothing had ever happened.

"That's disgusting! Get off me!" Mike struggled to no avail, starting to yell obscenities at Hooch. "You fucking fag! Don't touch me!"

Hooch didn't relent, kept his full body weight on Mike, pinning him against the wall, mashing his face into the grotty wallpaper for good measure. He didn't move nor did he say anything, letting the little piece of shit rant through an entire arsenal of homophobic hatred.

"Done yet?" Hooch eventually commented, when Mike was forced to draw in a breath.

"No, you fucking bastard!" Mike tried to spit, but Hooch slammed his head twice more against the wall.

"Now?"

Mike wailed, spittle flying. "You fucking fag are getting what you fucking deserve!"

"And that would be?" Still appearing calm, deadly and dangerous, Hooch could have killed the guy and would have only felt a modicum of satisfaction. Every fiber in his body strumming with anger and adrenaline.

"Dishonorable discharge!" Mike yelled.

Hooch lost it. With a roar he grabbed Mike by a shoulder and hip, and flung him half across the room, where he crashed into a rickety low table

Mike screamed in pain and flailed, struggled to sit up slowly, badly bruised and disoriented. "What the fuck do you want?"

"What I *want*? I want to wipe scum like you off the face of the earth." Hooch snarled. "Wrong question, try again." He took a couple of steps towards the guy on the floor.

Mike's eyes narrowed, finally getting it, or at least some part of it. Still too full of himself and his nasty little scheme to give up. "If you want the photos, It'll cost ya, like I said. Bet there's a few guys on base who'd find that photo very interesting."

"See, that's where you got it wrong." Hooch had himself back under control, once more the ice cold man who kept his fury locked down. He took another step, now close enough that his boot touched Mike's leg. "It's not going to cost me anything at all, because I don't play the games of little shits like you" With another all-too quick movement, he bent down, twisted his fist into Mike's grimy t-shirt, and pulled the guy up, as if he weighed nothing.

"Fuck, man," Mike gasped, "you can't do this. I'll call the cops." Realizing too late, that doing anything at all was going to be difficult with a very tough, coolly calm man holding the front of his shirt.

"Wrong again." Hooch gave Mike a shake as if he were a puppet, despite them being the same height. "Not only can I do it, I actually *will* do it." Mike never saw the knee cap that connected sharply with his groin, before Hooch dropped him.

Mike squealed as he fell back, landing heavily on the stained carpet. "You'll never find it," he covered his groin, face distorted into a grimace, "and you'll never know how many copies I've made."

"Perhaps." Hooch delivered a swift kick, and Mike howled in pain when the boot connected with his fingers that had been shielding his cock. Another kick and Mike's legs were spread apart. Hooch stepped between them, and placed his booted foot onto the groin, pressing down hard. "I'll make sure you'll never show it to anyone. You understand?" Increasingly adding weight onto his foot.

"You can't make me." Mike tried to move and to throw Hooch off balance, but instead Hooch delivered a well-placed kick between Mike's leg. Short, sharp, and utterly precise.

This time, Mike screamed and nearly passed out. "You fucking maniac!" he spat, curling into a ball from the pain. "You fucking fag, who do you think you are?"

"I'm the man who is going to stop you from ever blackmailing anyone again." Adrenaline was surging inside of Hooch, burning with a fury he didn't allow to show. "So. Where's the disk? You have three seconds, before I kick your face in. One…two…"

"Hey, hey, hey, hey," Mike held up his hands, "blackmail? You're the one who's breakin' the law, man, I thought I'd be a-decent like and give you right of first refusal-like."

"Decent. I see. As decent as someone who picks out a girl, flirts with her, and pretends to be into her, because he'd figured she worked at a place that might have to *fags* he could blackmail to get him some bobs. Am I right?"

When Mike didn't answer, just stared at him bug-eyed, Hooch took a step forward, which made Mike frantically edge away.

"Listen, you dickhead, your stupidity stinks so badly, I could follow the trail of the foul smell right to this place." Before he had finished the last word, Hooch straddled Mike as he went down on the floor. Knees clamping Mike's sides, both his hands fixing Mike's above his head and to the floor. Are you telling me it wasn't you? Are you telling me you didn't plan it right from the start?"

For the first time—far too late, Mike realized just what real danger he was in, and his eyes bulged out as strained but was completely unable to move.

Hooch could feel the moment the guy realized it was over. Mike's whole body sagged in defeat.

"Then are you telling me that it *was* you?" This was almost too easy. Hooch needed a fight, wanted a reason to wreak more damage, and to feel the pain of fists, boots and bodies clashing.

But all Mike gave him was a slight nod.

"What," Hooch leaned down, face to face, "cat got your tongue?"

"Y-y-y-yes," Mike stuttered, desperately cringing away. "Yes, I've got it. I swear nobody else has it, nobody knows about it."

"Good, but what assurances do I have that you'll destroy everything after you've handed me the disk?" Hooch shifted his upper body so that his elbows ground into Mike's biceps. "I want to be sure that you will leave Matt, me," more weight bearing down, "and Mandy alone."

There was death in those eyes, Mike realized at last. He'd run into some nasty types before, drug dealers and the like, but nothing came close to this. "Look man, you can check anything you like, it'll all be gone, I promise, and I never saw a thing and I'll never come near you again and I'll tell the broad it's me and not her, and it'll be as though this never happened. See?" he scrambled desperately, while panting against the pain.

Something deep down inside of Hooch, beyond deadly and above human, wanted to hear a scream tear out of this little piece of shit. "I want a guarantee or I'll come back"

"Anything!" Mike pleaded, "anything you like." The first a shout, the second a whisper.

"You will send an email to Mandy, telling her you are a stinking rotten bastard and that you will never bother her life again, and apologize. Then you will hand me the disk and any copy you might have made." Hooch still wanted a fight, but he needed a worthy opponent. Only the thin tethers of society rules held Hooch back from destruction. "Most importantly, I give you two days to move out of the area and far away. If you are still here after that, I will finish what I've started today."

There was wetness beneath Hooch, and he realized that Mike had wet himself in terror. A defeated, pathetic cur under the gaze of the contemptuous alpha wolf.

Hooch lifted his hips, his face showing his disgust. "Up." He moved off the body on the floor, made one small hand movement. "Email. Disk."

Mike scuttled away towards the computer in the corner, as though trying to make himself as small as possible.

Hooch stood close, arms crossed in front of his chest once more. He checked the email over, then nodded once. "Send." Another economic gesture. "Disk."

Mike fumbled, handing the small flat square over, and then, in a show of initiative, demonstrated on the nearby camera that the offending photograph was deleted from the camera's memory.

"Well done." Pocketing the disk, Hooch turned to walk to the door, unconcerned by showing his back. "Remember," he opened the door, "two days. I'll check."

Mike slumped back into his chair, trembling, staring at the door. After a moment, he got up, went to the bedroom, and started frantically throwing his belongings into a bag. He loaded everything that would fit into his car that very night and headed out on the highway, going west. He could cancel his lease and everything else away from Fayetteville. Very, *very* far away.

* * *

Hooch returned home straight away, while everything inside of him screamed out for a different course of action: to find a way of letting off steam. He needed to find a way to dissolve the tension from a fight that hadn't been a fight and an opponent that hadn't been worth it, but he forced himself to ignore the demand.

The gym was closed by the time he got back—it wasn't worth opening late early in the week—and Matt was upstairs in the apartment. The door opened before Hooch reached the top of the stairs.

"Hey." Hooch forced himself to remain calm, not allowing the darkness to show. "Here's the disk." Holding his hand out with the disk in the palm of it.

Matt took it, turning it over in his hand. Such a small and nasty thing. He looked up at Hooch. "Mike?"

"Broke up with Mandy by email, and is moving out of Fayetteville." Hooch closed the door behind him. "Probably right now, considering his state. He pissed himself while I talked to him."

Matt nodded. "Good." He looked at Hooch, seeing the tension. "Food?" He looked down at Hooch's groin, momentarily puzzled by the slight dampness visible even on the dark denim, and then remembered Hooch's last words. "Or bed?"

"Bed." Thank fuck for Matt and his perceptiveness. "Definitely bed." Hooch pulled the t-shirt off, before opening the buttons of his denims. "I need…" Damn. He couldn't say what he really needed. Pain. Anger. Aggression. Fight. "You." No lie. He needed Matt, always would.

Matt smiled, just a fraction of his normal one, but a genuine one, free from tension. "Come on, then." He was already halfway into the bedroom, shedding   his   clothes   as   he   went. Hooch was like a barely contained force of nature, and only Matt, as strong as Hooch, was able to match him in give and take, and sheer, unrestrained need. It was a side of Hooch that Matt rarely encountered: powerful, demanding and rough, a side of him that Matt knew Hooch consciously kept from him. In the end they were both sore and strained, bruised and battered, but relieved, and they slept soundly that night, knowing they had dodged a bullet.

* * *

Afterwards, it seemed that things went back to how they had been, and on the surface it was as though the blackmail attempt had never happened, and that life would continue in their peculiar version of normal.

Except that one afternoon in the last week of August, a young man appeared at the front desk when Mandy was on duty. He introduced himself at Lt. Jeff Sullivan, from the 82nd Airborne. He was tall and good looking, just a little shy, and from his accent a Yankee lost and bewildered in the South. He had a shoulder injury, he explained, that had healed but still didn't feel quite right, and Captain Bozic from the base had suggested that he come to the gym and make an appointment with ex-USMC PTI Mr. Donahue for an alternative PT program to the one he was getting up at Fort Bragg.

The result, perhaps, was predictable. The officer stayed far longer than anticipated, leaving not only with an appointment with Matt the following week, but also with Mandy's phone number and a lunch date that weekend.

Matt looked suspiciously at Hooch when he came home that evening. "Matchmaker," he accused him.

Hooch stared at him with a blank, mock-innocent look. "I couldn't leave things to chance, could I? I'd rather not have a repeat of Mike."

Matt snorted. "I bet that's why it's taken so long. How many did you vet before you decided on him?"

"Seventy-nine." Hooch retorted. "Number eighty struck lucky."

"You know, I can well believe that, and if my guess is right, he worships the ground you walk on, so even if he were to guess—and he's not likely to because he's got the imagination of a brick—he'd never say a word. I guess he's the sort who just needs someone to take him in hand and organize his life outside the military as much as it's organized in, and then he'll make Colonel."

"You're damn right, except for one thing: no one worships any ground I walk on. Crazy idea." Hooch cracked a grin.

Matt answered it with one of his own. "One good turn, I suppose. You know it's been ten years since Dan told me to go to the safe house back in Saudi while he was off to Thailand on R&R?"

"Ten years? Fucking hell." Hooch proceeded to push Matt up the stairs, with the intention to get him into the bedroom. "Celebrations are in order."

"No re-creating the first date, though," Matt joked, letting Hooch propel him forwards. "I was so fucking freaked you wouldn't believe, and that bed was fucking uncomfortable too."

"You did a damn fine job at hiding your freak-out." They were upstairs, the door shut. Hooch swiveled Matt round to face him. "Why exactly were you freaked out anyway?" He grinned, a normal, almost sunny grin.

The wide smile was rare enough that Matt couldn't help returning it. "Twenty-one years old, in the middle of the desert, when it was worse than DADT, fucking a crazy Brit merc on the sly, being sent to meet goodness knows who by crazy Brit merc and having a fucking Delta show up. What do you think?" He shook his head. "How the hell did Dan convince you to go out there?"

Hooch laughed. "Simple. He told me he had something waiting for me in the safe house that was of interest to an opportunist. He said I'd like it unless I had something against Jarheads."

Matt couldn't help it, he had to laugh out loud at that. "Fuck," he said when he could breathe, "what a fucked-up comedy we are, and you know what, I wouldn't have it any other way." He shucked off his clothes and threw himself on the bed, on his back, the way Hooch preferred, the expression on his face not so much 'come hither' but 'fuck me'.

A demand that Hooch was all too willing to fulfill.

The sex was slower than usual, but no less satisfying. Matt happily fell asleep afterwards, but Hooch lay awake, something itching inside of him, even though his body was replete. A something which raised its ugly head and flexed its razor-sharp claws whenever the silence caught up with him.

SEPTEMBER–NOVEMBER 2001, FAYETTEVILLE

The mellow season of the end of summer and the beginning of fall in the South was shattered by the crashing of planes in New York, Pennsylvania and Virginia, and the ensuring chaos afterwards. In the days and weeks that followed, Fort Bragg was thrumming with nervous energy, as there was a flurry of movement to and from Bragg and Pope Air Force Base, which had all personnel on edge.

Hooch spent more and more time on base, only rarely returning home, and when he did, he was tight lipped and grey with exhaustion. Even more silent, and even more obnoxious and difficult than usual. Matt could do nothing but watch, helpless as time went by, as Hooch withdrew further and further into himself.

It got even worse when the first planes carrying the coffins with his boys started coming back.

They tried to wage a war against an enemy that had no clear battle lines nor visible targets. It wasn't the long hours, the lack of rest, the fact that he had to stay behind, not even the sheer futility of it all, but the utter idiocy from those in charge, which poisoned Hooch's very self.

No one was listening to the guys on the ground, and as a result men were killed. His men. The young men he'd trained and who were being sent into impossible situations. It was like fine-tuning high spec weapons, only to waste them in suicide missions.

The itch inside of Hooch, which had never vanished since the blackmail attempt, had become an ever consuming presence that ate him up from the inside out. He knew he had no choice but to capitulate to the darkness eventually. The restless energy that gnawed at his guts, and the ever increasing tension that threatened to impede his ability to function, had to be silenced somehow.

He had to let off steam, the only way out he knew, before he imploded and destroyed what remained of his sanity.

* * *

They'd insisted that he took a few days off in November, marked it clearly into his diary, told him well in advance, warned him that everyone he worked with had been told and he was barred from the base. The first evening of his enforced leave, when Matt was downstairs in his office, Hooch made a mental calculation of the time difference, and called New Zealand.

The phone rang at least a dozen times before it was picked up.

"Aye?" Dan's slightly breathless voice was at the other end.

"Hooch here," he paused. "How are you?" going through the pleasantries.

"Fine, fine." The sound of a cigarette being lit. "You want him, aye?"

"Yes." Always direct, that was what he liked about Dan.

"Sorry, mate, he's bloody drugged out of his mind. Slipped a disk, now flat on his back floating on cloud nine." Another inhale, "I'm doing butler duties."

"Shit. How long's he out for?"

"Doc said at least a couple of weeks, but reckons he mustn't do anything physical for a hell of a lot longer. It's the same disk, he really has to take it easy now." A dry chuckle, "as if. You want him to call back when he's off his cloud?"

"Yeah." The veneer of civility, while the darkness clawed up his insides. Weeks at least; possibly months. No way he could wait that long. "Send him my regards, okay? I gotta go now." Hooch ended the call before Dan could reply. This was it. No other way out.

The sound of steps coming up the stairs, then Matt opened the door, yawning. He stopped in mid-movement when he looked at Hooch. Something in the expression on Hooch's face. "Anything I can do?"

"No." Not a lie. Nothing Matt could do. "Sorry. I just..." Hooch shook his head. "I'm going out for a bit. Don't wait up." He was on his way to the door quicker than Matt could grab his arm.

"Shit, what the fuck's up?" Matt skidded towards the door, blocking Hooch's path with his body.

"I need to go." This was not the Hooch Matt knew, but an extreme version of the man. "I just need to go!" Hooch gave Matt a push, far harder than necessary, to get him out of the way.

"Not until you tell me what's got into you!" Matt was caught off-balance, and his attempt to grab Hooch met with thin air as Hooch wrenched open the door and ran down the stairs. Thankfully, there was no-one in the gym as Hooch passed the reception area and went out into the icy chill of the parking lot towards the garage.

* * *

Hooch drove for while, until he was out of Fayetteville, stopping at a nondescript building in a run-down area. It had been years since he'd been here, and he hoped it was still what it used to be.

He got out, looking around and listening for anything suspicious, but there was nothing but crumbling buildings and a few cars discreetly parked in the shadows.

The place looked like it had three years ago, only shabbier. The clientele seemed the same, too, or at least similar. Hooch made his way through the people, a black clad hard-faced man with haunted eyes and a tense jaw, on the prowl for something he couldn't hope to find, yet so desperately needed.

Another man, just as hard-faced, leant against the bar, half-hidden in the gloom, watching the bodies writhe. He caught Hooch's eye—deliberate, calculating—then tilted his head.

Hooch lifted his chin a fraction, keeping his eyes on the other man's. He didn't back down nor look away, and gave a miniature nod after a moment. He was a masochist, but he was hardcore. He wasn't submissive. He made his way through the bodies that separated them, shouldering through the people as if they were nothing but meat.

The other man peeled himself away from the wall and out of the shadow. Hooch's height, but bulkier. Muscle, not fat. Cold, dark grey eyes. "You're new."

"No." Hooch appraised the other man with a swift glance, feeling the forced-down heat unfurling at the sight of the cold eyes that promised no mercy. "I'm not the usual client."

"No," the man agreed. "You want more."

"I don't play." Hooch's chin went up a fraction again, the heat now clawing at his insides, as if the darkness was an entity with its own life, feeding on the blood it was sniffing. "I don't do safe words."

Nostrils flared. A small, cruel smile. "Neither do I." A pause. "Not here. I know another place."

"Where?" One word, all that was needed to negotiate a pact that had no rules, no safety. The beast was raging inside.

The man tilted his head towards the back door. "Near."

"Walking distance?"

"Short drive," came the answer. "I'll lead."

Hooch nodded, following the man. Every single one of his soldier instincts screamed at him not to do this; not to go down that path of utter insanity into an unknown situation without backup, but his instincts were silenced by the beast. Now that he'd handed over the reins, the creature was full-out flaring, impossible to control.

He watched the other man get into a sleek black car, then followed several miles down the road to a row of abandoned warehouses.

Hooch didn't hesitate as he killed the engine and followed the stranger. He only had a rough idea of where he was, and he was going to give himself over completely. No backup plan, no safety net. The thrill of danger, and the anticipation of promised pain flooded his system with adrenaline. At last he'd be able to satisfy the darkness he'd been holding at bay for far too long.

The other man's footsteps were quiet on the gravel as they approached the door of the nearest warehouse. He fished out some keys from a pocket and unlocked the door, opening it and motioning Hooch inside.

Hooch peeled out of his jacket as he stepped through the door. As was his habit, nothing but cash in his wallet, his cell phone and the car keys, no ID, no bank cards, nothing. Flinging the jacket to the floor, he walked into the middle of the wide open space and stopped. The cold air made him shiver in his thin t-shirt, but it didn't matter, it'd be worse after stripping off anyway. Neither man said a word, not even when Hooch stood naked and the other man pointed to a spot above Hooch's head. When he lifted his gaze he saw chains hanging from a rusty steel girder, ending in manacles, high up in the ceiling. Looking back down, Hooch spotted the iron rings that had been set into the rough concrete that was wet and ice cold beneath his bare feet. The sound of chains rattling over a makeshift pulley and lever filled the empty space all of a sudden, a sound so loud, and his need so urgent, Hooch never heard the three other men entering the room through a door in his back.

* * *

By the time Matt arrived downstairs, Hooch had taken off like a maniac into the night, leaving Matt with no idea where he was heading. No way could he contact anyone for help, no way could he risk alerting Hooch's work. Cursing profusely, he went upstairs for his car keys, pushing aside the momentary hope that Hooch just needed some time in the truck alone, because that was fucking unlikely. He started his search along Hooch's favorite open spaces around the city, which would be deserted now in the cold. He tried, without much hope, at Hooch's usual drinking haunts, those few which were still open at the late hour. With increasing desperation, he went to the hospitals asking if there had been a man matching Hooch's description brought in. Frantic with worry, and exhausted from lack of sleep, Matt returned home, defeated, in the pre-dawn gloom. He snuck in the back door of the gym to avoid the early-birds coming for their workouts. Stumbling into the kitchen, he made himself a large mug of coffee and stared at it in his hands.

* * *

The sense of a throbbing, all-consuming ache in his entire body was the first thing Hooch noticed when he came to on the ice cold concrete floor of the warehouse. The next one that registered, was a cacophony of sharp, intense pain in several places on his body. No, not just on. In his body as well. His mind, usually awake within a moment, was sluggish to catch on, as he forced himself back to consciousness. He was freezing, shivering, naked, the sensations blended together into a dissonance of damage. Eventually, he managed to open his eyes, both of them almost swollen shut, his broken nose blocked with dried blood, but he could see enough in the pale grey dawn to take stock of himself. Covered in dried cum and blood. Bruised, in a lot of places so badly, the skin that hadn't been torn or whipped raw had turned almost black. He tried to move, but a frightening sound, that of an animal growling in agony, stopped him short. I took him long moments to realize he'd been the one who'd made the sound, and that he was alone. The four men had left.

Four men who'd known no limits, no mercy, and no safe words. Just like he'd wanted—with one, not four. They had used him, beaten him, cut and whipped him. They had fucked his ass and throat, had never taken no for an answer, not even after he'd been taken beyond the threshold he needed to quieten the beast, and he had finally begged for his life. Hooch looked around, spotting some clothes in a heap and his cell phone nearby. Nothing else. The jacket was gone, and so were his boots. No keys, no wallet. There'd be no truck either. It took him an agonizingly long time to reach for the cell. He couldn't think beyond the very real need to survive, and in order to do so he had to get out of that place. He knew only one number to call, the one he had on speed dial.

The shrill, annoying tone of the cell phone jarred Matt from his contemplation of his cold coffee. He only barely glanced at the name before answering it. "Where are you?"

"Not…sure…" Hooch's voice was low and slurred, raspy from screams he couldn't remember. It took all of his strength, whatever little was left of it, to recall the last street name he'd seen. "Abandoned…warehouse…" The cough that wrecked his broken body sent him into a spasm of pain. One side of his upper body was in agony, and only lying on his side eased the pain and made breathing easier. He dimly remembered steel-toed boots kicking his ribs. "Need…help."

Fuck. Fuck, fuck, *fuck*! Matt feared the worst at the broken voice as well as the tone and the words. "I'm coming," he said, unable to keep the trembling from his own voice. Hooch had only been wearing a light jacket when he'd gone out, so he grabbed his own long woolen overcoat. Heading down to the gym, he thanked his lucky stars that it was still early, that Mandy wasn't in, and that it was the reliable, but not-the-brightest-bulb early shift receptionist Danni on duty, as he got out one of the big first aid kits from his office and went to his car. He drove on auto pilot, through early morning traffic, passing the named street sign, getting more and more frantic until he spotted the warehouse fitting Hooch's description. He all but ran from the car, heedless of any remaining danger, but the sight that awaited him made him freeze for a moment, before he rushed to Hooch's side.

Hooch had tried to dress himself, but all he'd managed was to drape the t-shirt across his groin. His body was in a worse mess it had ever been in, short of the torture during capture, and nothing could have prepared Matt for the sight.

Matt's mouth moved, but no sound came out. His face set in grim lines as he slid the coat underneath Hooch and started to look at the worst of his injuries. No way they could go to a hospital, or even call an ambulance, not without some very awkward questions. There was little that Matt could do in the warehouse, except to bandage the worst of the cuts and scrapes, before wrapping Hooch firmly in the coat and all but carrying him out to the car.

Hooch was quiet all that time, except for some groans he couldn't suppress, and that told Matt more than he ever wanted to know. When Hooch failed to remain stoic, then things were worse than they seemed—and they seemed fucking horrendous. During the car ride, Hooch kept his swollen eyes closed and his lips slightly parted, unable to breathe through his broken nose. He was half curled up on his side to ease the pressure on his ribs, drifting in and out of consciousness. His mind stuck on one memory, one thought and emotion: fear. He'd been scared. He'd experienced panic in different ways than ever before. Not even during captivity had he felt that sharp, blinding sense of fear and helplessness, the knowledge that he would die and there was nothing he could do about it. He knew with absolute clarity that the reason for that fear was sitting right beside him. He'd been frightened that he would die without Matt knowing where he was, what had happened, and, most of all, why he'd gotten himself into that situation.

Hooch knew what he'd done, but the enormity of that knowledge overwhelmed him into silence.

Somehow, through sheer luck, Matt managed to manhandle Hooch through the back entrance and up the stairs. He answered Mandy's shocked look with, "idiot crashed the truck and won't stay in hospital." Which she seemed to accept, and if she didn't, Matt was past caring because he knew that Mandy would not say a word in any case. As he closed the door, he heard Mandy remind Danni that nobody was to disturb Matt that day, and all phone calls were to be diverted away from the apartment to the answering machine in Matt's office.

All but carrying Hooch into the spare room, and onto the bed, Matt took his time washing away the dried blood and the cum, mouth set in increasingly grimmer lines as he had the time to take in the damage. Taking care of the injuries properly, unsure whether to lay Hooch on his back or his front, because both were so badly damaged that it had to be agony either way. He settled him onto his side, as Hooch leaned towards it. At least it would help with the breathing, and the ribs seemed cracked, not fractured. Matt thanked small mercies that it didn't look like he had concussion, at least.

Hooch drifted off while Matt tended to him. Finally, what seemed to be hours later, Matt picked up the basin of dirty, bloody water, and looked down at Hooch.

"You fucking idiot." He said without heat. Weary rather than angry, he went to dump the water before coming back to sit in vigil by Hooch's side.

* * *

Matt woke him every hour to check Hooch wasn't slipping into full unconsciousness, and fed him as many painkillers as he felt were safe. It took all of that day, until the hours of darkness, before Hooch stirred on his own. Attempting to force his swollen eyes open, he blinked sluggishly.

Matt's own eyes were red with strain and lack of sleep as he came closer with water, offering the straw to Hooch. "Nothing's broken, I think, except the nose," he told Hooch. "Should probably get someone in to have a look at that."

Hooch took a few labored sips. Even the water burned in his abused throat. He didn't say anything, despite the thoughts battering at his mind. Thoughts for which he couldn't find the words to say out loud, and emotions he didn't know how to deal with, let alone express. Everything had been different the night before, and while the beast was silenced, he'd lost more than he'd gained. He wasn't just responsible for his own life anymore. He was responsible for another's life and wellbeing, and all it entailed, but he had no clue how to deal with that realization. So all he did was look at Matt through slitted eyes and nod slightly.

"I told Mandy that you crashed the truck," Matt said into the gloom, "and I'll tell the doc that too." The words hung in the dim room, with only one of the bedside lights on. The rest of what he wanted to say could wait until Hooch got a little better. "Shall I tell your work the same?"

"On leave…this week." Hooch managed to get out. Every word was a struggle, but he didn't pity himself. Never had, not even after captivity, but least of all now. This was his own making. He would not dream of blaming the beast, because he should be able to control it, but he had failed.

Matt nodded. "Figures," he said, half to himself.

* * *

The next week passed in a blur for both of them, as Hooch slept and healed and Matt ran himself ragged tending to Hooch. That included lying to the doctor, tense throughout the whole examination in case the man was more perceptive than he hoped. He thanked his lucky stars that everyone swallowed the story of the accident so easily, and there were no enquiries about the truck, for once grateful that Hooch's habitual driving habits meant that everyone took the lie at face value.

*　*　*

It was the night before Hooch was due back on base. He still looked horrendous, but not half-dead, and was able to walk.

Matt stood at the window, facing away from him. He was looking out into the parking lot below, full of movement even at this hour. "I think," his voice was level and calm, and somehow defeated, "it would be a good idea if we had a break from each other."

Hooch sat on the couch, leaning into the bad side. He had hardly said anything all week, not knowing how to find the words, not even where to look for them. 'I'm sorry' was pathetic, 'forgive me' sounded shallow. It took a long time before he replied, because every single thing he meant to say felt wrong. Everything. In the end he gave up and simply agreed. "If you wish."

"For a little while, so we have some space," Matt continued, as though he hadn't heard. "And you can decide whether this is what you want. This living together. With me. If I'm enough for you. And I can figure out whether I can keep doing this, the next time if this happens, when you need to...work off steam." He turned around to face Hooch, and he looked paler and more drawn than Hooch had ever seen him. "I don't think I've ever been more scared in my life. The way you've been lately, the way you took off. Running around town looking for you, the waiting. Not to mention what you did, and what happened, and what's still going on." He braced his arms on the windowsill behind him. "Not being able to get you proper help, not being able to get the doc to do more than he did, because what possible fucking reason could I give him that a guy who's just been in a car accident needs a fucking blood test for STDs?" He braced his arms to control the trembling.

Hooch met Matt's gaze straight on. Every single word hit him square and fair, right where it counted. 'If Matt was enough for him'. Was he? Could he? Who or what could ever be enough, and yet the thought of losing Matt had been ripping a bleeding wound into Hooch these past days. So deep and painful, he didn't know if it would ever close, if—no, when—he was going to leave. He had to leave, for Matt's sake. What guarantees could he give, and how could Matt ever believe him, when Hooch couldn't trust himself. And yet...the fear he'd experienced, of knowing what he was doing to Matt if those men had decided to kill the raw meat that he'd become in that warehouse; the memory of that fear hadn't left him. Still as clear as it had been, the moment when he'd known that this time he wasn't in it only for himself.

"Matt..." Hooch started and trailed off. It was pointless. He couldn't find the words. Every thought and regret unspoken, each plea and each emotion unsaid.

"Just for a while," Matt said, misery incarnate. "I'm sure you've got heaps on at work anyway. We both need to think, and being cooped up here together isn't the place to do it."

Hooch remained silent, all words inside swallowed up by that gaping wound. He'd never experienced loss before, and the heartache that spread through his very core made the beast and the darkness seem like nothing. It hadn't been worth it, and he should have been in control.

Hooch nodded, and with that one nod he gave himself over to the inevitable. Defeated for the first time in his life, and it was all his own doing. He'd been his worst enemy all his life, and now he'd lost the one battle with the highest stakes.

"Jeff's offered to take you back to base tomorrow morning," Matt's gaze was somewhere over Hooch's shoulder. "Smashed truck and all, and the contractors coming in for the install."

Hooch nodded again. That was he could do: agree, and to try control the damage he'd done to Matt.

* * *

Neither slept at all that night, not Matt in their bedroom, nor Hooch in the guest room. Early the next morning, Jeff arrived at the gym, dropping Mandy off before helping carry Hooch's pack and a large gym bag to his car. He wasn't anywhere near as talkative as Mandy during the short drive to the base, but he made all the right noises of sympathy about car smashes and losing much loved trucks. His was a pleasant enough voice to fill in the silence on the road, for all of his dropped 'r's that made Hooch long for another voice, one with a completely different accent.

Again, helping Hooch out of the car and carrying his bags, Jeff accompanied him as far as he could go. He let him know that he was spending most of his free time at Mandy's apartment or at the gym these days, and would be more than happy to give him a lift back any time until Hooch got around to getting a new car; all Hooch had to do was let him know.

Which he didn't.

Jeff spent that weekend at Mandy's, but there was no sign of Hooch at the gym.

The next weekend, there was no sign of Hooch either, and neither did Jeff see the man while on base. Hooch kept busy, did his duties to a fault, kept honing men in their deadly skills and sending them out. Not allowing himself to grieve when they didn't return alive, because there was no space in him left to mourn. Every part of him had been consumed by that open wound.

* * *

Hooch was working late one night in his office when he was interrupted by a knock on the open door. Looking up, he found Jeff there. "Sir?"

"Yes?" Hooch's eyes narrowed slightly, unsure what to think of the unexpected visitor. "Lt. Sullivan."

"Can I come in, Sir?" Jeff looked nervous.

Hooch nodded and pointed to the chair in front of his desk.

Looking like he was about to step into the lion's cage, Jeff entered and closed the door behind him, before placing a small plastic box on the desk in front of Hooch.

"They're from Mandy," Jeff said, sitting down where indicated, "she said they're your favorite."

Hooch's eyebrows raised as he recognized the contents of the transparent box. Red velvet cupcakes. "Thanks."

An awkward pause, as though the younger man had no idea how to begin a conversation. "She says that everyone's missing you at the gym."

"Everyone." Hooch made it a statement, not a question.

"Everyone." Jeff replied firmly, meeting the gaze directly, hoping that it didn't look as difficult as it was. Mandy had said that Captain Bozic was a 'pussycat' but it felt more like being locked in a very small room with a very large and very unhappy panther. Jeff bit his lip, considering. "With respect, Sir, I have been there more recently than you. Whatever's happened, they do all miss you down there. You could just call and let them know you're okay."

"No." Hooch shook his head. "No, I can't do that."

"I'm going down again on Wednesday for my session with Matt," Jeff tried again. "Do you want me to pass on any messages?"

Hooch's eyes hardened with suspicion. "Why would I want to do that?"

Jeff gulped. They said the Airborne was full of terrifying hardcases, but none of them had anything close to who was facing him across the desk. He attempted what passed as confusion, "'cos you're roommates and buddies, and your stuff's still there, and no-one's heard from you in weeks." Biting his lip and barely holding back a twitch, before he warily made another foray. "Do you want me to bring your mail back?"

Eyes still narrowed, Hooch nodded. "Yes to the mail, but what do you know about my stuff being there?"

"You only had your pack and a sports bag when you came to base two weeks ago. You haven't been back, and you've been living there for three years. You can't not have stuff there still?"

The tension left Hooch's face, but the desolation never did. "Yes, I do. Don't need it, though. Got my uniforms."

Jeff nodded, then changed the subject. "I never thanked you for the recommendation down there. Shoulder's all fine now." A pause, "thanks for setting me up with Mandy. She's a great girl."

"Anything else you'd like to thank me for?" Hooch tilted his head.

A look crossed Jeff's face, as though he was swiftly praying to someone. "Just her. It's…well, listening to the guys, it's hard to find someone who understands the job, willing to put up with all sorts of stuff, that's kinda special. Don't think I'd ever want to let her go without a fight, I mean, you know," he corrected, realizing how the words could be misinterpreted, "just that having someone who's prepared to stick it out for the long haul, that's…nice."

"Yeah." Hooch fell silent again, until Jeff thought that was it, but then Hooch added, "don't fuck it up."

Momentary silence, then, "I'll try not to, but I guess I'm luckier than a lot of others already." Jeff left the sentence half-finished. Adding, as though all subtlety had been used up, "when we have fights with each other, we both get it all out into the open."

"Lucky you."

It was like poking a panther through the bars of a cage, and getting nearer and nearer to the claws every time. "I guess," there probably was no budging him, and Jeff dreaded the unsuccessful report back to Mandy. "I can come back for the box on Wednesday, if you like, Sir," he stood up. "It is quite miserable down there, though they're trying to hide it," speaking in the neutral and the plural.

Hooch took in a sharp breath, holding it in his lungs, before he stood up and audibly expelled it. "I can't go back. I am not saying that I don't want to, but I can't. I fucked up." He was giving more away than he'd ever done before, but it seemed the only way of shutting Jeff up. "Say thanks to Mandy for the cupcakes. Also, tell her you make a shit undercover agent."

Jeff gave a small smile in reply. "Now you know why they haven't picked me for your lot. But you'd be surprised just how many guys on base are really good at keeping secrets, and not just the classified ones, but ones that really shouldn't matter and that people really shouldn't give a damn about, Sir."

He turned and went to the door, opening it and walking out into the corridor before Hooch could react.

"Wha..." Hooch never finished the word, staring speechlessly at the retreating back. What the fuck had just happened? There was no way he could have misread Jeff's words, only one possible interpretation of that which was unsaid and yet said so clearly. Secrets that shouldn't matter. Shit. Hooch slumped back onto his chair and buried his face in his hands. He'd fucked up and thrown away the one thing that had mattered.

✳ ✳ ✳

Thanksgiving passed, marked only with a delivery of pumpkin pie and an anxious look and a few pointed questions from Mandy. Matt threw himself into the gym, taking more classes, working early and late on proposals for the new year, and keeping himself busy. Anything to take his mind away from the empty spaces in the apartment, on the couch, at the dining table, in his bed. More strange with most of Hooch's things still there, as though he'd just gone on a long, classified exercise without communication. The place was silent, even though Hooch was so quiet most of the time.

While Hooch took little interest in food, except perhaps a good steak, the effort of proper cooking for one seemed too much, and one evening he was poking at the remains of his half-finished dinner, uncaring of the carbs in the pasta, when the phone rang.

The voice on the other end was warm and familiar, and didn't bother with preliminaries. "Matty, darling, why weren't you and Hooch *really* here for Thanksgiving?"

"We've been busy," Matt stalled, "especially Hooch at work."

"I know, darling, that's what you told me before the holiday, but I'm your mother, and I know when you lie. Do you remember the time you shoved Billy Haddington off that bike because he called you a fag?"

"How could I forget?" The memory was painful, but nothing compared to the present. Matt took a deep breath. "We're having a break."

"I thought so," Anne's voice softened. "Care to tell me why?"

"It's…" he trailed off, "it's been tough since September."

"Aftermath of the attack?" Anne probed gently.

"Yes," Matt confirmed. "His boys." That much at least, it would take a complete idiot or a shut-in hermit not to know that the operations in Afghanistan would involve Hooch's boys.

Anne made a soft sound of thoughtful agreement. "Which one of you wanted the break?" Always straight to the point.

"I," Matt confessed. Knowing that it made him sound like a heartless bastard, but no way could he tell his mother the full story.

"Matty, I know I'm biased, because I'm your mom and I love you and think you are the finest man to walk the earth, but I know you wouldn't ask for a break for no other reason than the man you love being difficult while that man is going through a hard time." She left the field wide open for him.

"Not just that." Matt didn't know if he should curse or thank his mother, who never failed to get to the bottom of everything, "also other things." Like driving off into the night like a maniac, going to goodness knows where to wind up half-dead, riddled with unknown infections and diseases, and closing off completely since. He hadn't expected a long, detailed explanation—this was Hooch, after all. But a "I'm sorry," and some hint of what madness was going through him would have been nice.

"Can you tell me a little about those other things?" She asked gently.

He opened his mouth and it almost came out, but shut it again, breathing deeply. He couldn't. "Just…stuff."

"Alright, dear," her voice remained gentle. "If you can't talk about it, perhaps I can ask some questions?" She paused a moment, "do you think Hooch still loves you?"

Matt almost answered with the first thing that came into his mind, which was 'as much as that crazy bastard loves anyone', but that would just raise more questions. The answer was simple, and yet not. "Yes," he breathed, knowing that he was telling the truth, "but sometimes that's not enough."

"Then he did something that hurt you very much?"

"Yes," let her think what she would. He only barely bit back a snort when he realized that she was partially right. After all, going out and getting yourself fucked by God-knows how many men, beaten up, chained, and tortured, probably counted as 'cheating.' They'd never agreed to be monogamous, even though they had been for the last few years. Too much risk otherwise, they'd more or less decided in that way that they had, without words.

"I see." Her voice was even gentler than before. "But you still love him?" She continued straight away, "and don't tell me that sometimes that's not enough, because if two people love each other, then they have to do everything they can to make it work."

"Yes." He loved that crazy, silent, maddening bastard more than anything. He was worth the lying, the worry, the Marines. But whether he was worth the pain of a repeat, the pain of the not-knowing, when he was out doing mad-assed crazy shit to himself, he still didn't know. "It's been a long road," Matt said at last, "so we're thinking about whether it's where we both want to be going." Knowing that he was lying, knowing that he wanted Hooch for the rest of his life—and that Hooch wanted him for most of it—except the bits where he had that urge to go out and get himself hurt so badly that he was barely human.

"Are you, dear? Are you both thinking that?" Anne let out a soft sound, like a tutting. "Have you two actually talked about this?"

He couldn't lie, but she knew Hooch. "No," he had to say. "Hooch isn't one for talking."

"Yes, I figured that, but darling, have you actually tried? I'm not saying this to defend whatever Hooch did, but you know better than I do that he is quite a broken man."

"Broken?" How the fuck could she know about his...thing?

"I talked to him, darling, remember? And I haven't been a mother to all of my brood for nothing. I can sense a very lost child a mile wide."

Only she could see that in Hooch, Matt thought, where everyone else saw the finely-honed killer. Hooch, who never spoke more than a word about his family if he could help it, who never spoke of his past. Who had been to Texas once or twice in the last three years, only when he could not avoid it, and scarcely more than a couple of days. Hooch, completely lost the first time when he visited Matt's family. "What he does takes a lot out of him," Matt said at last, noncommittally.

"Yes, I can imagine. While I don't claim to know anything about the sort of thing your jobs entailed, I can imagine that it's not something most people could do. But darling, don't you think you should at least try to talk to him? It seems to me that if you don't, you will regret it for the rest of your life."

"We will," Matt said vaguely, "we need to sort stuff out either way." Looking at Hooch's things around the apartment. Not that there was all that much of it, but each was a painful reminder: the coffee mug on the bench, the tattered paperbacks on the shelves, even the meticulously ordered clothes still in the wardrobe. All brought a pang. A repeat was unthinkable, but so was life without Hooch.

"Good." Anne managed to convey her disbelief in that one soft word. "I'll call you again. Send my love to Hooch when you talk to him."

"I will," Matt said quietly. "I will." more to himself than to her, as he finished the call and put down the phone.

* * *

It was a lonely Christmas and New Year. Hooch volunteered for duty over the holidays, watching the base empty of everyone who had managed to get leave, while those remaining grumbled about staying on base. He'd spent holidays on base before, letting the men who had families and actually wanted the time off take it, but this year felt far bleaker. No Matt kissing him awake with his customary enthusiasm on Christmas morning, no stupid joke presents, no New Year's celebration in the apartment, nothing.

There were Christmas-tree shaped shortbread cookies from Mandy, delivered by Jeff, who made half-hearted attempts to make him call the gym again, sensing it was hopeless. Jeff seemed wary of him after the last disclosure, as Hooch realized that he and Matt were possibly the worst-kept secret in Fort Bragg.

He got a call from New Zealand at the start of the holidays, and Hooch managed to be evasive, but when he ended the call, he realized that the gaping wound of missing Matt had not closed in the slightest over the past weeks. As raw and as painful as ever. He now knew what heartache was.

It was just as lonely in the gym during this quiet time. Even the most committed members decided to take a few days break for the holidays. With Mandy going up to Boston to meet Jeff's family, the remaining skeleton staff were professional and friendly, but nevertheless distracted by their own holiday thoughts. The gift for Hooch from his sister arrived at the gym the usual three days before Christmas, the beautifully wrapped box whose contents Hooch would stash away and never use, as always. Accompanied by a card that he would read once and then quietly put away. Matt sent the package up to base, no further note attached.

The day after New Year, Matt's private phone rang. It didn't show a number, but the caller became clear at the unmistakable voice with its Scottish accent and the customary exhale of smoke.

"Right, kid." Dan charged straight into the fray without a word of greeting. "I probably should be doing the Happy New Year shit, but I've been driven crazy by the Russkie's worrying. What the fuck is going on your way?"

He should have expected this at some point, Matt thought. "Hooch and I are on a break." It sounded feeble even for him. What was it now, two months? Almost that.

"Really, is that it?" Another deep inhale at the other end of the phone. "And that's why we are thinking about mounting a rescue mission?" The inevitable exhale of smoke. "Come on, mate, you can do better than that. Tell me what the fuck happened and I might get a decent night's sleep in the near future."

A moment's thought, a sigh, but this was Dan, who Matt owed more than anything. Dan, who had brought Hooch into his life. Dan, who had helped him get information about Hooch in what had, until now, been the worst moment of his life.

"You know what they do when they get together, don't you?" he asked, unnecessarily, because of course Dan would know.

"Aye, and I also know that Hooch called a couple of months ago. That's a bit of a coincidence."

Fuck, if that didn't make perfect sense. "It is, isn't it?" Matt stalled, while things slotted into place.

"Aye." Dan gave Matt a moment, during which he took another audible drag of his obligatory cigarette. "Does that mean you are finally going to tell me what the bloody hell happened?"

"He went to get himself worked over somewhere and rang me the next morning to get him, when he was three-quarters dead." It sounded awfully cold put like that.

"Well, shit." Dan's comment came out like a bullet. "That's serious crap, but only part of the story, aye?"

"It was the fucking last straw," the heat in Matt's voice surprised him, as it finally hit. "He's been fucking unbearable since September, more so since the fuck-ups began, and we got blackmailed over the fucking summer and then he went and pulled this shit."

"Crap." Dan retorted, with feeling. "I'd be pissed off to hell and back, too, but what does he have to say about it?"

Dan had a way of demanding the truth, even half a world away. "Nothing," Matt said, after a pause. "We haven't spoken since he left."

"Well, color me surprised. Not." A last exhale and the sound of a cigarette butt being violently stubbed out in the ashtray. "Look, mate, I get it. Talking is shit. It's a worse torture than being raked over glowing coals, but not talking in that situation? For two bloody months?" Dan raised his voice, *"are you two fucking stupid?"*

What a redundant question. "I guess we are."

"Bingo. You and Hooch score the jackpot." A faint raspy sound as Dan seemed to rub his hand over his face. "What a mess, and there wasn't even any KGB involved."

"No, I think we managed fine on our own." Matt felt the misery claw at him from the inside.

"I'm no expert on relationships," Dan huffed a laugh, "far from it, but you two really take the biscuit." He paused, "look, I'm going to talk to Hooch, aye? I'll tell him he's a fucking idiot, and then we'll leave you two to your own devices." An unspoken expectation that those devices were expected to be more communicative than they had been. "Alright, mate?"

"Alright." Apprehension, and more than a bit of bleak amusement. Dan had got them together to begin with—no wonder he took such an interest.

"Don't think I do that for you two. I'm selfish, remember? I want a decent bloody night's sleep." Dan chuckled, "bye."

"Bye," Matt smiled despite himself and his misery. Dan had a way of doing that. He put down the phone, and very firmly went and placed Hooch's coffee mug into the cupboard, where it belonged.

* * *

Back on base, Hooch's cell rang. "Yeah?" He answered warily, not recognizing the number.

"What the fuck do you think you are doing?" Dan's voice battered through the phone.

"With what?"

"Throwing your one chance away by not having the courage to do that talking shit."

"I...can't." Even that was hard. "I don't have the words."

"Okay." Dan calmed down somewhat. "I get it, I really do. I can guess what you did out there after you called a couple of months ago, and in what state you ended up in, but I've been through the shit, had my heart ripped out, and the one thing I learned through that? That if you don't communicate in whatever way you can, you're so fucked, you could just about throw your life away, because that equates to the same thing." He paused, during which Hooch felt his breath hitch. "You're not enemies, Hooch." Dan's voice had softened, "you're not on two different sides. You might think you are fucked up, but hell, you didn't have someone torture the last shred of self out of you. So, yeah, you're a masochistic bastard, and you got issues a mile wide, but you don't have anyone actually physically holding you back to pick up your damned phone and call the one person you love. Because you love Matt, don't you?" He didn't allow Hooch to get a word in edgewise. "Aye, I know that you do, even though I bet you've never said it." Dan was on a roll now. "If you don't have the words, then tell him that you don't have them. If you can't tell him what you feel, then show him. If you have to beg to be allowed to show him, then bloody well do it! Don't be as stupid as we were, because you're more clever than that and you haven't got most of the world against you. Goddammit, Hooch, do you get me?"

"Yes," and fuck, he did. Too caught up in his own pain and misery, too aware it had been his own making.

Dan let out a deep breath. "Thank fuck. Then take that chance and go for it. At least, if it doesn't work out, you tried. Whatever shit you did, I guess you figured out a few things in the meantime, aye?"

"Yes." That all the fear, the terror, the pain, the guilt—nothing was as agonizing as the thought of losing Matt.

"Get your arse in gear, soldier, because I hang up now." True to his word, the line went dead.

Hooch kept staring at the phone in his hand for exactly ten seconds, before he hit the speed dial for Matt. If he thought about it for too long, he'd realize once again how unequipped as he was with emotional tools, but cowardice wasn't an option any longer. He had nothing to lose, and everything to win.

He listened to the ring tone of Matt's cell.

"Hi." Matt's voice. Level, unsurprised. Wary? It was hard to tell.

"Can I see you?" Hooch sounded nervous even to his own ears.

"Yes." A pause, "do you want to come down? Do you have a new truck yet? Or should I come up?" Questions, so many questions.

"I bought a truck a month ago." All the little things that had hurt in new ways, such as the simple task of buying a truck and not telling Matt. Every little thing had fed the wound. "I could get a stand-in and come to the gym." Not 'your place', certainly not 'our place', carefully neutral instead.

"Yes," there was a soft exhale, "that would be good. It's still closed for the holidays so we'll have privacy."

"Thanks, Matt. I'll be there as soon as I can." Hooch cancelled the call and stood in his room for a moment, looking at the bare wall. He was shit-scared, because he still didn't have the words, but he'd had a long time to think, and he was going to try to communicate those thoughts, even if it killed him.

Staring at the phone in his hand, Matt took a deep breath before putting it down. Twenty minutes at least to work out what he was going to say. Twenty minutes before he'd have what felt like the toughest conversation of his life. Coming out to his parents was easy compared to this. He opened the door and went down into the deserted gym to wait.

For once, it actually did take Hooch twenty minutes, not the fifteen he usually managed with his maniac driving if there wasn't any traffic. His silhouette visible in front of the frosted glass door, as he rang the bell. One outside, one inside, and neither could see through to the other.

Matt opened the door."You look..." 'like shit' was what he was about to say, but he bit it back as he stepped aside to let Hooch enter

"Yeah, I guess." Hooch replied. He stopped once he'd entered, and turned to watch Matt lock the doors behind them. Matt. Fucking hell, it hurt to see him, as it all came rushing towards him, the loneliness, and the misery of knowing how he'd fucked up.

"Coffee?" Matt asked, heading towards the door to the apartment. Even now, in the deserted post-holiday silence, not worth the risk to be seen from the parking lot, just in case. No longer paranoia, but the caution that bit into everything with Hooch's career.

"Thanks." Hooch followed Matt up the stairs. A subdued version of the Hooch Matt knew. Once upstairs, Hooch took a quick glance around, but everything was just like it had been as he left.

Matt fiddled with the coffee machine, producing two cups, the way they preferred. Making a point of using Hooch's usual mug. "So," he began, "Dan phoned you, I guess."

Hooch's gaze lingered a while too long on his old mug. "Yeah, he did." He took the mug and then a first sip, looking at Matt from under his eyelashes as he glanced over the rim. "Told me I was a fucking idiot." He ploughed on before Matt could say anything. "I don't...don't know..." and fuck, if that wasn't exactly what he had been dreading. He huffed in frustration and grimaced.

"You don't know what?" Matt prodded.

"Words. I don't know how…shit." Hooch set the mug down on the kitchen counter and dragged a hand through his short hair. "For two months I've been trying to find the words, but I'm no closer to finding them."

More misery in Hooch's dark eyes than Matt had ever seen, even more than after the torture. "I see." Most, but not all, of the anger had burnt out of him, replaced by sadness and the Hooch-shaped empty space inside. "I know," what did he know, really? He tried again. "What the hell did you think you were doing?" No need to specify further, they both knew what he was talking about.

"I wasn't thinking." Hooch gestured to the couch. "Could we sit down?"

Matt nodded, put his coffee down too and sat on the couch.

Hooch followed, but he was no less tense sitting, as he had been when standing. "I never tried to explain my masochism to you. Thought I'd deal with it on my own. I was wrong, I tried to ignore the need and I fucked it up." Hooch sat straight, palms on his black clad thighs. How was he going to explain something so overwhelming—something he didn't understand himself? "For the first time…" slight shake of his head, he tried again. "I was scared. I'd never been scared before like that. Not for me, but…" he looked up and at Matt. "It wasn't just about me. I was scared to leave you, what it'd do to you. Scared, because I realized I had responsibility for someone else's wellbeing, and that wellbeing was more important than anything else, and I had fucked it up. I was a selfish bastard and fucked it up." Hooch looked down at his hands, fingertips lightly strumming on the denim of his trousers.

Matt blinked. Feeling what it must have cost for Hooch to say those words, more agonizing, he guessed, than any physical hurt that he'd ever suffered. The darkness in him, that he kept away from Matt—and truth be told—part of Matt had been relieved that he did. As though ignoring meant that he didn't have to deal with it. "Yes, yes you did," he said softly. "So what now?"

"I've been missing you." Hooch said quietly, still looking at his hands. "I never felt like that before. Didn't get better. It hurt, still does."

Matt exhaled a breath he didn't realize he'd been holding. Hurt. And not the physical. Like how he'd felt inside. "I'm not sure I can do that again," he said at last, "the silence, the brooding, the taking off, the not-knowing all night, and then finding you." For all he loved that maddening bastard, there were lines he wasn't sure he could cross again. "If…" he paused, "if you want me, like how we've been the last few years, we'll need to work out how we deal with it." And how that stuck in him, in a way he hadn't realized, that there was something Matt couldn't, or *wouldn't* (where had that come from?) be for Hooch.

Hooch nodded. "Matt," he lifted his head to look at him, "I am not making promises, because that's not enough. What I will do is give you my word that I will never do anything like this again. I understand those words are hard to believe, but I don't have anything more convincing, except for giving myself to you for the rest of my days, to show you that I mean those words." Hooch paused, drew in a breath. "I will talk to you, try to explain, tell you what I need when…I'm not asking you to do anything you don't want to do, but I will tell you." He'd been thinking about this, plenty of time in the last two months. "Perhaps there's a club or something, something safe, where I could go regularly. Perhaps that would stop the…the…" he still didn't have a word for it, so he went back to one of the old ones, no matter how inadequate, "before the darkness gets too overwhelming."

Matt nodded thoughtfully. "That's a start, at least." He paused, "I have missed you, but," always but, "I think we might want to ease back into this slowly. Think it over. Weekends perhaps, and we see how it goes."

"Yeah." Hooch's posture relaxed slightly. "It's not that I didn't want to talk to you during the past two months." Everything else unsaid, but even though Matt could hardly believe himself, he saw pleading in Hooch's dark eyes. Asking for understanding.

"No," Matt agreed, and stopped. "One more thing, though. No sex for a while. We need to wait to see if you're clear, and we've always just had sex—great sex—rather than sort out shit." Much as he'd missed it, missed Hooch's weight in the bed, the warmth of the body, this was important. It had always been too easy to just tear at each other like animals, forgetting everything else when they were sated and exhausted.

"Yeah, I understand." Not just the safety part. "Guess I used it," Hooch said hesitantly, "sometimes." He ran a hand through his hair again, matter of-fact in the face of the truly uncomfortable. "I went to a private lab, had tested what they could. All clear for STDs. Will go back in four weeks to get tested for HIV."

Matt let out a breath he didn't know he'd been holding. "Good." Hoping that the chances were good, that if the guys Hooch had been with hadn't given him anything else so far, they wouldn't have given him HIV either.

Getting to know each other again, Matt thought, without the sex that had been the beginning and the tie that had kept them together for so long—before the friendship, let alone the love, that was going to be different. His hand went to cover Hooch's on his knee. The first time they'd touched for two months.

Hooch looked at the hand, hesitated for a moment, before he covered it with his own. It felt to him like the most romantic gesture he'd ever done in his whole life, and he lifted his head to smile at Matt. Tentative, but there. "I have to be back on base in three hours tops. Did you," searching for normality, "did you tape the game by chance?"

The mountain of tapes of games that Matt rarely got a chance to watch before taping over them again, a private joke. "Yes," he said, standing up and going to the TV cabinet to rummage through the pile, picking one more or less at random from the most recent and slotting it in. "Drink?" he asked, going to the fridge, looking at Hooch.

"No, still on duty. Got a Coke?" Hooch moved across to the part of the L-shaped couch that was facing the large TV screen. He had marginally relaxed, but only a hard physical session in the gym would get rid of all of the tension for now.

Matt nodded and got a coke from the fridge. Full-calorie, not diet.

Watching the game, unseeing, in silence. But a comfortable one.

They sat close together, almost touching but not quite, a synonym for their relationship.

* * *

The following Friday evening, a surprised but delighted Mandy saw Hooch enter reception, his daypack on his back, like he used to.

She looked like she wanted to give him a hug, but hesitated out of discretion, and settled for a huge smile. "He's in his office," she pointed in that direction. Continuing her discretion, she quickly vanished somewhere else in the gym.

Hooch nodded his thanks and went through to the office, where he hesitated. The door was ajar, but he decided to knock.

"Hey," Matt looked up from the pile of accounts on his desk, "how're things?" The little bits of conversation they'd rarely bothered with in the past.

"Hey." Hooch stepped inside and let the pack glide off his shoulder. "Better than last week. I'm here."

"Yes, you are." A new awkwardness, as Matt shuffled the papers, then locked them away. "Up?"

"You want to order pizza? I got a six-pack of beer." Hooch lifted the backpack and pointed at it.

Matt smiled. "Yeah…but pizza?" The uneasiness at this 'new them' obvious.

Hooch flashed a grin. "Come on, Matt, some carbs and a beer won't kill you."

Matt gave in with a chuckle, and they went upstairs into the apartment. When they got into the living area Hooch stopped, unsure where to put his pack. He decided to leave it at the door, then proceeded to pull out the beer.

"How was your week?" He handed a can to Matt, opened one himself. This small-talk thing was damned difficult.

"Good, good, especially considering the weather." Matt didn't miss Hooch's hesitation, felt equally awkward. "Yours?"

Hooch shrugged. "Long hours, I'm tired." He took a long draught of his beer then walked over to the couch to sit down. He really was bone tired, but nothing would have kept him from driving back to the apartment. "What pizza do you want?"

"Anything, just no anchovies." Matt opened his own beer and sat next to Hooch. It felt oddly surreal.

Like the 'dating' phase they never went through, retro—and ill-fitted now.

"Okay." Hooch went for his cell and dialed the local pizza place he still had on speed. He ordered a classic one and a salad, the latter to appease Matt's health concern. When he was done he turned to Matt.

"So," Hooch stifled a yawn, "what now? Movie? Game?"

"Game?" Matt asked. He picked up the remote, flicking at random until something suitable came up.

Neither of them enjoyed watching war or action movies, except for classics: all the mistakes were too annoying. And stupid comedies seemed inappropriate.

Hooch kept stifling a yawn, but perked up during a couple of passes in the game, until the delivery guy arrived. He was ravenous, eating too fast and washing the carb laden food down with beer, until the pizza was finished. He slumped back against the couch, eyes on half-mast, trying not to fall asleep, but the drowsier he got the more his control waned, and he kept slowly sliding towards Matt.

A hand on his shoulder, firm and warm. "Hey, looks like you're about to drop."

Hooch, more asleep than awake, leaned into the warmth of Matt's body, rubbing his face against Matt's shoulder while sleepily mumbling, until he suddenly froze. Eyes open, he sat back up straight. "Sorry." Matt wasn't 'his' any longer, and Hooch felt the painful sensation of having intruded into territory he no longer had the right to. "Yeah, I'm tired."

"Bed, then." Matt stood and cleared away the boxes and the cans, then stood awkwardly in the middle of the room. "I've made up the spare room for you."

"Yeah, okay." Hooch acquiesced. He was too exhausted to argue, and he had expected it anyway. He had to give this time, this…them. Besides, wasn't the spare room officially his anyway? "Thanks." Without further comment, Hooch went to get his pack, then vanished in the bathroom, only to emerge soon after to head to the spare room. "Good night." The door closed behind him.

Matt finished tidying the living area and went into their bedroom, closing the door behind him softly.

Even though he'd slept alone for two months, never had the bed felt so cold and empty.

✳ ✳ ✳

Hooch woke with a start, the room dark and silent around him. Thoughts fuzzy, still caught in a dream woven from scary memories, his heart was racing and his mouth dry. Disoriented, as his mind frantically tried to supply where he was, and to gauge if he was in danger or not. Trained reflexes pushed him to high alert: this wasn't his bunk, nor the shared bed, and he had no recollection of the place he found himself in. His hands searched blindly, and he almost knocked over the lamp when he finally found the light switch. He could make out the spare room in the light, told himself he was safe, but his heart continued to race for a while longer, and the sweat felt sticky on his skin.

There was no point staying in bed, so he got up and quietly made his way to the bathroom to wash his face, and then to the kitchen for a glass of cold water. The couch seemed as good a place as any, and in the gloom of the light coming from the open door to the spare room, he sat on the couch, head back, glass of water half-drunk in his hand.

The other door opened quietly. Matt, backlit from the lamp in the bedroom, stood in the dim light, dressed in long, loose pajama pants—another change, when he'd always slept naked before. "Hey," his voice hung in the gloom, "the dream?"

Hooch looked up, letting his head turn until his cheek rested against the back of the couch. "Not sure." He was about to shrug, but aborted the movement. "Disoriented." He inhaled deeply, before slowly breathing out. "Matt…"

Matt came closer, and fumbled with the light switch on the reading lamp on the side table, before sitting down side-on to Hooch on the L-shaped couch. Elbows on knees, waiting for Hooch to continue.

"I can't do this, Matt." Hooch leaned forward to put the glass onto the table. "I can't pretend the last ten years didn't happen."

A tilted head, as Matt followed the movement of the glass, then turned back to look at Hooch. "How so?" Having a good idea of the answer, but pushing Hooch to put it into words.

"This." Hooch made a vague gesture between them. "Not touching you. I don't mean the sex, I can accept that it's off right now, but I can't not touch you. It's all wrong."

A hand, warm and firm on Hooch's bare knee was the response. "You're freezing." The hand was removed just as quickly as it had come, as Matt disappeared into his own room for his robe—Hooch had never really accustomed himself to one—and came out to fling it over Hooch's shoulders. It was several years old, slightly threadbare, and smelt of Matt.

Matt was like a dog with a bone, wouldn't let go. "How?"

Hooch rolled his eyes at Matt's 'mothering', but pulled the robe closed around him anyway. He hadn't noticed how cold his skin had become until the soft, worn cloth covered it with warmth. He was about to say something about Matt trying to force him to find words he didn't have, when he inhaled and the familiar scent of Matt surrounded him. Hooch closed his eyes and took another deep breath. "This. This is how," he said quietly.

Matt took a long look, as though knowing these were already more words than Hooch was really comfortable with, then nodded. He held out his hand. "Come to bed, then."

Hooch looked up, surprised, but took the offered hand. The robe slid off his shoulders as he stood, but neither man cared, as they walked into the main bedroom.

The bed was still warm, and Matt settled in behind Hooch, pulling the blankets over them both. Matt, the solid presence at his back. Hooch thought that nothing had ever felt so right, as Matt held him closer, body-warmth seeping into him.

Hooch huffed softly. "I'm the little spoon now, huh?"

It was more a rumble in Matt's chest than an answering chuckle, but the amusement was clear. "I guess. Sleep, then. I'll take watch."

Hooch was about to say something in reply, but thought the better of it, and just placed his hand on top of Matt's that rested on his chest. Enveloped in the familiar warmth and scent, he didn't even notice when he fell asleep, it was that quick.

* * *

Hooch woke to milky winter sunlight streaming into the room through a gap in the curtains. Matt's arms still encircling him, Matt's body pressed all along his back, and the hardness of Matt's morning wood digging into him.

Matt muttered sleepily and snuggled closer, into the warmth, until he realized that Hooch was awake and deliberately staying still. "Morning," he yawned, pulling away slightly.

"Does a hand job count as sex, or as helping out a buddy in need?" Hooch murmured.

Matt's hand on Hooch's hip stilled. Not moving away but neither moving closer. Clearly thinking, considering Hooch's question. He finally snorted softly into the nape of Hooch's neck, and his hand moved forwards, having made a decision. "I'll let you get away with it this time," slightly grumbly, but with a smile, as he shifted to allow Hooch to roll over.

Hooch had a small grin on his face as he pushed Matt's PJ bottoms down. "Honestly, I'm just helping out a buddy in need," he muttered as his calloused hand closed around Matt's erection. He knew Matt so well, every stroke was perfectly set. Two men familiar with their bodies, no second guessing necessary.

It didn't take long before Matt came, bodies close together, his head buried in the juncture between Hooch's neck and shoulder, teeth scraping against Hooch's collarbone as he shuddered.

He pulled away as soon as he had his breath back, close enough to see Hooch's still-dilated eyes in the faint dawn light. "Return the favor?" he asked, quirking an eyebrow in an unconscious imitation, his hand already going to the waistband of Hooch's shorts.

"No." Hooch said softly, voice a little hoarse with desire. Gaze fixed on Matt's flushed face, he gently circled Matt's wrist with his hand, sticky with cum, and smiled his ghost of a smile. "Not yet. I want the test done first."

A hesitation, then a nod. They'd been through this before, and Matt bit back the memory of—what was it now—nearly four years ago, back in his old apartment. The same worry from Hooch, but for a far different reason. "'course," he murmured, not making an attempt to pull away, instead burying himself further into the bed. It was near-freezing in the room, because they'd forgotten to turn on the apartment's rarely-used heater.

"You lying in the wet spot?"

Matt snorted, "it's all over you, and you know it." He paused and sighed. "We have to talk, you know."

Hooch wiped the cum off himself with a corner of the duvet, then settled back down. "What about?" Which of the many things they'd never talked about.

"You. Me. Us. This." Matt exhaled, then elaborated. "What you need as a masochist. What you expect of me, and what I've been assuming these last few years. The things we've been letting slide because we've been getting settled here, into your new job, into the gym, into living together."

Hooch closed his eyes and let out a soft groan. This was what he had anticipated, and definitely feared, yet he knew he had to do this or he would lose Matt for good this time. He opened his eyes, and his serious expression was proof enough for Matt that Hooch was willing to talk. "It's too big, Matt, the whole masochism thing. I don't know where to start; how to explain...how to find the words. Can you break it down?"

Matt nodded slowly, considered asking whether Hooch would be more comfortable getting up, but then realized if there was any place that Hooch was going to be able to talk it was right here, together, in the bed. Thinking, thinking about what it was, until he came to the answer. The selfish one, perhaps, but it was a place to begin. "What is it you don't think that I can help you with?"

"Do you enjoy inflicting pain? Do you get off humiliating others?" Hooch asked without hesitation.

A start, and a shudder Matt couldn't repress. "No," he answered truthfully. He trailed a finger down the length of Hooch's nose, slightly straighter now than it had been before. The doc, too used to patching up the aftermath of bar fights, had evidently had his own idea of aesthetics.

"It's a necessity for the really dark stuff."

"But that's not all?" Matt asked eventually.

Hooch tried to follow the finger, ending up cross-eyed. "What do you mean?"

The finger disappeared. "It can't be all the pain and humiliation," Matt clarified, leaving aside the 'really dark stuff' for later, though not too late. He felt anxiety he hadn't even suspected was there, that he didn't know where it came from, or why. Jealousy? He had never felt that in all the years that they had been together: knowing he was 'Central Station' at first, and then Hooch had come home to him. He'd been convinced that was all he had wanted or expected.

Hooch exhaled softly and audibly. Suddenly, a few things became clear in his mind. Truths he should have noticed for years, but had never looked at. "I knew Dan was jealous for a while, back when he fucked up his knee, but I'm a selfish bastard, because I never thought twice about it. I knew I was only in love with," he hesitated, realizing he'd never actually said the words, "only with you. I never even wondered what you felt about anything."

Matt clamped down on the fury that rose automatically, but his anger with Hooch had burnt out, and now they needed to sift through the ashes. "I figured...I figured it was just something you did," he said at last. "I never thought about it much." He stopped. Honesty, of course, needed to go both ways. "I didn't, because it hurt too much. That there was something you thought I couldn't give you."

"Fuck." Hooch exclaimed softly. "Jesus fucking H Christ, I never considered your feelings." What the fuck had he been doing all those years? Even after he'd claimed he didn't take Matt for granted anymore? "This is not an excuse, Matt, because there isn't one, but I'm trying to explain. To me, the time-out somewhere far away, never counted as having *sex* with someone else." Hooch paused, "it was easy to compartmentalize."

With anybody else, Matt would have thrown them out of bed. But with Hooch—with all his secrets and the big chunks of his life that were classified—it actually made sense, albeit a painful one. "I guess it was," he said noncommittally. Their heads were so close on the pillows, it was impossible to turn away. "But it can't all be pain and humiliation for a week?"

Hooch cupped Matt's face, letting his thumb stroke gently, trying to take some of the hurt away he could see in the handsome face before him. He'd never felt like a rat bastard before, not even after his last stunt that had got him almost killed. Now, though, he truly realized that he'd deeply hurt the one person who meant more to him than anyone or anything—and all because he'd never bothered to think beyond the obvious and the convenient. "It is, Matt. It is all about that."

The "Why?" slipped out before Matt could stop it. Much to his dismay, it was almost plaintive.

"I don't know." Hooch said softly. "There is something in me which gets wound up tighter and tighter the less I have control over events and the longer it goes on. Back when I was out on missions, the more often I had dodged death or seen destruction, the tenser I got. It was worse when I couldn't prevent losses." He hesitated as he tried to explain to Matt what he couldn't fully understand himself. "It's like something that eats me up from the inside; like millions of fire ants racing through my guts and crawling under my skin. I feel like I'm about to snap, and I worry I can't trust myself anymore, that I'll be unable to function like a human being and instead become someone unhinged, who wreaks havoc because he can; because he can't bear anymore what he has seen and done." Hooch took a deep breath, this was taking more out of him than he'd ever imagined. Never before had he tried to put the darkness into words. "It's a compulsion I cannot escape from, because if I try to, I stop being able to function. I can't relax, can't sleep, can't think, can't eat, can't breathe, can't interact, until I get taken apart and until I break. Until I can't take it anymore and yet I get taken that one bit further." Unlike those men a couple of months ago who had taken him too far beyond. "That's when I can finally let go." Hooch ended quietly, barely above a murmur.

Silence, then Matt put out his hand to Hooch's face, mirroring the earlier caress. "I can't pretend I understand right now," he said at last, "but thank you for telling me. I'll try to get it." His hand went to the back of Hooch's neck. "That was why you called New Zealand in November," he knew the answer already, but needed confirmation from Hooch. "You were already past breaking point, and you couldn't wait the time it took to set something up, the way you usually do."

Hooch nodded. "Yeah, that's right. I've been thinking about how to avoid getting to that point of no return when I don't care about anything anymore. I won't do that again, because I do care about you. I need to find a way of never getting to that point in the first place."

Matt had been thinking about it too, about alternatives. "What did you use to do before?"

"I went to bars or clubs, preferably outside of the US. That tied me over."

It was as Matt had suspected, and probably not something that was as feasible now with Hooch's job, but he'd been researching one option, ever since an overheard conversation in the wet room between two of the longest-standing gym members. "Have you ever thought about a members-only club?" he asked. "Something with strict confidentiality rules?"

"Do you think that exists? Here? Not exactly gay central, huh?" Hooch gave a wry grin.

"Well, probably not here." Matt conceded, trying, and failing to imagine such a place. "But Charlotte, maybe. Raleigh, probably. They're near enough for a weekend. Asheville definitely, but that's too far."

"Seems to me you did some research already." Hooch gently mock-punched Matt's nose. "But that's not all, is it?" Echoing Matt's earlier question.

"No," no getting away from Hooch, nor the question at the back of his mind. Matt hesitated, "I suppose this is when we talk about other people. Having sex with other people, I guess. What counts, what doesn't. We've never actually talked about this; not at the beginning when it was fun, and not when we moved in here. To be quite frank, I've been so busy the last few years with the gym, I don't think I'd have noticed anyone, even if I'd wanted to."

"Would you want others?" Hooch smiled slightly. "To me, any of the sex in a 'scene' is just part of the whole humiliation and pain infliction that I crave at that time. It's not sex in my mind, which probably sounds crazy. I don't care who fucks me when I'm out of my head. The man's just a body, then. I don't want to have sex, just sex, with anyone else, but if you do, I don't mind. Sex is just that."

Matt gave a thoughtful look. "No, not recently." Truth be told, with Hooch around and his work, he'd been too exhausted to consider exploring further afield, though there were speculative glances aplenty at the gym. In a bizarre way, what Hooch was saying sort of made sense—once you managed to remember that it was Hooch the crazy bastard saying it.

Hooch's stomach suddenly rumbled and he cast a wry grin at Matt. "Before I beg you to let me out of this torture-talking-rack to get some breakfast, I want you to know it's okay if you ever wanted to experiment with me and my masochistic side. Anything and anytime."

There was a chuckle as Matt automatically reached for his robe before remembering that it was in the living room. "I think I may just hold you to that." There was a gleam in his eye as he left the bed and went hunting for a sweater, only barely remembering to pull up his PJs before he tripped over.

Hooch watched him, relishing the ease of how they interacted. He braced himself and jumped out of bed, braving the cold in his slightly damp shorts and nothing else. "First one in the bathroom gets the hot shower."

Matt laughed, and abandoned the hunt for the sweater in favor of taking advantage of his position nearer the door to head to the bathroom.

＊ ＊ ＊

Hooch left to return to base on Monday morning, feeling like a weight had been lifted from his shoulders. Yes, there was still a chasm between them, but at least they had started to fill it in. He didn't know how long it would take, but he did know that he would shovel for as long as he needed to.

The next weekend passed much the same as the previous one, except now there was no question where he would sleep. He was back in their bed, with Matt wrapped around him—the spooning reversed. Though being so close to Matt, his determination not to permit so much as a hand-job until they were sure he was clean, grew increasingly difficult.

The following weeks passed in much the same vein, save that Hooch's self control was worn to a thread by the end of the month. He supposed that one benefit of staying on base during the week was that he had a chance of regaining mastery over himself, and not pouncing on Matt like he wanted to.

He waited until the appointed time on the first Friday in February, when he went to the clinic to pick up his test results. Once in his truck, he held his breath as he tore the envelope open. His eyes scanned over the lines, until he got to the test result itself. He read it once, twice, forgetting to breathe. After he'd read it a third time he turned the ignition of his truck, and sped with squealing tires out of the parking lot and towards the gym.

Hooch barely managed to maneuver the truck into the garage without damaging Matt's car parked in its reserved slot beside his, before all but hurling himself out of the vehicle. He stopped, breathing hard, forcing himself under control, before walking to the back entrance of the gym. Hooch let himself in, knowing that it was the shortest and most unobtrusive way to Matt's office, the most likely place where he'd be on a Friday evening.

He was so focused on his mission, that he walked straight into Mandy, who'd been carrying a stack of papers, which scattered all over the floor. "Sorry," Hooch snapped, "Matt in the office?"

"Uh…yeah?" Mandy blinked as Hooch moved past her, even brusquer than normal. But at least he was here, and Matt wasn't sulking anymore, what was a bit of scattered paper compared to that?

Hooch nodded, then barged into Matt's office, knocking at the same time as he opened the door and stuck his head inside. "You. Upstairs. Now."

Matt looked up, stared at Hooch, eyes narrowed. Mentally calculating dates, then standing up and, for once, not objecting to the curtness of the order. Without a word, he locked his office door behind him.

Hooch was already in the apartment, and the moment Matt stepped inside, Hooch simultaneously kicked the door shut and grabbed Matt. He shoved him against the nearest wall, descending onto him like a ravenous beast. Hands clawing at Matt's t-shirt and shorts, kissing hungry, open-mouthed, and close to biting.

Too shocked to object at first, it took a while for Matt to get enough leverage on Hooch's chest to shove him to arm's length, struggling against Hooch's weight and strength. "I take it you're clear?" he gasped, pulling away from Hooch's determined attack on his mouth, neck, collarbones, any area he could reach.

"Yeah." Hooch nodded, going once more in for the kill. He needed Matt, needed to feel, needed to fuck. He didn't realize he'd said that out loud.

"Christ, me too," Matt agreed. He returned the desperation and the hunger in equal shares, practically throwing himself at Hooch until they were on the floor, tearing at their clothes.

It was anything but coordinated, and everything like mindless rutting. Hooch thrust against Matt's thigh, groin, wherever he could reach, swearing when he couldn't get his pants open and down quickly enough; cursing even louder when their bodies and cocks aligned, wildly thrusting against each other while biting and sucking at skin.

It seemed like seconds before they were a damp, sticky, half-undressed mess on the living room floor. A miracle that they hadn't knocked anything over, as they fought to get their breath back. "Ergh," Matt wrinkled his nose as he sat up. He hesitated, as though he couldn't decide to make some pretence of pulling up his shorts before getting up or just giving up and stripping properly. "Shower?"

Hooch grinned with the sated expression of a breathless but very content Cheshire cat. A rare expression on him. "Yeah, shower. Then food. Then fucking."

A snort, but an affectionate one, accompanied by a gleam in Matt's eye as he decided in favor of stripping. "Dinner's in the crockpot." He nodded at the new appliance that his mother had mailed over, complete with a book of recipes. "No cooking required."

He made sure he stuck his ass in Hooch's face as he got up and headed to the bathroom.

"Hey!" Hooch grabbed for the tantalizing display, but narrowly missed him. Stripping out of the remainders of his clothes, he was hot on Matt's heels. "How long before you get it up again, kid?" He smirked, as he stepped into the shower cubicle to join Matt.

Matt took advantage of Hooch's momentary distraction when the water was turned on to shove him against the tiles, so that Hooch could feel him, half-hard already and definitely interested. "Faster than you, old man," he teased.

"Good." Hooch drawled, rubbing against Matt. "That means I can take advantage of you." He slid down the length of Matt's wet body, until he was on his knees on the porcelain floor. Hands on Matt's ass, he pulled him forward under the steady stream of hot water, and swallowed the half-hard cock without further preliminaries.

Matt only barely managed to stay upright, hand on the wall tiles as he watched his cock disappear down Hooch's throat. So long since they'd done this, and the sight itself was driving him out of his mind, even before the sensations. He groaned as Hooch started to move.

It would take longer, with the first edge taken off, but Hooch didn't care, because he craved being on his knees, sucking Matt's cock. He used every trick, everything he'd ever known about his partner's body, not to make him come as quickly as he could, but to draw it out even longer.

Even knowing it was coming, Matt only managed to give a warning before he came, feeling his cum run down Hooch's throat. Hooch sucked him dry, making sure he got every drop, letting his tongue run over Matt's slowly softening cock in long luxurious strokes, until he ended in delicate laps, barely feathering across the wet skin.

Hooch pulled himself up eventually, cherishing the twinge in his knees from the hard surface. He grinned at Matt with an even more satisfied, and decidedly wet cat appearance. "Your ass is mine now." He gestured with his thumb vaguely in the direction of the bedroom.

"Always was," Matt returned the grin tiredly, turning off the water and all but stumbling out of the shower, slightly wobbly at the knees. He made a half hearted effort at toweling himself dry before heading to the bedroom, barely moving the covers aside before flopping down on his front. "You'll have to do all the work, though," he threw over his shoulder, "you've wiped me out." But he gave the little wriggle that always made Hooch pounce.

"Gladly." Hooch grinned and fulfilled Matt's expectations by attacking him with lips and fingers. Pushing his legs between Matt's thighs to open them up, he only stopped to find the lube in the bedside drawer.

The fuck was much slower than Matt had expected, despite the months of missing. Hooch was mindful of Matt having just come twice, and his entry and strokes were long and drawn-out instead of the rough and hard he thought he'd receive. When Hooch came, a string of soft curses mixed with Matt's name and breathless groans filled the room, before Hooch collapsed on top of him, with his arms wrapped tightly around Matt, nuzzling the back of his neck.

Matt lay still, relishing the familiar weight on him, and groaned a little in protest as Hooch recovered and withdrew. Hooch lifted himself off Matt, but quickly collapsed back on the bed again. "I'd get you a wet cloth if I could move." Hooch murmured, too sated to talk any louder. Reaching out, he let his hand caress up and down Matt's spine.

Matt made an inarticulate sound at the caress, something between a rumble and a purr. "Missed this," he murmured into the pillow, before the change in his breathing told Hooch that he'd conked out completely.

Hooch chuckled at Matt's coma, he was used to him passing out after really good sex. He dragged himself out of bed and to the bathroom, brought the promised wet cloth with him and cleaned up the sleeping man as best he could, before falling onto bed for a post-coital nap. Keeping contact with Matt's skin and Matt's body. This had been a close call, he was determined it would never happen again. If he lost this, he knew now, he'd lose everything that had ever meant anything.

Hooch fell asleep, thinking what a lucky bastard he was.

* * *

When Matt woke up from his cat-nap, Hooch was still asleep. Matt frowned as he was able to get up out of the bed, rearrange the covers over Hooch, pull on his clothes and leave the bedroom for the kitchen to start dishing up dinner, without Hooch waking up. Testament to how much strain Hooch had been under that he didn't move a muscle at the disturbance.

Matt got out the plates and flatware and set the table, waiting for a sound from the bedroom.

Eventually, the bedroom door opened and a bleary-eyed Hooch emerged with his short hair standing up in all directions. He was dressed in shorts and a t-shirt of Matt's, which was too wide in the shoulders for him, his body leaner. "How damned long did I sleep?" he groused, running a hand through his hair to smooth it down. "Hasn't happened to me in forever."

Matt glanced at the clock. "Less than an hour." He dished out the food, pleased that it hadn't all lost shape. "Needed it, though."

Hooch flashed a quick grin. "You saying I'm getting old?"

Matt gave him a look. "You?" he snorted, "you'll be still running rings around those youngsters in ten years." He found Hooch's Tabasco sauce, put it on the table, and sat down.

"Good to know." Hooch turned towards the bathroom with a, "be right back." He emerged a few moments later, his face still damp, while his hands smelled of soap.

"No ketchup?" He sounded disappointed when he sat down.

Matt smiled and shook his head at Hooch's desensitized taste buds, legacy of years of eating pretty much anything, and got the rest of the condiments out of the pantry, regardless of whether they went with the food.

He waited until Hooch had poured a liberal amount of ketchup over the chicken breast, before saying: "I've looked up a few clubs."

Hooch's fork was halfway in his mouth when he froze at Matt's statement. "What?" The fork went back down onto the plate.

"I've looked up a few clubs for you," Matt repeated. "You wouldn't believe how many there actually are, just in Raleigh. More in Charlotte. And, if we really want to get out of state, sky's the limit." He could have been discussing the football scores.

"Clubs. Clubs for me." Hooch repeated, more dumbfounded than he had any right to be. "You looked up clubs for me." He drew in a breath and held it for as long as he could, to keep himself from making any further comments that would potentially upset Matt. "Okay." He finally let out that breath.

Matt made a noise of confirmation as he speared a cube of sweet potato. "You said it yourself: it's something that you need sometimes, and, as we've agreed, we need some other outlet, if we're going to go back to living together. I'm not sure I can go as far as you need," Matt was honest, "at least not now. Maybe never. So we need to find something else."

The repeated 'we' had no emphasis, as though Matt was stating a perfectly obvious fact: they were in this together.

Hooch, though, had picked up on this immediately. "We?" He still hadn't continued eating, a frown steepling between his eyes. "And no, you can't. We've established that." He was on the defensive, walls building back up in nanoseconds

Matt's look was firm. "We," he used the emphasis, "because I am going with you to look them over and decide. We are going to pick one, and when you get...antsy, you are going to go there."

"I am, ain't I?" Hooch's eyes narrowed, shields in place.

"Yes." Matt pressed his point. "And when you are done, you can come back to me." He held the gaze, purposefully silent for a few moments. "You need it, I may or may not ever be able to give it to you, that's why we find something that means I do not ever have to pick up your carcass from an abandoned warehouse at the crack of dawn."

Hooch had locked himself into a battle of stare-down, but at the last words, he broke the gaze and lowered his eyes. "Okay."

Matt nodded, tension leaving him, as he went back to his food. "There are two public clubs with a private members area, and one solely members-only club in Raleigh. If we decide on Raleigh, the members-only one has the least risk of running into someone you know. If we go further, we can probably be less paranoid in Charlotte and there are more to choose from."

"Okay." Hooch hadn't taken his eyes off the plate and was swishing the now-cold piece of abandoned chicken repeatedly through the ketchup.

A hand descended onto his wrist. "Stop that." Matt increased the pressure until Hooch looked up. "I don't particularly like this." He said at last. "I hate that I can't be for you what you need. I hate the thought that someone else is going to be hurting you, humiliating you. But you need it if you're not going to crack. You know that this is the best—heck, probably the only—option that won't screw things up."

"You hate it." Hooch stated, dark eyes betrayed his turmoil. "How is this going to be anything but screwed up, if you hate it."

Matt's turn to look away. "How can I not, when I can't be what you need?" he said at last, repeating himself. "When it's taking huge risks in more ways than one? But," he met the dark, burning eyes again, "we need to work it out."

Hooch shook his head ever so slightly. "The more you want to be part of this the more you hate it, because you know more. It won't work. Let me do this alone."

Matt took a deep breath, knowing that his words were going to wound. "No fucking way. You did it alone last time. I. Am. Not. Letting. You. Do. That. Again." Each word clearly articulated, Matt's determination absolute.

"I need to," Hooch pulled his hand out of Matt's grip, "need to be alone."

Matt let him go to his study.

"Well, that went well," he said to the thin air, as he gathered up the plates and started to clean up.

He washed the dishes slowly, taking far longer than usual. Thinking, and keeping one eye on the closed study door. Never easy living with Hooch, but at least he only retreated further into the apartment, instead of taking off like he had in the early days.

Or as he had more recently, for that matter.

With an eye on the clock, Matt thought for a moment, then turned the oven on, letting it heat, while rummaging in the freezer for the apple pie he knew was there.

Half an hour later, the air was heavy with the scent of cinnamon and cloves when he saw the door to the study crack open, slowly opening further to reveal Hooch with his nose crinkled and sniffing the air.

"There's some ice-cream to go with it." Matt said, deliberately casual, feeling like a zoologist trying to lure some rare big cat out from its lair. Not too far from the truth, actually.

Hooch took a step further into the room. "Did you chuck out the chicken?"

"No, it's in the fridge." Matt sounded mildly horrified at the thought of throwing away perfectly good food. "I've got a couple of bread rolls heating up in there with the pie." White bread at that, which was usually forbidden at the table, a measure of the lengths he would go to lure Hooch out.

Another step, Hooch looked as if he were a puppet, pulled closer by the string that was the scent of food. "Do you have butter?"

"Yes." It was already on the kitchen bench, beckoning.

"Salted?" Hooch looked like a kid at Christmas.

Matt nodded. No way was he going to admit to Hooch just how many lonely dinners he'd had of full-fat macaroni and cheese on the couch in front of the television, his mother's recipe made for feeding hordes of active children.

Hooch padded across to his usual chair, still sniffing the air. He watched Matt heating the food, a pensive look on his face. "Never thought anyone would look after me. Never thought I wouldn't hate it."

"Sometimes shit really surprises us," that was as close as Matt got to philosophy. He opened the oven and took out the tray with the bread rolls, tipped them on a plate and put them in front of Hooch, before going back to the microwave for Hooch's chicken. He was nowhere near as assured as he sounded, evidenced as he absently took one of the rolls for himself. "You need looking after. I like doing it."

Hooch didn't seem to notice Matt's carb-fuelled faux pas, as he thickly buttered a hot roll. "Am I really that pathetic?"

"No," Matt's smile was back at the expression on Hooch's face. "Just human."

Hooch was thoughtfully chewing with a fairly blissed out expression on his face at the dripping salty buttery goodness. "Not quite. Seems to me most humans can look after themselves."

Matt snorted, "if they could, we'd all be hermits. And extinct." He brushed over the contradiction. "But like it or not, you are one extraordinary human being. You're not 'most humans'. You need someone to keep an eye on you, and that's me."

"Right." Hooch cut off a generous piece of chicken and chewed it, before he said anything else. "Is that your way of saying I'm off the 'normal' scale?"

Another snort. "Delta are all off the normal scale." Matt had just a smear of butter on his bread, but he was chewing it thoughtfully. "What sort of normal person would go through what you go through? Much less pass it? Voluntarily, at that?"

Hooch let out a huff of dry amusement. "Yeah, guess you're right. I can feed myself, though. On roots, hunted wildlife, insects…" He flashed a grin.

Matt wrinkled his nose. "If that's an offer, I think I'll keep on doing the cooking, thanks." He went back to the oven to turn it off and take out the pie so that it could cool slightly.

Hooch kept eating in silence for a while, until he had polished off all of the food. "Been thinking."

Matt raised an eyebrow, urging Hooch to go on. He took out the tub of ice cream from the fridge, a silent encouragement

"Do you want me back?"

Matt, who had been getting the ice cream scoop out of the drawer, straightened up in surprise. He had certainly not been expecting that. "Yes," he said, the simple truth, "but you can't keep running away."

"Not even into the study?" Hooch kept his gaze fixed on Matt.

Steady, meeting Hooch's eyes calmly. "It's only got one door, you can't fit through the window, and it's not difficult to lure you out. Retreating into the study I can deal with."

"If I give you my word I'd never run any further than the study, can I come back?"

Matt's smile grew as he reached out and grasped Hooch's hand. "Yes."

Hooch grinned back, taking the offered hand in a firm grip. "Promise me carbs and butter and ketchup in return?"

Matt laughed, "only in moderation, and as part of a balanced diet." He let go his grip and went to cut up the pie.

"I can live with that." Hooch watched Matt scooping the ice cream onto his pie. "I guess that means I'll have to get back to 'the talk' again, huh?"

"Did you honestly ever think I was going to let you off?" Matt put the bowl in front of Hooch. "My mistake in tackling it without feeding you first."

Hooch sighed, but Matt had put an extra large portion into his bowl, and that somehow eased the dread. "Can't I just leave it all to you and you tell me what to do and when and where to go?" Adding after a moment's hesitation, "with you." He'd accepted that Matt wasn't going to let go and this was Hooch's way of admitting that he'd been an ass.

Matt shook his head. "No." The feeling, almost like a thrill; the rare moments when Hooch was like this with him, like he'd managed to get a panther to walk at his heel, something so dangerous and powerful bending to his will. "This is for you, and we need to find a place that will give you what you need—or as much of it as possible, and where I'm satisfied that you'll be safe."

Hooch drew in a deep breath and nodded. He attacked the pie and ice cream to keep himself from dwelling on it too much. "The Raleigh place, then. The private one."

Matt nodded, though he knew that Hooch probably only saw the movement out of the corner of his eye. "Good, we'll start there, and move on to the others if it's not right."

"Can we change the topic now?"

Matt had to smile at Hooch's plaintive tone. Some things never changed. "Mandy's been moping around like a wet rag for the last week, but Jeff's still coming here at the weekends. Is there something happening on base?" Focusing on someone else other than themselves, and knowing that if Jeff had told Mandy something, it certainly couldn't be classified.

"Yeah, they'll be off in a couple weeks. Half a year at least." Hooch shoveled more half-molten ice-cream into his mouth. "If she's moping now, she'll be unbearable soon."

Matt closed his eyes at the thought of Mandy sulking for months. "Is this what people do when they're not worried about getting a dishonorable discharge?" it slipped out.

"Openly moping?" Hooch shrugged, "I guess."

Matt snorted. "We'll have to put up with it, I suppose. Problem with her being an army brat is that she pretty much knows exactly what could happen, so lying to her about it isn't going to make her feel any better."

"I never understood why anyone would want to be lied to." Hooch scraped the last of his dessert out of the bowl. "Better to face the facts." He put the spoon down and looked expectantly at Matt. "Is there any more?"

The pie dish with the rest of the pie was easily visible from Hooch's seat, as was the almost finished ice cream tub, but Matt had to smile at Hooch's attempt at subtlety in the face of sugar, as he obligingly pushed both over.

Some things, he thought, would never change.

Hooch flashed a grin as thanks, and tackled the remains of the dessert with dedication.

* * *

A week later, after Hooch had settled properly back into the apartment, Matt entered his study.

Hooch looked up from the laptop screen, squinting a little after staring for too long at the screen.

"So, I made an appointment."

"With whom?" Hooch frowned, trying to remember what kind of appointment Matt was talking about.

"With the club." Matt said calmly, as though he'd just made an appointment with the dentist.

"The club." Hooch repeated slowly and entirely unnecessarily. "Which one?"

"The private one in Raleigh, like we said. I've checked your diary, you're off on Monday, so if it doesn't suit we can have a look at the other two as well."

"You're better at organizing than I ever was, getting my team in and out from behind enemy lines." Hooch cast a wry grin and rubbed his tired eyes. "You got more intel on the club?"

"Mmmm," Matt made a noise as he waved a few sheets of paper he was holding his hand. "Application form and an introduction to the club, just a one-pager for that. Most of the information comes during the interview and tour of the club."

"Application form." Hooch commented. "Of course." He reached for the laptop and shut its lid before getting up. "Let's get on with it."

The first part of the application form was deceptively short, and, after the usual questions—contact details, age, gender, allergies—they came to a halt.

Hooch stared first at the form then at Matt. "What does that mean? 'Do you consider yourself to be D, M, s(u) or s(a)?' What the fuck's all that?"

Matt shook his head in bewilderment. "I'm not entirely sure. I think 'D' might stand for…" he trailed off. "No, not something that we should be getting wrong, I don't think. Leave it blank?"

"Yeah, I put n/a. Makes no fucking sense to me." Hooch scanned through the rest of the questions. "That one's easy: 'men only'." He glanced across at Matt, "you're filling it in, too?"

Matt nodded. "When I called, they said partners too, if there was one, whether they were going to join or not."

"Okay." The latter made more sense to Hooch. "Did they say anything about preferring couples attending to single attendees?" He put another n/a beside the questions regarding preference of leather, PVC or rubber.

Matt shook his head, "only that they were quite firm that if one of a couple was going to be coming, that the other had to know what was going on. I suppose the last thing they want is an outraged spouse trying to break in and screaming the place down."

Hooch huffed a short laugh. "Sounds like fun to me, would make the place livelier. So far it sounds as hot as a stockbroker's canteen."

"I think," Matt replied dryly, ticking the box next to 'leather' after few moments thought, "that lively is likely to bring the cops, and all sorts of interesting questions that don't generally get asked in stockbrokers' canteens." His pen hesitated at the rest of the page, as he left a great many blank.

"Good point. Score one for you." Hooch quickly filled in his stats. Height, weight, hair color, eye color...then hesitated. "How hairy or not hairy am I, you think?"

Matt looked up from his contemplation of the same question, where he'd made a mark near, but not at the 'smooth' end. "Somewhere in the middle," he said, after a moment's thought. "We could take some off, if you feel like it, but putting more on is a bit difficult."

"Why would I want to take any of my body hair off?" Hooch shrugged. "I shave my balls, that's enough. Smooth suits you though." He dutifully put his tick in the middle. "Piercings? Hell, no."

Matt continued down the page, ticking the appropriate boxes, leaving blank the ones with the incomprehensible acronyms, before finishing. Hooch was still working his way methodically down the last page, so Matt picked up the page where a summary of the facilities and services was listed, and scanned it briefly, eyebrows climbing to his hairline.

"What?" Hooch glanced across at Matt's expression, as he finished the last of the many n/as.

Matt handed the piece of paper over. "It's...comprehensive..." he choked, mind boggling. He wondered how big the building had to be to fit all those possibilities in.

"Not a fucking clue what most of that stuff is. Sounds more like a fashion mall than an S/M club."

"There's got to be something that you like there." Matt worried a lip as he pondered just how many members there might be, if that much was on offer. The thought that anyone from the base would be in the same position as Hooch did not make him feel any better.

"It's not about liking things, Matt. I don't care what the place looks like, what props they have, none of that bullshit." Hooch shrugged. "Does it say how many members they have?"

Matt shook his head. "No," he paused, "but since they do emphasize confidentiality and discretion, I wouldn't think that they would." He sighed and put the piece of paper down, looking at Hooch. "Beer?"

"Beer." Hooch confirmed. "Can't say I'm looking forward to that interview. Stop me from punching the guy if he gets too annoying."

"Will do," Matt agreed, getting up and going to the fridge. "Sounded English," he added, "posh, like their officers back in the Gulf."

"Does that mean I have to dig out my upbringing?"

"I have no idea," Matt said honestly, as he sat back down on the couch and handed Hooch the second bottle. Rare enough that Hooch made any allusion to his childhood and the wealth he'd left behind. There were occasional phone calls, and a present each Christmas from Hooch's younger sister, but otherwise there seemed to be no contact with his family except for the odd summons back to Texas that Hooch obeyed only if it could not be avoided. The presents were luxurious and tasteful, but things that were very much not Hooch, such as cashmere scarves and sweaters, expensive sports watches, or exquisitely crafted cases and bags for his electronic gadgets that said, more than anything else, 'I have absolutely no idea what you like or what you are like.'

"He's looking for paying members for his club, not dinner party guests." Matt pointed out.

"How much is the fee anyway?" Hooch clinked his bottle against Matt's.

"Scaled," Matt hedged, "depending on what you're after."

"Right…" Hooch took another mouthful of his beer. "That's vague. What's the scale? The starting point?"

Matt waited until Hooch had swallowed before giving him the figure.

"Holy fuck!" Hooch blurted out. "For that much I can expect getting my dick gilded."

"For that much you can expect that nobody finds out," Matt retorted.

"Score two to the golden boy here." Hooch raised his bottle to indicate a salute to Matt. "Thank fuck I got money." He suddenly laughed, a deep, throaty chuckle. "Damn, if that isn't the best of it all."

Matt looked at him in confusion.

"The money." Hooch said, as if that explained everything.

"You've lost me." Matt put the beer bottle down, wondering what had set Hooch off.

"My inheritance." Hooch finished his beer. "Did I not tell you about it?"

"You've never said anything about your family." Matt pointed out. "I'd always thought they were off-limits."

"I have nothing to say about them. My sister's alright, but not sure where she lives now. The rest are a bunch of dickheads who think money and social status are all that counts. And looks, for the ladies." Hooch shrugged. "My family made big bucks in cattle and oil. Hardly ever saw my mother and father as a kid, business, society events, all that shit. Couldn't care less about them. Inherited stuff from my grandfathers. Couldn't stand either of them, but then they didn't give a shit about kids unless they promised to take over the family business. I wasn't having that." Hooch fell silent, then, "as far as I remember I've got shares, cash, investments, bonds, and land."

Matt's jaw dropped open as he sat up straight. "So you're telling me you're loaded?"

"Guess so. Don't know how much, haven't checked in years. I could call my financial adviser."

Matt shook his head. "I finally get why you were so insistent on trying to put money into this place," his hand took in not just the apartment but the whole gym. He paused, realizing what Hooch hadn't said. "They don't know what it is you do, and they don't know you're gay, do they?"

"They know I'm army, which pissed them off when I enlisted. They were angry because I didn't take over the family business and I didn't even study, nor go for commission. They don't know anything else, told them it's classified. They've never asked." Hooch tilted his head. "Sofia, my sister, she knows I'm Special Forces, but nothing personal. As for my sexuality, any idea what that perfect Texan society pair would do if their good family name was tainted that way?" He let out a humorless laugh. "I'm not going to be responsible for their early graves."

Matt felt a rush of gratitude for his own family, the acceptance and love, and how they'd welcomed Hooch unquestioningly, for his sake. Clearly there had been a reason that Hooch's family had been off-limits for so long. He put his hand on Hooch's now-tense arm, a comfort more than any words could bring.

Hooch gazed down at Matt's hand, and when he looked back up, he had visibly relaxed. "That's why paying with my family's money for getting off by having the crap beaten and fucked out of me," he smiled to placate Matt, "made me laugh. It's probably enough to pay for a lifetime of club membership, I'll check tomorrow."

Matt exhaled as Hooch seemed to come out of the low mood. Clearly yet another thing that would take careful handling in the future. He smiled, hand not leaving Hooch's arm. "Good." He looked at the time. "I'm starving. Do you want some food, too?"

"Let's go out for food." Hooch stood up, "I pay."

Matt laughed in reply. "Why not? I've had a sugar daddy all these years and never known—might as well make up for lost time."

The club looked like a low-rise office building, several levels and a basement parking lot that was card-access only. New, with lots of steel and concrete and tinted one-way glass. The automatic doors opened to a small reception area, which would have been claustrophobic had it not been open the entire height of the building, and lit by a false skylight that gave off a diffused glow. The security/reception desk looked like any other security/reception desk anywhere. The very attractive female receptionist, who greeted them and asked them to wait on the low black leather banquettes that surrounded the walls of the reception area, was wearing a beautifully-cut suit that was clearly made to fit her like a glove, and razor-sharp stilettos—she had the legs and body to carry both off.

The narrow black leather choker around her neck looked like a fashion statement, a contrast against the deceptively conservative outfit.

No hint of what this place was. Sleek and modern, with polished chrome, glass and steel, black leather and white tiles, it looked like some dot-com that had cleverly sold out at the top of the market and then invested the windfall into something even more lucrative and far more substantial. The windows, in the reception area at least, were covered by plasterboard from the inside so there was no chance of seeing in, or out.

One of the wall panels facing the main door pivoted and a young man came out. Like the receptionist, wearing a tailored suit that fit him exactly, but without a tie—so that the plain black leather collar was prominent against the crisp whiteness of his impeccably ironed shirt. "If you will follow me, please?" he asked, indicating the opening that he had just emerged from.

Behind the wall was a wide corridor. Like the reception area, it had been painted and tiled an off-white, with doors spaced on either side. At one of the doors the man stopped, knocked, and after a precise three seconds, opened the door and entered the room, holding it open for Hooch and Matt to follow.

The large office—though it was likely that the actual administrative work was done elsewhere—was, like the rest of the interior, sleek and modern. There were two large desks towards the end of the room, on a slightly raised dais. One aggressively tidy, as though it was just for show, and the other had a woman sitting behind it.

There were a number of low, black leather and chrome sofas in the middle of the room, and a man sitting on the one that faced the door.

Hooch's eyebrows had raised considerably by now. What he thought of the whole thing was written clearly in his face, but for Matt's sake and for the promise he'd made, he kept quiet and forced himself not to turn round on his heels and leave.

The impeccably dressed and equally perfectly groomed gentleman stood up as they entered. He took a couple of steps towards them, and with the poshest English accent either Matt or Hooch had ever heard, he greeted them while holding out his hand for a shake. "Good day, gentlemen. I am Mark Robertson, the proprietor of this establishment."

He didn't introduce the woman behind the desk, who kept her eyes downwards and on her work at all times.

A glance showed that Hooch wasn't going to be doing anything, so Matt stepped forward to take the offered hand. "Matthew Donahue. This is Hubert Bozic."

"Pleased to meet you Mr. Donahue." Robertson cast a quick glance from Matt to Hooch who hadn't moved yet, and seemed to come to a conclusion. He let go of Matt's hand and addressed him again. "May I?" Indicating with an elegant hand movement to Hooch, who stared at Robertson in disbelief and confusion.

Matt's eyebrows echoed Hooch's and his expression was completely bewildered. "May you what?"

"May I shake Mr. Bozic's hand." Robertson explained mildly, with just the slightest bit of surprise, as if he hadn't quite expected Matt not to understand his request straight away.

"Why the fuck is he asking you?" Hooch looked at Matt, his voice low and—only known to Matt who knew him so well—rather menacing.

Matt was feeling like he was in a play where everyone else had the script except him. He blinked. "Um, I think that's up to him?" He hated how his voice went up at the end of the sentence, betraying just how confused he was.

"Ah." Robertson made a delicate sound as he nodded his understanding of the situation. "Perhaps we should go through the application form in that case." He held his hand out to Hooch, who shook it briefly, purely out of ingrained manners, then let go as quickly as he could, as if that finely manicured hand was poisonous. "Gentlemen, would you like to follow me?" Robertson gestured ahead and to a door, which led to a smaller room. Far more intimate, with equally modern, but more comfortable furniture: a U-shaped sofa arrangement of white leather and chrome with a low glass and chrome table in the middle.

Matt started to open his mouth, but decided that the morning was quite weird enough as it was and followed, nudging Hooch in front of him to make sure he didn't slip away.

If Robertson noticed the nudge he didn't let on as he closed the door behind them, and waited for his guests to sit down first. "Beverages will be brought in three minutes." He smiled graciously. "May I take a look at the forms?"

Matt had them in a folder and handed them over, feeling more apprehensive than he'd ever been since seeking this place out. However weird it was, though, anything had to be better than a repeat of the disaster back in November.

Hooch leaned back on the couch, looking deceptively relaxed, but Matt could read the tension lines all along his body and in his carefully neutral expression.

"Thank you, Mr. Donahue." Robertson pulled out the forms and cast a quick glance over them. His face didn't show anything other than politeness. "Perhaps we should look at Mr. Bozic's form first?"

Hooch shrugged.

That very moment, exactly three minutes after they had entered, the woman who had been behind the desk came inside after a knock. Eyes kept downwards, she entered with a tray with a variety of hot and cold beverages, which she arranged pleasantly on the table, including a plate of small, exquisitely looking British biscuits. She walked back out quickly and quietly, with Hooch staring at her as she walked to the door and out backwards, in unbelievably high stiletto heels, their ankle straps fastened to her slim ankles with small padlocks. She never presented her back to them, and the door closed as softly behind her as it had opened.

"Please, gentlemen, help yourselves." Robertson said, before studying Hooch's form.

Matt had been staring at the closed door, and blinked several times before turning back to Robertson.

This time it was Hooch who nudged Matt, before he reached for the delicate china coffee pot, pouring into two equally delicate china cups. Cream and milk were in polished silver vessels, and so was the sugar.

"Well, gentlemen," Robertson looked up from the form with a courteous smile, "I see there are quite a few questions that were answered with 'n/a'. Do I understand correctly that neither of you has been a part of the scene yet?"

"No," Matt shook his head, taking the cup from Hooch. "New for both of us, though it'll be Hubert who'll be coming, as I said."

Hooch groaned. "Do me a favor, Matt. Not Hubert." He took a sip from the far too dainty cup and focused on Robertson. "It's Hooch, and no, I've never been into any 'scene'. Looks like a lot of bullshit to me."

Robertson inclined his head with a mild-mannered smile. If he was shocked at Hooch's language, he didn't let it show. "Hooch it is, then. Please do call me Mark, we like to have a friendly relationship with our members." He looked at the form again. "Am I correct in assuming that you might not be familiar with the terminology on the forms?"

The expanses of unticked boxes and neat 'n/a's on both forms were fairly obvious, but Matt nodded in agreement nonetheless.

Hooch just rolled his eyes in silence.

"In that case, let us go through the form together. Hooch, would you call yourself a dom, or a master, or a sub or a slave?"

"Huh?" Was all Hooch managed.

"And you, Matt?"

"I don't think we're any of those," Matt said warily.

"If you don't explain what all of that means you'll never get an answer." Hooch challenged.

"Of course, my apologies, gentlemen." Robertson never stopped smiling politely. "A dom is someone, male or female, who enjoys dominating others, male or female. This may or may not include physical domination such as bondage, inflicting of pain, verbal and/or physical humiliation, sexual domination, or a combination of any and all of the above." Robertson nodded slightly, unfazed by the narrowing of Hooch's eyes. "A master or mistress is someone who enjoys dominating others, male or female, but in a more intimate and possessive way. They tend to own a male or female as their slave, and the relationship tends to be formalized and often 24/7. Does any of this strike either of you as fitting?"

Hooch's reply came without hesitation. "No way." He glanced sideways at Matt.

"No," Matt was in full agreement, "absolutely not."

"Well, then," Robertson still didn't show any surprise, "perhaps I should explain s and s. A sub enjoys to be dominated with any or all of what a dom does provide. They do not seek a 24/7 formal ownership situation, like a slave usually does. Does any of this strike you as fitting?"

Matt hesitated. "Definitely not a slave situation, but sub...sometimes?" He turned to look at Hooch, not quite sure how to articulate. How could he explain that Hooch could never fit into anyone's tidy, well-thought-out form, or any neat boxes?

Hooch shook his head. "No."

"No?" Robertson asked, for the first time showing a little surprise. "May I ask what you would see yourself as?"

"I'm a masochist. Simple as that. Can't do with all the frills and bullshit." Hooch frowned, his tension up a notch.

"I'm afraid in this club we do have to have certain classifications, it helps run the establishment smoothly and ensure the safety and discretion of our members."

"I won't let you fit me into one of your damned boxes." Hooch growled.

"Hooch," Matt placed a hand on Hooch's arm before it got out of hand. He turned to face Robertson, "I didn't talk about this on the phone, but we've come here even though we're not interested in 'the scene' because we—Hooch—needs a higher level of discretion. He's a masochist," Matt repeated, was that the first time he'd said it out loud? "and I can't give him what he needs, not at the level that he needs. We can't risk a public club."

Robertson looked at Matt then Hooch, taking in the hand on Hooch's arm, and how the latter seemed to calm down, as if holding himself back for the younger man's sake. "I think I understand." Robertson nodded before reaching to pour himself a cup of tea out of the china tea pot. "I suggest in this case we forego the forms and have a chat instead. I will have an individually customized file drawn up for you." Adding a splash of milk to his tea, he thoughtfully stirred it with a finely crafted silver spoon. "We do keep our members' professions and special requirements regarding their personal context on file, but not computerized, merely on good old fashioned cardboard." Robertson took a sip. "Under lock and key, of course, in a safe. The reason why, is so that we are aware at all times and no mistakes can be made, while greatest security is guaranteed." He took another sip. "I take it you are military, Hooch?"

Hooch nodded when he was addressed directly. "Fort Bragg."

"We have a number of military members, but none based at Fort Bragg at present," Robertson told them. "I assure you that we are well accustomed to the sensitivities."

"I'm also gay." Hooch glanced at Matt and added, "obviously."

"Ah, yes, I see that on the form." Robertson pointed to a tick on the top file he'd put onto the table. "Exclusively men." He had found his gracious smile again. "How are you planning to join the club? Will both of you be visiting us?"

A quickly exchanged glance. "Just Hooch, at this stage," Matt answered, "this is for him. Unless he wants me there. I'm…" he hesitated, "I'm not really into this sort of thing. Pretty much vanilla."

Robertson inclined his head, appearing to be deep in thoughts for a moment. "I understand." If he did or did not was impossible to figure out. "In that case, I assume you will prefer to wear your partner's collar, Hooch?"

Hooch's eyes tore open and his upper body snapped forward. "What?"

"Collar?" Matt blinked, hard.

"Oh." Robertson let out softly. "Did you not read all of the materials that were sent to you at time of application? At the club, we have a simple way of identifying what those who are seeking to be dominated," he carefully emphasized the word, to make clear he acknowledged that it was meant to stand for the wide range that included Hooch's masochism, "are looking for. Members who are slaves to other members usually wear collars, in many instances as an everyday adornment to signify the complete ownership. Some subs who come with their partners do not wear them, because their dominant partner will be here to guide and order, so there is no room for error. Slaves hardly ever come here on their own, and if they do, then their owner will have made arrangements beforehand, such as loaning them out to other members, so that the slave is always taken care of. Subs who come on their own and are seeking the possibility of a more formalized or closer relationship with a suitable dom, those won't be wearing a collar, to signify they are not owned in any way. However, someone such as yourself, Hooch, you are in a partnership, thus you are owned and not seeking. Therefore you should be wearing Matt's collar, so that it is clear without room for misunderstandings, that you are not seeking any kind of relationship with a dom. Besides, the collars are our ways of indicating what someone who seeks to be dominated is looking for: red for females, blue for males, both colors on collar-flashes if both genders are sought. Any other preferences will be made available to fellow members in an internal file. Such as penetration, or CBT, or flogging, or electro shocks, and so on."

Hooch was staring at Robertson when he had finished. There was only one word his brain had latched onto. "Owned?"

Matt, less stoic than Hooch, was doing a credible imitation of a goldfish, and couldn't get so much as a syllable out, and just stared at the two of them mutely.

"You are, aren't you?" Robertson looked kindly from one to the other of the men sitting opposite to him.

Matt choked, "I...er...I..." he trailed off.

Hooch turned his head and stared at Matt.

"Well, gentlemen?" Robertson smiled, taking a sip of his tea.

Matt closed his open mouth shut with an audible click. "I don't think so," he backed away, much as the mental thought of Hooch wearing a collar, and nothing else, was strangely arousing. "But that might be best, yes." He hid behind his teacup, a slightly comical sight in such a large man.

"We'll talk about that later." Hooch's voice lacked any inflexion. He looked back at Robertson, face neutral but a new set of determination on his face. "Yes. I will wear a collar. No, I am not interested in any kind of relationship with anyone else in any way shape or form. Nor am I interested in any fetish clothing or ritual or anything at all. It's ridiculous." He leaned forward and came closer to Robertson's face than the man very obviously liked. Right into his personal space. "To make this clear, I want pain. I want humiliation. I want extremes. If that means I get to be the attraction on stage so be it. If that means I have to wear a collar with blue, or camo, or polka dots, or any other bullshit, then so be it. No marks ever outside of what my uniform covers. Everything else: I don't care. As long as I get what I need so I can go back home and be the partner to Matt that he deserves. So, no amateurs and no beginners. I don't take kindly to anything but the best." He sat back.

Robertson had lost his polite smile, and his speech as well, it seems. Visibly flustered. This was not how any sub was supposed to behave. But at the back of his mind was the thought of just what an attraction someone like this was going to be for the hardcore doms. He nodded, trying to keep his equilibrium. Fort Bragg. It wasn't difficult to guess what Hooch might be. He nodded. "I'm sure we can accommodate." He made a few notes about the uniform. "Do you have any medical issues you haven't put on the forms?" he asked, "Pre-existing injuries?"

"Fractured pelvis. Healed but might cause trouble." Hooch looked at Matt. "Anything else?"

Matt gave Hooch an affectionate, if exasperated, look and recited the long list of other 'minor' old injuries, the broken bones, the sprains, the other bits and pieces of Hooch's body that were evidence of a long and hard career.

Robertson was making notes, having found his balance once more, not batting an eyelid at the long list of injuries. Eventually, he put the expensive pen down. "We require monthly STD screening for those of our members who prefer to forego condoms, which are, as you can imagine, most. I trust this meets with your approval?"

Both Hooch and Matt nodded.

"Very well." Robertson smiled. As odd and unsettling as this Hooch was, Robertson could increasingly see the attraction and potential. His club would undoubtedly profit from this new member. "Is there anything you absolutely do not do?"

Hooch thought for no longer than about a second. "No. Except for shit."

A scratch of the pen as he picked it up and made a final note. "That's the most common one," he said conversationally. "Would you like a tour of the facilities before we come back to finish the administrative details? I imagine you might want to stretch your legs."

"Why not." Hooch answered, looking at Matt to see if he agreed.

Matt nodded and stood up, feeling a rush of relief that the interview seemed over, or at least suspended.

They followed Robertson out of interview room and back into the large office, which led to the reception area. A door with a keypad led through to a corridor with several doors leading to the left and the right. Everything was scrupulously clean and gleaming. "We have all sorts of themed rooms. Medical examination rooms, fully stocked from enema kits over speculums and TENS units to a vast variety of needles and syringes; we have a medieval torture chamber with associated dungeon and cages, including suspended ones. The replicas are all made to the highest specifications. We have a salon emulating the sensory impressions of the eighteenth and nineteenth centuries, for those preferring the old world charm of ritualized slavery," at that Hooch almost let out a groan of disbelief, but caught himself and rolled his eyes at Matt instead. "We have a variety of modern rooms and even one specializing in blood play, but our main attraction is what I like to call the theatre." Robertson opened a set of black double doors that led into a vast room with seating, tables, a mind boggling array of bondage equipment and bondage furniture, steel chains and manacles from walls and ceiling, and in pride of place, at the very centre of the room, a round, raised stage.

Matt had been trying not to gape at the rooms. One thing to have them neatly laid out on bullet points on a one-page factsheet that looked like one from a fancy hotel, quite another to see it all laid out in front of him. He stepped into the 'theatre' with a slight sense of trepidation, and turned to look at Hooch. Here, he suspected, was where he'd spend most of his time.

Hooch took only one look at the vast room and its stage, then kept his eyes on Matt. He reached for Matt's shoulder and gave it a squeeze. "It's okay. I've seen enough." He looked at Robertson, but didn't step away from Matt. "I can see that the steep fee is warranted. I'd like to set up payment one year in advance. Can this be arranged?"

Robertson blinked. He couldn't remember the last time he'd been quite so taken aback by a new member. He nodded quickly. "Of course." A pause, "shall we go back to the office to finalize matters?"

"Yes." Both Hooch and Matt replied at the same time and Hooch added, "as quickly as possible. I've had enough of formalities for now." Whenever he showed a veneer of manners, he seemed to need a dose of bluntness to counteract. They followed Robertson back into the office, where Hooch informed him that he didn't feel like filling in any more forms and if anyone wanted to know his preferences they just had to try.

The rest of the details were sorted out quickly and efficiently, and Robertson watched them exit through the main doors and to the public car park opposite on the security cameras. He was rarely flummoxed, but they had to be one of the oddest pairs he'd seen in a while. Bozic was certainly the most interesting prospect he'd come across in a long time. Military, he'd bet either high ranking or a very vital job, or both—extreme masochist—and completely under the thumb of his partner without realizing. A partner who didn't know that he owned Bozic. Obviously substantial financial resources, too. A puzzle indeed. Robertson tidied the notes and put them in a new file, before locking them away in the safe.

Hooch and Matt sat in silence in the truck, until they were out of Raleigh and well down the highway back to Fayetteville.

Hooch set the truck onto cruise control and turned his head towards Matt. "So."

"Will it do?" Matt asked, somewhat redundantly, given the amount of money that Hooch had just paid. There had been much to think about, not least all those odd assumptions by that really odd owner.

Hooch shrugged, eyes back on the road. "Will have to. At least it's secure." He drew in a deep breath, holding it for a moment. "I just don't get it, though."

"Get what?" Not as though Matt didn't suspect. "The way they have all those rules and frills and fancy equipment?"

"No. I get that one. It's for boring people who have to pretend they aren't boring." Hooch scrubbed a hand over his face. "The ownership thing. The collar."

"It worries you?" Matt asked. It certainly worried him, with Robertson's automatic assumption that Hooch was somehow his possession. "That was weird," he agreed. "Do we give off freaky vibes?"

Hooch didn't answer for a long time. When he eventually did, he kept looking ahead at the road. "You built the gym and the apartment, you chose how it looks. You organize our everyday life and you make me eat healthy stuff. You gave me an ultimatum to go seek a club, you sought the club for me, and I will be going there. I cannot imagine a life without you because those two months were unbearable. I left without argument when you told me to. I asked you to take me back. You tell me off when I behave like an antisocial bastard. You talk for me when I'm too much of that bastard to function in polite society." Hooch finally glanced at Matt. "Anything else?"

A momentary stunned silence. "I think that just about covers it." Matt replied, then paused to think. "I look after you," he said, repeating what he'd said the night he'd taken Hooch back, "because I like it, and you need someone to look after you." Letting it settle as the road passed under the tires. "That doesn't mean all the freaky stuff he was saying." Matt added, too quickly.

"Freaky stuff such as?" Hooch's voice didn't give away any of his thoughts or feelings.

"Like the ownership stuff, the slave stuff he was going on about," Matt said. "The whole asking me if he could shake your hand, as though you were a pet or something."

"Pet…" Hooch huffed a laugh. "Your pet Delta. Not that off the cuff, is it?"

Matt smiled, the first that day. "I guess." That thought again, of Hooch wearing a collar and nothing else, flashed through his mind. "I wonder where he gets all that stuff," he said, changing the subject.

"No way, Donahue, none of this." Hooch flashed a grin at Matt. "No changing of the subject. You made me go to that club, you sit through this talk. Don't like your own medicine, huh?"

Matt tried not to squirm. "Okay, fine, it freaked me out a bit—like that woman who didn't say anything and never made eye contact and was wearing those heels. How he was treating her as if she didn't exist. If that's ownership, that makes me…" he couldn't think of the word, "well, that just freaks me out." He was using that word a lot today.

"Yeah, but I guess it's that weird slave stuff they have going on." Hooch felt more at ease now than he had all day. Somehow a few things were falling into place. "I'm not slave material, and you're the first person to know that. I don't obey well at all, outside of work, and even there I've always had a reputation." Hooch indicated as he overtook another car, then slotted back into his lane. "One thing's true, though, I don't want anyone but you. When I was gone, those two months, I wasn't even alive."

"Neither was I, much." Matt was looking out the window. "Wanting you back and yet knowing I couldn't go through that again if you just took off. Feeling furious…and empty that I couldn't give you what you needed. Terrified what you would do without me there."

"Maybe we own each other." Hooch surprised himself with that statement, and it showed on his face.

Matt looked at him in shock, and then in contemplation. "Shit," he said after a long pause, "I think you're right." More silence. "Maybe it changes," he hazarded, "and he jumped to the conclusion because I was the one who dragged you there."

"Whatever." Hooch shrugged, "fact is I'm going to wear your collar." The word sounded weird in his mouth. "Any preferences?" he added, some part of him enjoyed seeing Matt squirm.

"Your choice. You're going to be the one wearing it," Matt retorted. Too quickly, hoping Hooch didn't notice just how much that disturbingly turned him on. "Where on earth are we going to get one? Should have got one back there," he meant Raleigh.

"No, it's going to be yours, so you choose." Hooch definitely did enjoy Matt's discomfiture.

A sign caught Matt's eye, thankfully relieving him of the need to answer straight away. "Stop here. I think we'll find what we're looking for right there, don't you think?" He pointed to a large barnlike building in a row of superstores. 'PetSmart' read the gaudy sign.

"PetSmart?" Hooch asked, but turned off the highway and into the parking lot.

"Pet Delta," Matt repeated Hooch's earlier joking words, "and where else are we going to find one without having to sneak in some dodgy back alley somewhere or risk some interestingly raised eyebrows from the post office?"

Hooch laughed. "Yeah, good point." He killed the engine and got out of the truck. "Does my neck look 'Rottweiler' to you?"

Matt snorted as he got out his side. "Thick enough, sure. Let's get this over and done with."

They were greeted inside by a young sales assistant. "Can I help you, Sirs?"

"Hi," Matt stepped in before Hooch's sense of humor could indulge itself, "looking for a collar for a dog. A big one." He determinedly did not look at Hooch.

"What breed?" She smiled at both. Hooch remained silent, hands in his pockets, and with an unidentifiable smirk on his face.

"Rottweiler cross," Matt said firmly. "Something sturdy, in black leather." Luckily, he still refused to look at Hooch, because the growing smirk would have made him blush or crack.

"Of course," the sales girl motioned for them to follow her to an aisle with dog collars. Every single type one could think of was displayed by increasing thickness and width. "Would you like to choose for yourselves or do you require help? Oh, and if you need a lead or a chain, they are behind you." She smiled at them.

"We'll be fine browsing, thanks." Matt hoped he didn't sound as choked as he felt.

"Just holler if you need any help." She cheerfully replied. "I'll be at the checkout." She finally walked off, just in time for Hooch to make an all too amused sound.

Matt watched her go and serve another customer before he glared at Hooch. "Not a word."

"Is that an order?" Hooch bared his teeth in a grin.

Matt just glared before selecting a collar off the display and glancing between it and Hooch's neck. "This one?" he asked.

"Let's see." Hooch took the collar from Matt's hands and without further ado, slipped it round his neck, to all intents and purposes about to buckle it closed.

The black leather looked disturbingly good against Hooch's tanned skin and plain white t-shirt, and Matt had to swallow before answering. "Yeah, it's the right size." He all but snatched an identical one off the same display and marched off to the checkout.

Hooch looked at Matt's quickly retreating back, then at the collar he had pulled back off his neck and grinned. Whatever wasp had stung Matt, he enjoyed the reaction. He put the collar back on the display and followed.

"Want me to pay?" Hooch asked.

Matt was already fumbling with his wallet. "No, I've got it." Handing over the cash and answering the small talk about the non-existent dog. Which was apparently, according to him, very large, absolutely ferocious towards those who threatened the family, but a complete softie with those he knew. He didn't glance at Hooch as he picked up the bag with the collar, refused a catalogue, and retreated to the parking lot.

When Hooch opened the truck doors for them, the grin was still firmly in place. "Ferocious, huh? Softie, huh?" He waited for Matt to climb into the truck before he followed. "I think I need to decompress from this crazy day of revelations when we get home."

Matt had his eyes closed and seemed to be forcing himself back under control. "I'm glad you find this funny," he said, half under his breath, and then realized that he was holding the collar in his hands. The thin plastic not much of a barrier, his finger tracing up and down its length.

"You don't?" Hooch steered them back onto the highway. He remained silent for a moment, pondering. "No, you don't. Something has you riled up. What is it?"

Matt still had his eyes closed. "It looked..." he swallowed, "really good. Trust me, I was about three seconds away from ripping your jeans off and fucking you in the aisle next to the kitty litter."

"I didn't expect that." Hooch voice had immediately slipped a notch into huskiness, and the steering wheel got a little jerk. He glanced at Matt. "I'll floor it home."

By the time they arrived back in Fayetteville, Matt had regained some of his composure. Enough that he made it through the gym, managed to exchange greetings with a few of the regulars, before heading upstairs, the bag with the collar held in a white-knuckled grip.

Hooch followed shortly behind, nodding a greeting at Mandy and a couple of regulars who'd been persistent enough in greeting him to kick his manners into being and to greet them back. When he reached the apartment, he locked the door behind him. Matt was standing in the middle of the room, back towards him.

Hooch stopped, dropped the keys in the bowl beside the door, took off his jacket and hung it up without a word. Unlacing his boots, he toed out of them, then took one step forward while pulling the t-shirt over his head and discarding it on the floor. He had opened the belt buckle and was about to unbutton the black denims, when Matt finally turned round.

He still had the bag with the collar in his hand. "Stop." A single word, voice shaking slightly, but Hooch stilled immediately. Fingers on the last button, he didn't move a muscle. Matt stepped closer, until he was close enough for Hooch to see that his eyes were almost completely dilated, just a narrow ring of green around the pupil.

Hooch's lips parted, but he didn't say anything. His dark gaze locked with Matt's as he stood perfectly still.

"Are you sure about this?" Matt's voice was slightly steadier now, but husky, as he took the collar out of the bag. Holding it with both hands, he never took his eyes off Hooch's.

"Yes."

Not a word, not even a nod, as Matt raised his hands with the collar and slipped it around Hooch's neck. He adjusted the buckle so that it fitted smoothly, not affecting Hooch's breathing but enough that it lay next to the skin.

Hooch swallowed visibly, the leather snug against his throat as he did. He'd never thought the symbol of the collar would affect like that, but it did, entirely unexpected.

Teeth at his neck, just nipping above the leather, as Matt's hands covered his at the buttons of his jeans, pushing them down. Hooch let his head fall back, giving as much access to Matt's teeth and the above and below the collar, as he could. His hands moved down, pushed the denims and briefs over his rapidly hardening cock, then stayed at his side, passive.

Matt's hands moved over Hooch's body, touch firm as they grabbed Hooch's ass, pulling him closer. Continuing to bite around the collar, pressing harder as Hooch writhed under his hands, reveling in the sensation, the coiled power under his fingertips, the metallic taste of blood in his mouth...

"Oh shit!"

Matt pulled back as though burned, staring at Hooch, at the bloodied mark on the side of his neck, before undoing the collar and practically throwing it on the couch.

"Wait here, I'll get the first aid kit." Matt darted off to the bathroom for the small kit they kept at the apartment.

"Wait!" Hooch called after him, but when he tried to follow, he tripped over the forgotten trousers round his ankles, and landed on his ass with a curse. "Matt!"

Matt was back, first aid kit in hand. "Shit, shit, shit," he cussed, kneeling down next to Hooch and dabbing at the small wound—only barely breaking the skin, but enough that it was bleeding. "Does that hurt? Oh crap. I think we'll get away without putting a dressing on it but oh crapthat'sgoingtoshow." He was dimly aware that he was starting to babble.

"Matt!" Hooch barked out the name like an order. Taking hold of Matt's shoulders. "Look at me, Matt, and shut up for a second. It's okay. It's nothing. You hear me? It's nothing."

"You're bleeding!" Matt was staring at Hooch's neck. "I bit you! I didn't even...I didn't even..." his voice trailed off and he looked at Hooch in bewilderment. "I didn't even realize I'd done it."

"You call that bleeding? Don't be ridiculous, hardly even a drop." Hooch cupped Matt's face and drew it closer. "You didn't realize you were doing it because you found it hot, as much as I did. That's not a problem."

Bewilderment turned to distress. "That'll show above your uniform," Matt repeated. "I…I…" his shoulders slumped as he pulled out of Hooch's grasp. "Well, that settles it. I'm really not cut out for this sort of thing."

Hooch was about to protest and try talk sense into Matt, but the dejected look made him realize it would be pointless. "Come on, look at me." Hooch moved so he knelt in front of Matt, ankles still restricted by his trousers. "Come on."

Matt obeyed, eyes still full of distress and the bloodied tissue held uselessly in one hand. "I don't get it," he said at last. "I really don't get it."

"It's okay." Hooch said in a far more soothing voice than a man like him should be capable of. "You are who you are and if you weren't you wouldn't own me." Before Matt could say anything Hooch continued, "yes, you do, so no comments on that one. There's no one else I want to be with and no one else I love. Got it?" Hooch covered Matt's fist with the balled-up tissues with his own hand. "I. Love. You. You better remember that, I won't say it often. I don't give a shit if we stick to vanilla or if you lose control or if you come with me to the club or not. I don't care, because I care about you and being with you, and if this crap here," Hooch gestured with his free hand at his throat, "if that upsets you, then we forget about it, because it's not worth it. I'll never get tired of sex with you, we don't need to go into stuff that freaks you out." Hooch drew in a deep breath. "I talked too much now and I really need some food and drink and to blow you. Not necessarily in that order."

Matt smiled at that, and leaned into Hooch for a kiss. "Depending on what order you want that," he was still smiling, "you either need to get some clothes on or I should be taking them off."

Hooch grinned, "or we could order in and stay both naked."

Matt laughed in reply, feeling much relieved. "Now that is an excellent idea."

FEBRUARY 2001, FAYETTEVILLE

A month later, Saturday lunchtime, Matt was waiting for Hooch to return from Raleigh. He knew when he'd left the club in the night, receiving a text at 3 AM stating simply "back at hotel," then got a text when Hooch was up a few hours later and heading for breakfast, then another when he'd got into the truck to head back home. He'd been surprised to receive those texts that recounted Hooch's whereabouts, they'd never talked about this previously. They had, in fact, not talked about much at all, only that Hooch would go to the club for the first time on a Friday night so he had Saturday and Sunday to recuperate. Matt hadn't asked any more questions and Hooch hadn't volunteered any answers.

Hooch entered the gym around the expected time, carrying a bag of takeaway containers.

Matt stuck his head around the door of his office, deliberately casual, and not at all as though he'd been watching for Hooch's arrival. "Hey," he said, "how was it?" Keeping it ambiguous, even though there was nobody within earshot except Mandy, and Mandy hadn't been paying much mind to anything except her work since Jeff had left for Afghanistan.

"Okay." Hooch said, looking relaxed, even though some of his movements were stiff. He smiled and held up the bag. "I got Thai, your favorite. Hungry?"

Matt nodded. "Upstairs?" He turned to Mandy. "You want any?" he asked, though it was largely useless.

The answer was, as it had been since Jeff left. "No, thanks, I'm not hungry." No exclamation marks, no bubbly enthusiasm.

"Doesn't matter." Hooch stepped towards the reception desk and opened the bag, looking for a particular container. "I got you some anyway." He pulled out the right one. "You think Jeff wants to come back to a wraith? He'll be starved of sex and affection when he's back, you got to keep in shape." He set the container down in front of her and gave her a look that would have made any recruit quake in their boots. "Eat, Mandy, or I'll get word out to the 'Stan about your moping."

She looked up at Hooch, blushed hard and obediently opened the container. "Thanks," she said, picking up the fork. "I know we're luckier than most—at least I can write to him and stuff and they'll let me know if anything happens to him. Thank you." Behind her, Matt smiled at Hooch as he started to move towards the door to the apartment.

"You're welcome." Hooch followed Matt up the stairs to the apartment, where he dropped the bag on the kitchen counter.

"Well," Matt asked, "how did it go?"

"Better than expected." Hooch pulled Matt into an embrace. "I tell you everything if you want to, if not, I won't say a thing, or keep it vague."

Matt exhaled and returned the embrace, reminding himself not to check Hooch for injuries too overtly. "Only as much—or as little—as you want." He bent his head into the crook of Hooch's neck. "Anything you want to get off your chest, or anything that I…" not 'can do', there was quite a lot he couldn't, "anything that I should watch out for."

Hooch cradled the back of Matt's head in his hand, guiding him to look at him. "Last night was all about me. Selfish bastard and all that. Now it's about you. I tell you—or don't tell you—what you want to know."

Matt exhaled, not entirely sure. On one hand, he wanted to know everything that had happened: what Hooch had done, or more accurately what had been done to him, but on the other, the thought of hearing about him hurt was painful in itself. "Just…briefly…" Matt said, after a pause, "an outline and some sort of idea and especially if we need to be careful about anything in the next week or so."

"Okay." Hooch smiled and slowly let go of Matt. "I can do that, but let's get the food before it's cold." He peeled out of his jacket and left it hanging near the door, then went to help Matt who'd started to dish out.

"I forgot to give you something." Hooch went back to the jacket and pulled an item out of a pocket. "Hand out, palm open." He placed the collar into Matt's hand. It had a blue color flash on it, and nothing else. The same collar they had bought a month ago, now with traces of wear, such as the indentation of the buckle on the top of the leather. "Yours." Hooch said softly while sitting back down.

Matt held it in his hands, the collar bought at the pet store, the collar he'd put on Hooch, claiming him as Matt's. "Mine," he echoed, before winding it up in his hand. "Where do you keep it?" he asked, genuinely puzzled. It had completely slipped his mind where it had got to after he'd thrown it on the couch the day he'd attacked Hooch's neck like some deranged vampire.

"In the bottom drawer of the bedside table." Hooch flashed a grin. "You never look in it, because the lube's in the top one." He started on his plate full of food, swallowed the first mouthful before speaking again. "I'd like you to keep it. It is yours, after all, just like I am."

Matt opened his mouth to say something, but couldn't find the right words. He nodded in agreement. "Yes, I will." His hands closed around the collar. Just a strip of leather, a metal buckle, but a wealth of meaning. Hooch, his, just as much as he was Hooch's. With or without the symbols.

Hooch nodded, eating in silence for a moment. "I'd like you to know that I made it a rule never to see anyone at the club. I don't want to know who they are and what they look like. I don't want anyone to be anything but anonymous to me, that's why I'm blindfolded at all times. It's in my file now." He continued to eat as if they talked about the weather.

Matt blinked and only barely stopped his fork falling from suddenly numb fingers. "Oh," he said. The thought of Hooch, bound, blindfolded, helpless—he didn't know what to feel. "Is that a new thing?" he asked, slightly warily, going into territory that he'd never gone before.

"Yes." Hooch swallowed his last mouthful. "Do you know why?"

Matt shook his head. "No."

"I wonder who's the blind one, then." Hooch leaned forward and poked his finger right in the middle of Matt's chest.

Matt looked at Hooch in surprise. "I've got no idea what goes on in your head most of the time and this is no exception."

"Why would I want to see anyone else? I don't care about anyone other than you."

Matt's brows steepled in confusion, because there was no doubt this was one of the times that Hooch simply made no sense. "What's that got to do with it."

"I can't explain it better."

Matt shook his head. "I suppose I'll get it in time. It's still all a bit new to me, but if you find it works for you…"

"Yeah. Yeah it does." Hooch was visibly closing back up again.

"What's it like?" Matt asked, after a few minutes of silence. "Not seeing what's being done?"

Hooch glanced up from his food. "It means I can't brace myself for whatever is coming, which makes it better. Most of all it means I can stay in my head and don't get distracted by other bodies and faces."

Not sure whether this made him feel better or worse, Matt continued with his food. "Do you think the club is going to be enough?"

"Yeah, it'll do." Hooch finished his meal and leaned back, arms crossed over his chest. "How do you feel?"

Matt exhaled. "I don't know. I know you need something, and I don't mind other men, it's not that, it's just…well, I'll get used to it in time." Matt's thoughts were all over the place. "I wish there was a better way, but we know there isn't." He finished, feeling that it was lame.

Hooch sat for a while in silence. Realizing eventually there was nothing he could say to make Matt feel better. He was fucked up, no way around it, and Matt had chosen this path for him, Hooch, to allow him to deal with that fucked up self of his while they stayed together. Only now, confronted with Matt's painful acceptance, did Hooch truly understand the magnitude of what Matt was giving him.

Hooch slid off the couch and onto his knees. Moving closer, until he nudged Matt's legs to settle between them. He reached for Matt's face, cupped it and gently pulled him close until their lips met. He tried to put everything he felt into his kiss: gratitude, love, respect, trust. Above all, love. More than he ever thought his broken self could feel.

Matt closed his eyes, just feeling. Thoughts and fears banished for now, with Hooch here, his. No matter what else, Hooch would come back to him, and that was the most important thing. It had to be.

He pulled back gently, his own hand on the side of Hooch's face, touch light. "It'll be okay," he said softly, not sure whether he was telling Hooch or himself. "It will."

Hooch nodded. "Yeah." The word not much more than a soft exhale. "Come to bed with me." Knowing full well that any bruise, any sore spot, any cut and scrape would be visible to Matt's eyes, but trying to hide the evidence of what he had needed, would only prolong Matt getting used to it.

Matt nodded, pulling away and taking the plates to dump them in the sink before returning. He took Hooch's hand, the only obvious sign of his insecurity. "Come on," pulling him gently, though Hooch needed no such guidance or encouragement.

Hooch slowly peeled out of his clothes; a more pliant and patient man than the one who had left the day before. He lay down in top of their bed and let Matt examine the damage that had been done to his body by men he didn't care about but needed.

Gentle hands moved over each bruise and scrape and welt. Matt winced even though Hooch did not, and each of Matt's gentle touches on his sore body reminded Hooch not of what he'd done the night before, but of why he was doing it: so he could be the man who was capable of being in this relationship.

"Love you," Matt murmured into Hooch's ear, "no matter what." Feeling the weight of Hooch against him, soothed into the sleep and the rest that his body craved so that it could heal.

2002

EARLY SUMMER 2002, FAYETTEVILLE

Hooch went to his club every month or two, almost always on Friday night and returning Saturday lunchtime. There were occasional phone calls, too, and a week once a year that Matt never commented on, just as he didn't comment on the club. That was Hooch's business, and Hooch's alone.

Perhaps forewarned by Mandy's observations, Matt began to notice the knowing looks in his direction from his clients. Less conscious of having to hide all the time, he surprised himself when he accepted the first frank approach from Greg, one of his personal training clients, and then some of the others after that. Usually after-hours in the gym, in the personal training rooms or treatment rooms.

Hooch called them Matt's 'nibbles', and seemed to be supremely comfortable with his occasional indulgence. 'Nibbles' was a good way to describe them—fun, temporarily satisfying, but somehow not feeding the hunger quite enough.

✳ ✳ ✳

"You realize that you've never so much as asked me in for a coffee?" Greg asked one Friday evening, putting on his clothes after their latest meeting. "We've been having some fun for the past three months, what's wrong with your bed?"

Matt froze as he was pulling on his t-shirt, and then forced himself to relax. "I'm not the only one in the apartment," he kept his voice light.

"So what? Your buddy's a homophobe?" Greg laughed, as if he'd just made the funniest joke in a decade. "It's not a secret you're gay." He shrugged on his sweater jacket and straightened back up.

Matt snorted, covering up the first reaction of relief that Greg was so completely off the mark about Hooch. "No, he's not. It's not that." He pulled down his t-shirt and then ducked under the massage table to retrieve his shoes.

"What is it, then?" Greg made a grab for Matt's ass and squeezed one firm buttock with an appreciative grunt. "You think military guys get the heebie-jeebies when in close contact with *two* gays?" he grinned.

Matt caught Greg's wrist firmly. "Leave it, Greg." His voice anything but joking. "He doesn't bring anyone up to the apartment, and neither do I."

"Hey, what's up with you?" Greg was taken aback and not a little put-out. "Lost your sense of humor? What the hell's wrong with you and your roommate?" His eyes narrowed as he pulled his arm out of Matt's grasp, calculating. "Or is it not just your roommate?"

"Nothing is 'wrong'." Matt pulled on his shoes, keeping calm despite the thudding of his pulse around his ears, knowing that he had to deflect Greg's thoughts before they went in the wrong—the right—direction. "He's my best friend," he said at last, "but that doesn't mean I let him know everything I do."

"Don't tell me you're trying to keep from him that you're gay." Greg sneered, which gave his usually handsome face quite an ugly distortion. "I've got news for you, buddy, that's too late That sounds like bullshit to me."

"Firstly," Matt began, tying his shoelaces with a nonchalance he didn't feel, "Hooch is neither blind nor stupid. I imagine he's worked out by now why I quit the Marines." He straightened up. "Secondly, I don't get why you're so pissed. This isn't anything more than a bit of fun."

"Yeah, I get that, but I'm not used to being a bit of fun that has to be hidden away." Greg frowned. "What the fuck's wrong with drinking a coffee together? That's part of being fuck buddies in my book."

"Let's go out for a drink sometime," at least the worst had been headed off. "It's no secret, but neither Hooch nor I bring anyone up. That's the deal."

The easy smile was back on Greg's face within an instant. "Okay, buddy, if that's the deal, that's alright." He took his gym bag and threw his towel on top. "Next week same time after cardio?"

"Sure," Matt nodded, glad the tension was diffused. No-strings fun was meant to be just that. "Have a great weekend."

"You too." With a wave of his hand and a last smile, Greg sauntered out.

The gym was deserted, and Matt quietly locked up and turned the lights off before heading upstairs. It was Hooch's Friday in his club, so he planned an early night with a few movies. When he opened the door to the apartment, he was taken aback.

The TV was on and Hooch was sitting on the sofa, bare feet on the couch table, a bottle of lager in his hand. He craned his neck as Matt entered and greeted him with a quick smile. "Hey."

Matt blinked. "Hey," he echoed automatically. "I thought you were going to the club this weekend?"

Hooch took a mouthful of the beer. "Got called into a late meeting. Couldn't be bothered to go to Raleigh after that." He hit the mute button on the remote. "Working late?"

"Nah, just meeting up with Greg after his session." Matt shook his head. "Just give me a minute, I need a shower. You had dinner?" he asked on his way to the bathroom.

"Had a burger on my way home." Hooch called after Matt, before turning his attention back onto the TV, the sound back on.

Matt ducked into the shower, washing quickly, then dashed to the bedroom for clean clothes, before heading to the kitchen to throw together a salad. He sat down on the couch next to Hooch. "Whatcha watching?"

"Soccer." Hooch glanced at Matt with a raised eyebrow. "The ball, the green field, the guys in shorts should have given you a clue."

"Soccer." Matt repeated, as he stabbed at a mushroom. "You going to the club next weekend then?"

"No, I'm okay. Don't need to, yet." Hooch leaned across a little to stare pointedly at the mushroom Matt kept spearing repeatedly. "I reckon it's dead by now," he commented drily.

Matt looked up. "Yeah, but you never can tell with the bastards." He shoved the mangled remains into his mouth, and swallowed without chewing.

"You don't act like someone who's just had some fun with a guy." Hooch finished the last dregs of his beer and put the bottle onto the table.

"He complained that we hadn't gone out for a coffee." Out loud, it sounded ridiculous.

"So he fancies you. That's not a surprise, is it?" Hooch hit the mute button once more.

"No, " Matt finished the salad and put the empty bowl on the table. "Just weird. It was never meant to be anything than a bit of fun, and all of a sudden he was getting pushy and asking to come up here."

"He's falling for you." Hooch shrugged, but a hidden line of tension in his shoulders betrayed the indifference . "One day one of your 'nibbles' would. Those guys aren't stupid."

Matt snorted. "You'd have thought they knew better. At least Greg seems to get that I won't bring him up here, even if he thinks it's because 'military guys get the heebie-jeebies around two gays'."

"Good one." Re-crossing his ankles on the table, Hooch projected a casual unconcern . "What should they know better, though?"

Matt frowned. Unusual for Hooch to be probing quite so much. "They should know better than to think it's more than just a bit of fun. It's not as though they don't know about the others, after all."

"Yeah, right, and they all think you're actually single. What's to stop any of them having a go at becoming more than a bit of fun?" Hooch rolled his head to the side, resting on the sofa's back, looking at Matt.

"How about me saying 'No, thanks'?" Matt met Hooch's gaze.

"Without a reason?"

"Would I need to give one?" Matt paused, "and why would you care what I tell them?"

Hooch shrugged. "Just figured you might get annoyed with a persistent one." Neatly avoiding the second question.

Matt scratched the side of his nose. "Greg took it well enough, and he's the only one who's pushed for anything so far. Neil hasn't been around for a bit, and Tom and Craig are only out for a bit of no-strings fun."

Hooch huffed a laugh. "You're collecting a stable."

"You said you didn't mind," Matt said doubtfully. "Do you?"

"Of course I don't mind." Nothing in Hooch's face, voice, or demeanor gave any signs to the contrary. "I've never in my life said anything I don't mean. You of all people should know that." He flashed a quick smile.

Matt answered it, relieved that the weirdness seemed over. "That's okay then. I'm beat, I'll wash this up and go to bed." He picked up his bowl and headed for the kitchen area.

Hooch didn't say anything while Matt did the washing up, and was still silent with his eyes on the game while Matt occupied the bathroom, but when Matt came out to make his way to the bedroom, Hooch hit the mute button again. "I guess you're not up for sex tonight?"

Matt stopped in the doorway and turned around. "I'd probably fall asleep," he said frankly. "Unless you want to do all the work?"

"Depends on you telling me what kind of work it is you want me to do."

Matt furrowed his brow. "You've lost me."

"I meant, is there anything you want me to do, or you want to do to me, which we haven't done yet? Things you get from the other guys but not me, or are the other guys just variety?" Hooch looked at Matt with open curiosity.

Matt blinked. Hooch had never said anything of the sort before, whether in terms of sex or other men. "No," he shook his head. "They're just a bit of fun, and I thought you were going to be out this weekend anyway." He stayed in the doorway, curious at what Hooch would come up with next.

"Okay." Hooch nodded and to all intents and purposes the case was closed. "I let you sleep unmolested, or don't you let them fuck you?"

Matt who was turning to go into the bedroom, paused for a second. "I don't think I have, no. Not even all that much actual fucking to tell the truth."

Hooch hit the off button on the remote and stood up. "I'm asking too much, huh?"

"Surprised me, is all." Matt turned back around. "You've never asked before, and I don't ask you about the club."

"I'm not you." Hooch walked towards Matt.

Matt stood, waiting. "No." He tilted his head. "Do you want me to stop?"

"No, I don't." Hooch squeezed Matt's bare shoulder. "As long as you don't fall in love with any of them."

Still a little perplexed at Hooch's sentimentality, Matt snorted. "Course not."

"Good, because you're *mine*. It works both ways."

Matt smiled. "You coming to bed?"

Hooch turned towards the bathroom. "Yeah, be with you soon."

Matt shook his head, wondering what had got into Hooch before sliding under the covers. He hadn't been lying, he was exhausted from a busy week and the enthusiastic session with Greg, and wanted nothing so much than a good night's sleep before the early Saturday morning spin class he was due to lead. By the time Hooch slipped under the covers Matt was already out like a light, snoring softly.

Hooch reached out to brush his palm along the smooth skin. Matt didn't stir, the touch too light, just as he has intended, and with the lights off, Hooch settled in to sleep.

The next morning, Hooch was back to his usual silent self, and didn't revisit the baffling conversation of the night before.

2003

SPRING 2003, FAYETTEVILLE

Things continued as they had been, the only small difference was that Hooch seemed to take particular care to greet the 'nibbles' by name if he saw them at the gym.

In early 2003 activity at the base intensified, and Hooch was back to working the long and intense hours as he had in late 2001, while the preparations for the invasion of Iraq built up.

In some ways it was easier than in 2001, because this was more like a war than an invisible enemy to be fought on unclear territory, but in others the stress of the insane workload was even greater. Hooch had stay on base again, not even managing to get back to the apartment every other weekend, and he once more felt the frustration and pull of wanting to go out there with his boys, be active, go on operational duty. That part hadn't diminished at all in the last two years.

He was simultaneously exhausted—physically and mentally—and full of tension, when he finally managed to get home one Saturday lunchtime.

Matt was in the kitchen, snatching a quick lunch in between classes. "How are you holding up?" he automatically went to the fridge to get out more food to prepare for Hooch.

"I don't." When Hooch entered the kitchen it was clear to Matt how frayed around the edges he really was, and how utterly exhausted. His usually tanned skin had a grey tinge and there were dark shadows under his eyes, which made it all too clear that despite his exhaustion, Hooch hardly slept. Or perhaps because of it. The last sixteen days had wreaked havoc on Hooch, who leaned against the doorway, arms crossed in front of his chest, still in uniform.

Matt's eyes widened as he looked at Hooch's worn-out state. "Food," he said firmly, pushing the plate of cold cuts in front of Hooch, "then bed." Words curt. "Do you need to plan anything?" he asked, remembering the last time Hooch had been under so much strain.

"Yeah. Yeah, I do." Hooch let himself be manhandled into a chair at the table, where he stared at the food for a while, as if unable to switch off enough to eat and not just stuff down fuel to keep going. "But I don't have much time."

"How long?"

"Back tomorrow at seventeen hundred hours." Hooch finally picked up some of the bread and cuts, layering a sandwich. "Not enough time to go to the club."

"Can you call him?" No need to mention who Matt meant.

"Yeah, I have to try." Hooch stared at the sandwich in his hand, as if he'd forgotten just how to eat. "It won't be enough." He looked up at Matt, the expression in his face ranging between demand and pleading. "I need you, too."

Matt looked at Hooch with surprise. "What do you need me to do?" Need, not want.

"I'll be given orders on the phone. Usually I do things myself, or it's in my head, but this time I need you to carry them out." Hooch finally bit into the sandwich.

Matt swallowed, feeling his fingers clench. Thinking of what happened last time, and how he could never, ever let that happen again. "Yes. When?"

"Tonight, or I won't be able to wind down enough to sleep." The 'again' unspoken. "If I can't get him on the phone, will you fuck me hard, really hard?"

Matt held back from making a flippant response, knowing that it was the last thing needed. He settled for a nod, not trusting himself to speak with his suddenly dry mouth.

"Thank you," Hooch said in a quiet voice around a bite of his sandwich, that tasted like straw.

Matt looked at Hooch, then at the food and said, "I'll order in tonight." Even though he knew that Hooch would barely taste it. "Why don't you have a soak in the bath? My last client finishes at 1700."

"Okay." Hooch nodded and kept eating, taking meticulous bites, in a robotic fashion. He suddenly looked up. "Matt?"

"Hmm?" Matt had to turn back to Hooch from where he'd been putting away some clean plates in the cupboard.

"I want you to know I'm not a sissy. I'm not just stressed like a pansy-assed loser. I want to go out there and it drives me insane that I can't. It's fucking unbearable."

Matt wanted to reach across the bench to touch Hooch, but that was the wrong move now. So he settled for words. "No, you're the furthest thing from one. " He looked at the clock. "I gotta go. See you in a bit."

Hooch watched him leave, his face stony.

✷ ✷ ✷

When Matt returned to the apartment after his last client of the day, still sweaty and in gym kit, he found Hooch sitting on the couch, dressed in a pair of gym shorts, staring into nothing. His cell firmly gripped in one hand.

"Hooch?" Matt called quietly, alarmed that Hooch hadn't seemed to register his entrance.

Hooch looked up, the sudden hyper-focus of his dark gaze on Matt. "He'll call back. They're out."

"Ah," Matt nodded. "I'll go shower first then."

"No!" Hooch's reply came as sharp and fast as a bullet. "Don't. I want you…" he was cut off by the cell phone ringing, and without checking who it was, he answered the call without saying a word.

Raising an eyebrow, Matt moved to the kitchen counter, keeping his eyes on Hooch who was concentrating on the call.

"Yeah." One word, sharp and cutting, then silence on Hooch's end once more, listening intently. Finally another "yeah," followed by, "understood." With that he put the cell down and turned his head towards Matt. "Can you keep me tied up for twelve hours?"

"Twelve…" Matt trailed off, looked at the clock, then at Hooch. Swallowed. "Alright. With what?"

"Anything you can find." Hooch shrugged, "as long as it's sturdy and I can't get out of it. Leather belts?" He stood up, his body so tense, every muscle appeared sculpted. "Gag me, and don't let me come, no matter what. Fuck me, with your cock, with a dildo, with anything you can find." Hooch's voice had become hard as shards of metal, and as cutting. "Just *fuck* me."

Matt swallowed, hard. "The bedroom, then," he choked out.

Hooch moved immediately, and without being told, he got onto the bed, face down, spreading his arms and legs.

Matt stood frozen for a moment, before going to the wardrobe and rummaging for something, anything that would do the task asked of him. Eventually, he found a handful of leather belts, and a large cotton scarf from goodness knows where. Opening the bottom drawer of Hooch's bedside table, he found Hooch's collar, and the toy collection he'd long known about, but never seen.

Hooch's hands were clenched into fists, and his long legs trembled with a tension he'd been holding in for too long. He didn't move, but sensing Matt's hesitation, he spoke quietly. "Anything, Matt. Anything and everything, no matter how much." He paused, and the emphasis on the last word was compelling: "Please."

"Yes." Matt moved, rummaged in the drawer, then shut it. A sound behind Hooch, then movement as Matt slipped a sleeping mask from an airline amenity kit over Hooch's eyes, the nearest thing he could find to a blindfold.

Hooch's breathing audibly relaxed once he was in darkness, for a reason Matt couldn't understand, and wasn't going to explore right now. He had been set a task, and he was going to help Hooch, keep him from being unable to function or—worst of all—from breaking his promise and go off again and perhaps get himself killed this time.

He picked up the belts next, turning them in his hands, contemplating what to do, before tying Hooch's wrists and ankles to the four posts of the bed. He was careful, never having done this before, but Hooch urged him on.

"Tighter." Hooch's voice was low, partly muffled by the bed sheets. "Make me hurt."

Matt gulped, but obeyed, stretching Hooch out as far as he could go. Picking up the cotton scarf, he brought it around Hooch's mouth, pulling tight and gagging him.

Hooch's body, spread and tense, was all rock hard muscles and sinews, fists clenched in anticipation and need for something Matt had promised to give without knowing what it would take.

Stepping back, Matt paused to admire the movement of muscles under smooth skin, the play of shadow amidst the fading light. "Should I put the lamp on?" he asked, before he remembered that he'd gagged Hooch. "No," he answered his own question. "No."

He moved closer, getting on the bed, and kneeling between Hooch's spread legs.

Hooch said nothing, did nothing, just waited. Remaining tense and wound up like a far too tight coil, ready to snap any moment.

Already half hard, Matt flipped open the lid of the lube and stroked himself, moving closer to Hooch, hand on the tense back. He could see how Hooch was doing the exact opposite to what he should: he didn't relax his muscles, clenched his ass instead, to get *more* pain.

He took a deep breath, moved forwards, hands spreading Hooch as far apart as he could, fighting against him, ready to force himself in. He could feel, rather than see, Hooch trembling under his fingertips.

This wasn't about wanting, not even about sex; this was all about giving Hooch what he needed, and Matt dug deep into his self to find all the anger he'd ever felt at Hooch's antics and how helpless it had made him over the years. He fucked Hooch, who didn't need *him* right now, but anyone who would do this to him, no matter who. He fucked him and tried to hurt him, which went against everything Matt ever was. He kept him tied up, re-tightened the leather that held Hooch's body spread, fed him energy drinks throughout the twelve hours, rammed the dildo into his ass until Hooch screamed and panted, and never let him come, not until it was dawn, and Hooch collapsed into an exhausted, sated, heap.

Matt was trembling too, as he untied Hooch's limbs and crawled into bed beside him, pulling up the covers before sleep claimed him.

* * *

It was after noon when Hooch woke up. His body aching, the skin around his wrists and ankles almost raw, and his ass stinging, still feeling the shadow of soreness deep in his guts. It was good; it was enough. The last twelve hours had given him a valve to let off the tension, allowing him to return to the core and find equilibrium, without tearing his own self apart.

He opened his eyes and turned his head towards the sound of steady breathing. Matt. Matt, who 'didn't have it in him' and yet he had done for Hooch what he'd asked for, and Hooch knew what that meant. He reached out to touch the short, tousled hair, stroking gently.

Matt woke, leaning into the touch. "Mmmmm?"

"Thank you." Hooch said quietly, far more in those two words than a whole speech could convey.

Matt blinked, calm. "You're welcome."

Hooch was silent for a long while, stroking Matt's hair. When he finally spoke again his voice was still as soft. "You hated it."

"Not my thing," Matt said at last. "But yours."

"Was there anything you liked?"

"You," Matt smiled. "Mine. All mine to do with as I wish." Leaning into the caress. "The tying up I didn't mind," he added, serious, "but something other than the belts, next time."

"Next time?" Hooch's eyebrows rose. "You would do it again?"

"If you wanted me to."

"I don't want you to do anything you hate, because if you continued to do that, you'd hate *me* one day."

Matt was silent for a while. "Maybe," he reached out a hand, touching Hooch, "but you're more important than that. We could give it another go, when it's just fun. And maybe you could do it to me."

"That would be a first." Hooch chuckled softly, his face visibly relaxing. "But I'll do it, for fun I can do anything."

Matt smiled. "For now, what I need is a couple more hours sleep."

"I'll see you when you wake up." Hooch leaned forward to place a ridiculously chaste kiss onto Matt's lips.

Matt laughed, and then closed his eyes and burrowed into the pillows.

2004

LATE SPRING - EARLY FALL 2004, FAYETTEVILLE

Earlier that week, Jeff had returned from a several-weeks posting in Montana. With Hooch being a lot less of an ogre than he had at first appeared to be, Jeff asked him to meet for lunch at the canteen, to check in with what's been going on at base.

They never got to talking about anything that had happened at Fort Bragg, because Jeff had started to enthusiastically describe the charity he'd seen at work close to the Montana base: Horses for Heroes. Even if Hooch had wanted to stop him, he wouldn't have succeeded without serious intervention, so impressed Jeff had been by the charity's work with the first waves of injured veterans returning from the Gulf. Working with the horses, getting the men and women into the saddle, had a remarkable effect on the veterans with issues ranging from amputations, over a diverse range of physical disabilities, to mental issues, such as the ever growing numbers of PTSD sufferers.

Hooch listened to Jeff's words with interest, and an idea began to form in his mind.

* * *

That evening, when he returned home, he was deep in thought and even less vocal than usual.

"What's up?" Matt asked, when Hooch didn't move nor greet him when he came through the door.

Hooch hummed, his only acknowledgment as he kept clicking away on his laptop, set up on the dining table. A long pause, a couple of clicks, and then he swiveled the laptop with a flourish, presenting the screen to Matt. It showed the website for Horses for Heroes.

"What do you think?"

Matt looked at it, and at Hooch. "You want to go to Montana?"

"Jeff told me about the charity." Completely ignoring Matt's question. "Would be good to have that here."

"And?" Matt realized that this was one of Hooch's weird-ass trains of thought where he expected Matt to be able to read his mind.

"Isn't that obvious? Horses." Hooch looked up, dark eyes alive, "horses, Matt."

"What about horses? Can you, um, start from the beginning?"

"What?" Hooch stared at him, dumbfounded. "You didn't know I…" he trailed off when realization hit him. "Damn. No, you didn't." He ran a hand through his hair then kicked back in his chair. "I spent my life on horseback, before I joined up. Pretty much all eighteen years of it, minus the baby stage."

Matt's eyebrows went up, but then it made sense. The passing reference to the ranch and the cattle money, back when Hooch had dropped the bombshell that he was loaded. "Ah," Matt nodded, "you want to start it up?"

Hooch didn't hesitate. "Yeah. I got the investment money for horses, equipment, stable, paddock. I'd need volunteers and at least one member of permanent staff. I know jack shit about the psychological stuff, but I know how to ride a horse."

"Are you going to talk to base about it?" Matt sat down at the dining table. "Got to be at least a few guys there who'd know something?"

"Good idea, but how the fuck do I go about finding the rest?"

Matt thought for a second. "I've got to have a ton or more of shrinks at the gym, and Mandy can scare up any number of volunteers for anything."

"Just need some proficient horsemen," Hooch added after a moment, "or horsewomen." He crossed his arms before his chest and looked at Matt. "This can work. I bet you anything that being on a horse is good for anyone. Was for me, I hardly ever got off."

Matt scratched the side of his nose, still slightly perplexed at Hooch's new train of thought. "Shouldn't be difficult, not here. I'll have Mandy put the word out." He paused. "Do you want me to do anything?"

"No, I'm alright. I better get on with it right away."

True to his word, Hooch threw himself into the idea with the same energy, dedication and excellent planning and executing skills, as he had always done for his military missions.

✳ ✳ ✳

Matt hardly ever saw Hooch off the phone or the laptop screen during the next weeks– when he was home at all. The reports he was getting were positive, and Hooch's tenacity and focus began to pay off quickly. Having the funds helped.

Hooch was out and about one Saturday, checking up on a few potential paddocks and sites for stables, when the landline rang in their apartment.

"Hello?" Matt answered warily. Not a lot of people had the number, and fewer would call on a weekend.

"Hello?" the voice at the other end was female, Texan. "Hubert?"

"Uh, no, it's his...roommate. I'm Matt." Matt frowned in concentration, and came to the conclusion this had to be someone from Hooch's family, but no one had ever called the landline. "Can I help you?"

"Oh, hello Matt," she paused, "sorry, I should have said. I'm Sofia, Hubert's sister, I was wondering if he was around? He's asked me to send him some of his old things and I was just making sure I had everything he wanted."

"Sorry, no, Hooch is out, probably all day." The 'Hubert' sounded so very wrong in Matt's ears. "Is his cell off? I could note down a message."

"Oh, thanks. I tried before but yes, his cell's off. Could you ask whether it's just his boots and belt and gloves and hat that he wants, or does he want the old ribbons and things as well? I'm so glad he's getting back into horses again. Ask him to call me if he wants anything else, otherwise I'll send all this off on Monday."

Matt's eyes had widened at the list, and he had to bite his lip not to ask any further questions. A roommate wouldn't be that curious. "Okay, I'll do that. I tell him to call you back before Monday." He added, "nice talking to you."

"Thanks." A pause, "nice to put a voice to a name, too. Bye." The phone call ended with a soft 'click.'

'Name'? Matt's brows shot up as he stared at the phone. He hadn't expected Hooch to ever mention him to anyone in his family. Still bewildered, he replaced the phone on its charger, then went to fix himself some lunch.

✳ ✳ ✳

Hooch returned a few hours later, short hair tousled, boots and black denims splattered with mud, but a satisfied look on his face.

"You look pleased." Matt observed redundantly.

"Found the perfect location. Stables need renovating, but foundations are intact, and paddock is large enough, complete with training yard." Hooch shrugged out of his jacket, before bending down to unlace his boots at the door. "Price is higher than I'd initially budgeted for, but have organized a call with my financial adviser in Texas, to see what can be done."

"Speaking of people in Texas," Matt began, "your sister called. She wants to know if there's anything else you want apart from," he paused and looked at his neat notes, "your boots and belt and gloves and hat, like your old ribbons and things. And she's glad you're getting back into horses."

Hooch looked up, one muddied boot in hand. "She did?" He stood still for a moment, thinking, before placing the boot down and working on the second. "I can't believe they kept the trophies. Stupid sentimentality."

Whatever Matt was going to say first, he bit back. He settled for: "trophies."

"Yeah, what about them?" Hooch hopped on one sock-clad foot, while pulling the boot off the other.

"What did you use to play?" Matt asked, genuinely curious. "You've seen all mine."

"Horses." Hooch huffed a laugh and walked over to the couch. "I'm Texan, guess what I did with them." He grinned, unusually cheerful.

Matt blinked. "I'm not sure I want to."

Hooch's response was a short, but full-out laughter. "Nothing more exciting than rodeos. I did bareback bronc riding."

Matt shook his head ruefully. "Figures, and now?"

"Now I'm too old and fucking worn out to fall off bucking horses and get back up without an ambulance." Hooch was about to sit down on the white leather sofa, but a pointed look from Matt at his muddy denims made him stop in his tracks.

"Off and into the laundry basket," Matt inclined his head towards the bathroom where said basket was located, "and call your sister." He called after Hooch's retreating back as Hooch stalked off.

"Bully!" Hooch's voice came from the bathroom, but—as expected—he did exactly as he was told.

∗ ∗ ∗

Hooch had quickly showered and changed into a fresh pair of black jeans, his staple civilian wardrobe, and a t-shirt. Sitting in his study, bare feet on the desk, he dialed Sofia's number on his cell.

"Sofia Bozic Callahan," the voice crisp and professional.

"You don't have my cell on caller ID?" Hooch's way of greeting, the good humor still lingering.

"Hubert!" the voice was surprised. "Perhaps it's because you don't call me more than once or twice a year. What on earth are you up to?"

"Maybe I don't call you more often because you insist on calling me 'Hubert'." Hooch re-crossed his ankles up on the desk. "I started a branch of a charity for veterans."

"Oh," she seemed momentarily taken aback, "you did?" Ignoring the comment about his name.

"Have you heard of Horses for Heroes? Deals with injured veterans. Figured that was a good idea."

"No, no I haven't…" she trailed off. "It sounds interesting and something that would suit you. Would you like me to send anything else apart from your old things? Is there anything I can do?"

"No, I got everything I need here and I don't want any of my old stuff. Throw it all away. My horse gear will do." Hooch thought for a moment. "Did they keep my saddle and tack?"

"No." Hey voice was regretful. "They sold it when they sold your horses."

Silence on Hooch's end for an uncomfortable length of time. Finally just one word: "Okay." If his voice was hard as steel and sharply cutting, it remained unmentioned. "Nothing else I want, then. Tell them to throw the other shit out."

"I will." Simple words. "Your roommate sounds nice. Another soldier?"

"He was. Runs the gym now." Hooch was starting to become cagey. All too quickly the good humored man was gone.

"Oh." Sofia paused. "Have you known him for long?"

"Why?"

"Just curious is all," Sofia had a touch of nervousness to her voice, "you've never spoken about any of your friends, and I'd never thought that you'd share an apartment off-base with anyone."

Hooch sat up straight, feet off the desk, and his back rigid. "You said yourself we talk twice a year on the phone. I forget your birthday and I forget everyone's Christmas. I only visit Texas when I absolutely have to. You wouldn't call us close, would you?"

"No," a pause. "I'll box up your things." Another pause, "and Hubert?"

Hooch frowned, hating that name, hating it more than he'd ever be able to explain to her without destroying some of her last illusions about her family. "Yeah."

"Is Matt the Marine who visited you when you were in hospital after your last mission?"

The smallest sound escaped Hooch as he pulled in a shocked breath, followed by a tell-tale hesitation he couldn't control. "You saw him." A statement, since a question would have been redundant.

"Well, yes," Sofia sounded confused, "I did, and he was the only visitor listed for you in the book. I've been wondering ever since you mentioned you were moving off-base."

"Wondering about what?" The sharpness and alertness remained at the front of Hooch's voice.

"Wondering if he was the same Matt you mentioned you were sharing the apartment with."

Another pause, too long for Hooch's usual quick wit. "Yes. He is." No other explanation, and there wasn't going to be anything else Sofia would be able to pry out of him.

"Oh," another pause. "I'll send your things on Monday." She knew that she had already got more out of him than expected. "Let me know if there's anything I can do for your new organization."

"You mean the offer? If yes, any help with the books is appreciated."

"Any time. I'll look into charity tax exemptions for you, too."

"Thanks. I'll send you the paperwork. And Sofia," Hooch added, "you'll find I'm using my inheritance for this. So you know."

An unladylike snort, but then a smile. "Thanks for the warning. I'll remember not to be in the same room when father finds out."

"Fuck him." Hooch shot out, before his brain had engaged.

A shocked silence. "I'll not mention it to him, then."

"Do whatever." The damage was done. "It's my money, not his. I don't care if you tell him or not." He wasn't going to retract what had slipped out, couldn't undo what he'd done. "It's not your problem, Sofia, don't worry about it."

Another long pause. "I have to pick up Martin from soccer," it sounded genuine, not an excuse. "But before I go—Hubert?"

Hooch groaned. "Yeah?"

"Look after yourself."

The hesitation this time was different, as Hooch slowly pulled in an audible breath and released it equally slowly. "That's no problem anymore."

"Good." The phone call ended with a soft click.

Hooch put his cell down, gently placing it onto the desk. He remained in his chair for a while.

* * *

Several weeks later, Hooch was at an equine rescue facility where he had arranged to inspect a couple of horses that had previously belonged to a bankrupt trail riding business. They were on the elderly side, which was why the company's liquidators had not managed to sell them with the rest of the horses, but gentle and quiet and calm, and perfect for what he had in mind.

After discussions with the manager, and making arrangements for the horses to be delivered to the property that he'd bought, Hooch was distracted by the sound of a shrill piercing neigh from the barn, together with the sound of frantic kicking against solid boards.

"What else have you got in the stables?" Hooch called the manager back. "What's up with that horse?"

Cyn followed his gaze and shook her head. "It's Lucifer. He came in six months ago, starved and horribly mistreated, he'd been locked up in a filthy tiny stall almost since he was a foal. We've tried all we can, but we simply can't place him or adopt him anywhere with good conscience. No matter what we try, he can't be handled by anyone, and he's too dangerous—we've already had any number of near misses." She gave a sad shrug. "We've just managed to get him into the barn to wait for the vet tomorrow." No need for her to say why.

"Lucifer?" Hooch's brows rose. "Who named him that?" He listened to another barrage of high pitched neighs and frantic kicks. "Can I see him?"

"It was 'Luke' when he came, but the longer name became quite appropriate soon after," Cyn's voice was dry. "You're welcome to, but mind any appendages. He's a big boy, and a fast one."

"Yeah, don't worry. I used to ride broncos." Hooch turned back to the stables, following the noise to a single box, where a dark, wild horse was rearing up, hammering against the box door in front and kicking the stable wall in the back.

Hooch approached slowly, letting the frantic horse see him coming. Pausing when the horse screamed and reared, but not retreating. Stopping at the door, while the horse backed into the corner, trembling, he leaned against, but not over, the door. "Hey," he said softly to the horse.

The horse's fear was palpable in the air. Fear fuelling aggression, the hardest kind, but Hooch just stood still. Close. Non-threatening. "Hey, Lucifer." Hooch kept talking with the same gentle voice. "Stupid name, huh?"

The horse shifted restlessly, but didn't rear or kick. A large horse, as Cyn had said, rippling with muscle under the glossy dark coat, which was drenched with swear. Ears pricked, listening to Hooch.

"You'd kill me if I tried to come close, wouldn't you?" Hooch said softly, with a chuckle in his voice. "So I won't, not now, but I make you a promise: I *will* get close, and I *will* ride you one day." He stood and watched the horse, taking in everything. "I never break a promise." With that he walked out slowly, without any sudden movement or noise, and looked for Cyn.

She was outside, waiting for him. "You're in one piece," she observed. "Crying shame about Lucifer. He's such a stunning colt, but we don't really have any choice, not when he's so dangerous."

"I'll take him." Hooch stated, and before she managed to get a word in, he raised his hand. "I know what I'm doing. I'll give Lucifer a home, he doesn't have to die. I know how to deal with wild and frightened horses. I'll take him."

She looked at him steadily, measuringly, before nodding. "The paperwork's in the office."

"Thanks." Hooch was about to turn towards the office, when he stopped. "You're welcome to check up on the horses any time."

"You may regret that. I'll probably be around your place all the time. Your idea sounds fascinating."

"Not my idea, I copied it from Horses for Heroes." Hooch smiled. "We need volunteers who know what they're doing."

Cyn smiled and scratched the side of her nose. "I'm sure I can find more than a few people to come by and lend a hand." They had reached the small building that served as an office. "It would not be a good idea to transport Lucifer with Daisy and Minnie, but we might as well organize it all now."

"I'll get some guys to help with Lucifer's transport later." Hooch agreed, as they went inside to deal with the paperwork, which took some time.

* * *

Later that day, after the first two horses had been safely taken to the new charity stables, and with Lucifer staying for another couple of days before Hooch could organize help with the transport, he finally made his way back home. Somewhat tired, definitely hungry, and surprisingly content.

Matt was in the apartment, working on an assignment for his nutrition course when Hooch arrived home, and raised his head at Hooch's entrance. "What are you so cheerful about?"

"I got myself a horse today. His name's Lucifer." Hooch grinned, unlacing his boots.

"Lucifer." Matt looked at Hooch steadily, "figures." He closed the textbook that he was reading from, then saved his work and closed the lid of his laptop, knowing that no more work would be done. "How did that happen? I thought you were going out to look at some retired old-timers to plod around in circles."

"I was," Hooch shrugged, "but there was this horse, dark colt, real good stock, but mistreated and frightened. They called him Lucifer, because he's out for everyone's blood." He left jacket and boots at the door, and walked over to where Matt was sitting. "The horse is aggressive because it's frightened. It was about to be put down. No one could handle him." He shrugged again, "so I got him."

Matt stayed still for a moment, before standing up. "You might act like the tough-ass Delta, but you're just a softie inside, aren't you?" Just a hint of a smile from him.

"I'm not!" Hooch was adamant, and he crossed his arms in front of his chest for good measure. "It simply made sense. I have experience in riding wild horses, have tamed a few, too, and that horse is going to be an excellent one when it's realized it has nothing to fear."

"Ah-hah," Matt nodded sagely. "Whatever you say." Clearly disbelieving. "Are you planning on taming and riding him?"

"Of course. Pretty pointless to own a horse otherwise."

Matt hummed thoughtfully.

"What?"

"You used to be thrown off wild horses, yes?"

"Sure," Hooch huffed a laugh, "that's the point of rodeos."

"That was *before* you fractured your pelvis…"

Hooch's grin immediately fell. "Ah, shit."

Matt hated the way Hooch deflated, and quickly offered, "I could research supportive braces for you. Just to make sure."

"Sure thing, buddy."

Matt chuckled at the 'buddy'. "When do I get to meet this demon?"

"We'll transport him to the stables in a couple of days, once I've organized some guys to help. Want to come along?"

Knowing he was being challenged, Matt rose to the bait. "Sure."

"That's sorted, then." Hooch's grin was back, "you'll like him."

Lucifer's transport turned out to be as much of struggle and hard work as his name suggested. They needed four men and all of Hooch's and Cyn's expertise to eventually get the frightened and aggressive horse into the trailer and after a short journey, into his new box in the charity's stables.

All of them were exhausted, but Hooch had taken the brunt of the work, staying the closest to Lucifer as was possible at this stage, without getting killed.

He leaned against the stable wall, pulled off a glove, and wiped his sweaty face with a satisfied grunt. "Thanks, buddies."

The others seemed ready to drop, and looked from Hooch to the still nervous horse, as though Hooch was insane. "Time for a drink, then?" one of them asked.

"Sure, I could do with one." Hooch focused on Matt who'd been staring at him in a strange way. "What about you?"

"Umm," Matt was uncharacteristically inarticulate, "yeah, that sounds good."

Hooch studied Matt for a moment longer, then pulled his other glove off. "Okay, guys, meet you at the bar in twenty. I'll finish off here." Everyone except Matt started to move. "Matt, I could use your help."

"Sure…" Matt was still sounding a little dazed.

As the others left to drive to the bar, Hooch opened the door to the washroom and beckoned Matt inside. "So," Hooch started as he closed and then locked the door, "why are you staring at me as if I'd grown horns?"

"You look…" Matt swallowed hard. "That was hot."

An amused grin began to spread across Hooch's features. "Does that mean you're into cowboys? I never knew that about you, Matt Donahue."

Matt blinked and came back into himself at the teasing. "Makes me wonder why I didn't know either." Stepping closer, until he and Hooch were nose to nose.

"So, that means skin tight denims, boots, broad belt and shirt do it for you, huh?" Hooch rumbled.

Matt's hands went to Hooch's chest, lying them flat against the sweat-soaked cloth. "I think they do." Matt's mouth so close that Hooch felt his breath, more than he heard the words.

"You want to do me, huh?" Hooch murmured, their lips touching as he spoke. "Right here and now. With my denims down enough for you to fuck me, huh?" Pushing forward, until he ground his crotch into Matt's, hard cock against hard cock.

"God yes." Matt pushed back, "against the basin, so I can see your face in the mirror."

"Looks like it's going to be a dry run." Hooch didn't appear perturbed by the lack of lube, just turned round and moved the few steps to the large basin, then gripped the stoneware firmly, and bent forward. Low enough for Matt to fuck him, and high enough for his face to show in the mirror. Dark eyes fixed on Matt through his reflection, urging him on silently.

Matt fumbled with both their belt buckles, tugging on Hooch's jeans, pulling them down with difficulty, before moving to his own. He pushed Hooch hard against the basin, who didn't say anything, but his breathing had become harsh and fast, bracing himself.

"Shit, no lube," Matt swore, panted, then spat into his hand. Not enough, but better than nothing, and Hooch relished the burn of a dry fuck.

"Doesn't matter." Hooch willed his muscles to relax, to ease the breach. "Come on!" Urging Matt, who obeyed, forcing his way in as Hooch shoved back against him, panting and plastering himself against Hooch's sweat-soaked back.

"So...good..." Matt groaned, going deeper, fingers clawing at Hooch's hips, pushing harder against the basin.

"Yeah, shit," Hooch gasped out, recklessly pushing back against Matt, while his own cock chafed against the stoneware basin with every thrust. "Fuck me!"

Hard and fast against the basin, reaching around to roughly take Hooch in hand, it seemed barely seconds before they came, and Matt crashed even more heavily into Hooch, crushing him against stone, forehead against the mirror, arms and hands shaking where they gripped the basin.

Hooch chuckled breathlessly, a rumble against Matt's chest. "If I'd known you react like that to my old riding kit, I'd gotten a horse earlier." Blindly reaching behind himself, he patted Matt's hip.

Matt panted, still catching his breath. "If I'd known, I'd have got you a horse myself." He slowly withdrew, pulling up both their jeans, but not cleaning either of them.

Hooch turned round and fastened his belt buckle himself. "I'm going to leak," he smirked, "sweat, cum, leather and beer." Hooch reached behind himself and pulled a Stetson off a peg. Battered, faded and worn, he tipped the hat down low over his face and grinned. "Doesn't get better than that."

2005

JANUARY 2005, FAYETTEVILLE

Right after Christmas and New Year, Hooch had been spending every free minute at the stables, working hard on getting the charity into full swing. He was rarely home, and when he returned at night, he was so physically exhausted, he fell asleep almost immediately.

He didn't notice that Matt spent more time downstairs with Greg, his time eaten up by the charity, and most of all by Lucifer, who he was training every day, if possible.

He didn't notice anything until he came home one night to find the apartment dark and deserted, no Matt there. A noise from the parking lot caught his attention—Matt, being dropped off by Greg after a night out.

Despite himself, Hooch looked out of the window, watching the two men in the deserted parking lot, illuminated by yellow street lights. They were laughing, and Greg pulled Matt back inside for what was obviously a kiss.

Hooch froze. The coke can in his hand crushed by suddenly tensing fingers.

Matt got out of the car, still laughing, and walked to the gym door, a spring in his step. Greg was waiting until Matt was inside, before driving off in his stylish little car.

Matt's steps were still light as he made his way up the stairs to the apartment and opened the door. "Hey," he sounded surprised, "you're home early."

Hooch was still standing at the window. "Hey." He turned round to face Matt. "You were out with Greg." A statement.

"Yeah," Matt dropped his keys in the habitual place, and Hooch saw that he was carrying a camera case, top quality, that he'd never seen before. "Photography masterclass."

"Are you in love with him?" The question came out as if shot from the hip: straight to the point.

Matt blinked, recoiled as though slapped. "No," he said too quickly, "just friends. You've never objected before."

"I've never before seen you together with any of your guys."

Matt thought for a moment. "You haven't? Ah, no, it's lunch usually, so you wouldn't."

Hooch hadn't left his position at the window, crushed can still in his hand. "Matt, I'm not objecting to you fucking other guys." He chose his words carefully, but each of them was as straightforward as the next. "Never have, never will, but what I saw didn't look like a fuck buddy. He's the same guy who a few years ago complained he'd never been up here, isn't he?"

"Greg? Yes, he was." A pause as though Matt was thinking. "Yes, he was." he repeated.

Hooch nodded. "Photography masterclass?" latching onto the other unknown.

"Well, yes," Matt was too used to the way Hooch's mind worked to be surprised at the quick shift, "been getting into it more lately, time I learnt how to use a camera properly."

Hooch's fingers relaxed their grip on the crushed can fractionally. "I asked you back then and I ask you now: is there anything you want me to do, or you want to do to me, which we haven't done yet? Which you think you can't get from me and need to get from others? Or are they things I can never give you, like being out openly?"

"Is that what this is all about?" Matt sat down heavily on the couch. "Course it sucks, having to stay in the closet, but…"

"No." Hooch finally moved from his frozen stance. He put the crushed can onto the table and sat down side-on to Matt on the L-shaped couch. "It's about me seeing you out there laughing with a guy with whom you've been out to a new hobby I didn't know anything about, who took you home, and with whom you've been having sex with for years. This is simply about me being…" Hooch hesitated, then used the most fitting word, no matter how that made him look, "worried you've fallen in love with someone else."

"Shit," Matt said, after a breath. "He's a good guy, sure, and we have fun, and he's a friend…but…no."

"Are you sure he knows that?"

"Course he does," the reply was a bit too quick.

"And what about the others?"

"The others?" Matt leaned back. "What's got into you?" he thought for a second, "but for what it's worth, there isn't anyone else at the moment, not since Tom took that new job in Turkey and Craig and Paul got together and moved to San Fran."

Hooch nodded slowly and thoughtfully. "I guess Greg knows that he's the only one."

Matt shrugged. "I suppose so."

"And he knows I've been hardly ever home lately."

"Not that he has any idea we're not roommates." Matt, as always, conscious of Hooch's safety, but now it was entirely the wrong thing to say.

Hooch froze, sitting straight as if he'd swallowed a rod. "Yeah, shit." Anything else he wanted to say got caught in his suddenly too-tight throat. He sat in silence until he swallowed hard, forcing the words through. "This isn't going to work."

"What isn't?"

"I could reassure you that I don't mind. That it's okay, no problem, I don't care who you fuck. They are your nibbles, nothing else. But it's not true, because I saw you together and it fucking…" Hooch stopped, taking a forced breath. "Anyway. I have no right to be jealous." The admittance that he was jealous, as unexpected as his return to Matt's apartment, so many years ago.

"You go to your club." Somehow Matt made it sound reasonable, rather than petulant.

"Yes, I do. That's why I have no right to…anything." Hooch could have pointed out that he had no idea who the men were who did things to him and his body, that he'd never seen anyone, didn't speak to anyone, didn't care about anyone, but he couldn't bring himself to do so.

"Do you want me to stop? The fucking or the friendship?"

Hooch shook his head. "I don't know. On their own they are fine, but together they are more."

Matt sighed, and got up to go to the kitchen for a glass of water. Silently offering the same to Hooch, who shook his head again. "Then what? It clearly pisses you off, no matter how much you try to hide it, and these last few months…"

"I've been away too much." Hooch finished the sentence for Matt. "Is that it?"

"Oh, please," Matt came back to the sitting area, "don't make me sound like I'm pining. The charity's important, and you're doing a great job with it. Just that I would have liked to know you still lived here, instead of being this shape in the bed that appears when I'm asleep and is gone by the time I get up." He turned the glass in his hand, staring at it, before looking up at Hooch.

"Then what do you want me to do?" Hooch was floundering. After all this time he still found it difficult to get to grips with everything a relationship entailed. "Give me some help, here."

"Want?" Matt slumped back. "What I want is to be able to go out with you in this town without having to watch every move we make; to not have to be careful about every word I say when I'm talking about you so it doesn't look suspicious. But we can't do that, I know. This," he made a vague movement vaguely taking in the whole apartment, "is the only place we can be together. And let's face it, I rather miss the sex lately."

"Yeah." Hooch's voice was low. "Is it just sex we have when we spend time together?"

Matt's smile was small. "It's never been just sex for us, has it, at least not since you turned up on my doorstep after we left the Gulf." A statement, not question.

"No, it's not. If it were I wouldn't feel…" searching for words again, Hooch had never felt like this before, and he didn't know how to describe that hurt at seeing Matt with Greg. "Anyway, it's not." He ran a hand through his hair. "But with your job here, mine on base, the charity I'm trying to set up, and your new hobby, how are we going to do that relationship stuff?"

Matt bit back a laugh. "Probably the same way that we've always done the 'relationship stuff'. For two people who live together we do less than we did when we weren't. And," he shrugged, "if you need a hand, I can come out to the stables. And…aren't you curious as to what I take photos of?"

"I guess if you come out to the stables to help, we could combine that with the sex thing." At long last Hooch relaxed. "So what are you taking photos of? Greg?"

Matt almost smiled himself, remembering the time in the washroom at the stables. "Not just," Matt answered the question, and reached for his camera. "Others, too." He turned it on, set it to view the photos and passed it to Hooch, who started to flick through the images.

Hooch didn't say anything for a while, took his time, looking at each and every of the shots: all of them of nude male bodies, and all of them amazing images, capturing the beauty of skin and muscles perfectly. He handed the camera back when he was finished. "Wow." That was all, and it came out stunned and clearly in awe.

"Thanks," Matt ducked his head. "Don't suppose you'd want to pose?"

"Would you like me to?"

A single word. "Yes."

"Then I will. Guess we could combine the photography with the sex stuff."

Matt laughed, "that's part of the fun."

"Want to get started now?" Without waiting for an answer, Hooch swiftly pulled his shirt up and over his head.

Matt fumbled with the camera, fingers suddenly clumsy. "Why not?"

Hooch bent over to pull off his socks, then opened belt buckle and buttons, and pulled the whole lot down by lifting his ass off the seat. His briefs followed the next moment, before he poured himself onto the couch. Leaning back, legs splayed open, a hand touching his cock that slowly began to show interest at the new scenario. "I guess you're not planning on showing my face."

"No," Matt shook his head, "nobody's. Just to be safe."

"In that case…do you want me hard? Want me to spread my ass? Want to fuck me and take shots of your cock inside me?" Hooch's slow grin spread, and suddenly Matt realized something about Hooch he'd never been fully aware of: the man was an exhibitionist at heart.

Matt had to stop his hands from shaking, or else he'd drop the very expensive camera. He swallowed, then tried to answer the grin. "All of the above."

"Then let's get started." Hooch pulled up one knee, opening wide, and began to stroke his cock to full hardness. If this was going to be how they spent relationship-time together, indulging Matt's new hobby, then he was damned if he didn't throw himself into it with all he had.

* * *

The following week, when he was due to meet Greg for lunch, Matt was ready for a difficult conversation. One where he had to be careful what he said, enough truth, and enough left unsaid, that Matt could not give Greg what he wanted, no matter Greg's protestations to the contrary.

Greg listened, his usual smile fading, angry at first, but reluctantly accepting in the end. Friends, still, but the sex was over. When Greg accused Matt of having a hopeless crush on his roommate, Matt did not deny it, and left Greg to his conclusion, knowing that it was the safest assumption for Greg to make.

It would keep Hooch protected, and their relationship as secret as it could be.

2006

JANUARY 2006, SCOTLAND

They were standing in the queue at Glasgow airport security, where Hooch had to mentally brace himself for being touched by the security staff. He glanced at Matt who seemed deep in thought. "Penny for your thoughts?"

"We should probably wait until we get to the lounge," Matt replied absently, "not something for a crowd."

Hooch's brows rose, but before he could ask anything, it was his turn to walk through the metal detector, get checked out, take his boots off, turn his pockets inside out and stand with his arms spread while being patted down. Gritting his teeth throughout. When he was finally released, got his clothes back on and had sorted his hand luggage, he waited for Matt to join him. They didn't speak until they reached the first class lounge where Hooch let out a breath of relief. That part was over, the one that followed was mainly the boredom of sitting in a plane. "So," Hooch settled in a comfortable chair, "what were you thinking about?"

"You, mainly." Matt replied."

"You thought about me." A statement. "What else than the obvious?" Hooch ordered a coffee and water when a young man arrived to ask for their wishes, and waited until they were alone again.

"About how I can be…" Matt paused as a well-dressed woman walked past their chairs, ignoring her batted eyelashes, "more of what you need."

"You are everything I *want.*" Hooch tilted his head, considering. "After all this time, you now want to be more of what I need?"

Matt didn't say anything until their drinks arrived and the waiter disappeared. "Let's just say I've been thinking about it for a little while."

Hooch took a sip of his steaming hot espresso. "What are your thoughts?" He held up a hand, "wait, let me guess. You are enjoying power and control more than you thought back when I first went to the club."

Matt gave a hint of a grin. "I've had some time to get used to it," he admitted, "and over the years, I've picked up little bits here and there. The phone calls are part of it."

"Does this mean you'll come with me to the club? Trust me, there's a lot of curiosity regarding the partner of the guy who refuses to see anyone."

Matt nodded thoughtfully. "Yes," he paused. "If you think I'm going to live up to the advance publicity."

"You don't have to do anything. Just be there, and you'll be regarded with awe." Hooch leaned back his seat as he finished the espresso. "I might have let slip how very much you own me without the need for any bondage or pain." The smirk that graced his face was positively evil.

Being in public, Matt knew he had to keep himself under control, and not make the retort he wanted to. "Sneaky Delta," he muttered, taking a sip of his mineral water, though that was nowhere near as satisfying. "When are you going next?"

"Three weeks. I'm off to supervise a training exercise for the next ten days."

"Hmm." Matt made an indeterminate sound. "Do I need to get anything before then?"

"That depends. You can wear what you want, but I think you'd look fucking amazing in skin tight leather." Hooch managed a ridiculous leer over the rim of his glass.

Matt snorted before he finished his mineral water, trying to hide how much that idea had interested him. "We'll see," he said noncommittally.

"You know that cock cage…" Hooch suddenly said.

"What about it?" Matt tried not to think about it, because thinking of Hooch's meticulously organized and edited collection of 'toys' in the bottom drawer of the bedside table was seriously inconvenient in the first class lounge, full of imminently respectable and staid looking people.

"I think it should be you who controls me wearing it." Hooch pasted on a smile of utter blandness, as if he was discussing the stock market.

Matt only barely restrained himself from gaping. As it was, he blinked hard and swallowed. "Can we talk about this at home?" he said in a low voice, with a nervous glance around.

"Sure, as long as you agree that it makes sense."

Matt thought for a while before he nodded. It seemed he wasn't the only person who'd had been having thoughts for a while.

"Thank you." Hooch said quietly and unexpectedly seriously. Before either of them could get another word in, their flight was announced.

They gathered their jackets and hand luggage, and walked to the boarding gate past the long queue. Turning left into the plane, they settled into the comfortable seats.

Matt declined the champagne, as usual, and took a glass of the offered mineral water. "Home," he said with a sigh of contentment.

"After a long and boring flight." Hooch sighed, closing his eyes. "Wake me when we land."

Matt snorted at Hooch's habitual phrase when they travelled, knowing that Hooch would no more than cat-nap, alert to every single movement and sound in the plane. He smiled at the cabin attendant as he returned his empty glass, put on his headphones and tried to find something on the entertainment system that didn't bore him to tears, ready for the long flight home.

JANUARY-FEBRUARY 2006, FAYETTEVILLE

The training exercise had been harder than previous ones, because Hooch hadn't had sufficient time to get rid of the jetlag beforehand. He wouldn't be Delta, though, if he hadn't just ignored the fatigue. Still, ten days later he was glad to be given a couple of extra days off, but before he could head home and to his well earned rest, he had to run a long-planned errand, organized by the inimitable Mandy, now Mrs. Sullivan. He texted Matt to let him know that something had come up and he'd be later than expected. It was long dark by the time he pulled into the secure parking and texted Matt to meet him at the truck.

Matt walked out quickly, curious. While being sparse with details was hardly unusual for Hooch, asking him to come out to meet him was sufficiently out of the ordinary for Matt to know that something was going on. "What's up?" he asked, as soon as he was in earshot.

Hooch stepped out from behind the truck, a leash wound around his wrist, and at the other end a gorgeous example of a greyhound. Sleek and elegant, well-trained and curiously looking at Matt while standing close to Hooch. "Happy early birthday, Matt."

Matt's jaw dropped. "You got me a dog?" he said, feeling dumbfounded, but coming closer and holding out his hand for the creature to sniff.

"Mandy's idea, she's been dropping hints like an Iraq shelling." Hooch watched the dog sniffing and wagging his tail in a friendly manner. "He's from the greyhound sanctuary. Ex-racing dog, and lazy as all fuck." He grinned. "His name's Rex."

"Hi, Rex." Matt reached for the dog's ears and gave them a thorough scratch, while the dog's whip-like tail swung even more wildly.

"Thank you," he said to Hooch. "Haven't had a dog for twenty years, not since high school."

"Here," Hooch handed Matt the leash, "plus you'll get some practice in."

Matt took the leash, looking at Hooch in confusion for a second before the penny dropped.

He looked at the leash, Rex, and then back at Hooch. "I suppose now it'll be less embarrassing going shopping at the pet store." Hooch got his toys online these days, but as always, the memory of buying Hooch's collar was burned in Matt's mind.

"Speaking of which," Hooch reached into the truck to pull out a load of dog owner paraphernalia, "I have an extra two days off. What do you think about a 'trial run'?"

Matt blinked. "What, now?"

"Why not?" Hooch locked the truck and headed to the stairs, arms full with kit and bags. "I've just been training a platoon of guys, pushing them beyond the limits of their endurance, while being jet lagged. It was tough, intense, and I could do with some letting go." He turned round to look at Matt, alone on the garage stairs except for the dog. "You don't have to do anything. Just let me wear the collar and decompress."

Matt was standing still at the bottom, Rex wagging his tail furiously while pressed against him. He looked up at Hooch and visibly forced himself to release the tension. "Have to start somewhere," he nodded, and followed Hooch up the stairs, with Rex gingerly padded beside him, carefully placing his paws on each step.

"I'll make it easy for you. No pressure." Hooch promised before they entered the gym's reception area. All hell broke loose the moment they stepped inside, with a delightedly squealing Mandy, who made a fuss of Rex and produced a custom-made coat for him with the gym's logo and name on, and several customers, who petted the dog who lapped up the attention like a sponge. Hooch, meanwhile, took the baggage upstairs, except for a spare water bowl that was to live in the reception area, and found spaces for the dog paraphernalia. Eventually, he went into the bedroom to undress, letting out a big sigh as the tension began to drain with every piece of clothing he took off, until he was naked and went for a shower to get himself cleaned inside as well as out.

Finally tearing Rex away from his new fan club, much to the disappointment of both dog and humans, Matt made his way up to the apartment. He unclipped Rex's leash, letting the dog explore his new home, noting where Hooch had placed the various bits and pieces. The running shower let Matt know where Hooch was. After a longing look at the couch, which Matt correctly interpreted and then returned with a suitably stern look, Rex curled up on the dog bed placed under one of the windows.

The water stopped just as Matt came out of the bedroom, having retrieved Hooch's collar from its usual place.

A couple of minutes later Hooch emerged with damp hair, freshly shaved face and balls, and trimmed groin and ass. He looked tired but fairly relaxed, less tense than Matt had expected. He glanced at the curled-up dog, the now empty food bowl, and smiled at Matt when he discovered the collar in his hands. "Thanks," he said while stepping closer.

Matt returned the smile as he slipped his hands around Hooch's neck, fastening the collar, leaning towards his ear. "I promise this time it won't end the way it did the first time," voice low and husky. The slightest brush of his lips above and below the collar, then the lightest sting of his teeth as he nipped, just a memory, before he pulled away.

"Well, it's been a few years." Hooch teased, then slid onto his knees and simply leant into Matt. Face pressed against Matt's stomach, breathing in deeply the familiar scent.

Matt's hands went to Hooch's head, lightly ghosting over the damp hair. "Do you want to stay out here or move to the bedroom?" he asked, before remembering that he was the one who was supposed to be deciding. "We should move to the bedroom," he corrected. More comfortable, given how tired Hooch was. Besides, having Rex's curious eyes on him felt distinctly odd—which was strange as he'd never felt any discomfort with having humans watch him.

Hooch looked up and nodded, before standing up. Matt took his hand and led him to the bedroom, where Hooch stood, waiting until told what to do.

"Undress me," Matt said simply.

And Hooch did. No hesitation, immediately following the order. Expertly taking Matt's clothes off with great care, from the trainers over vest top and shorts, to the briefs. He stayed on his knees when he was done.

Matt's hand went to Hooch's jaw, lifting it upwards. Contemplating whether to make Hooch take him into his mouth, knowing that Hooch would do whatever he asked. Turning his hand around, caressing Hooch's jaw with just the back of his fingers. "Up," he ordered, deciding against it, at least for now, "into bed."

Hooch's body gave him away, with his movements less fluid than usual, it talked of fatigue and exhaustion, but his face didn't show the relief he had to be feeling as he sunk onto the firm mattress. The look he gave Matt but simply calm.

Matt climbed in after him, pulling the covers over them both. He smoothed his hands down Hooch's body, ignoring his own arousal, which had been slow to catch on at first, but was now insistent. "Sleep," he soothed, "we'll continue this tomorrow." He watched as Hooch drifted off, obedient and relaxed. Matt waited until Hooch's breathing changed, and then got up and padded to the bathroom to take care of matters before slipping back into the bed.

He stared at the ceiling for what felt like long hours, thoughts racing through his head.

* * *

The scent of coffee wafting under his nose drew Hooch into consciousness. He opened his eyes to a room flooded with sunlight, and Matt standing in the middle of it. Dressed, holding a tray which he proceeded to put down on the bedside table, and which was loaded with not only coffee, but also what was usually banished from the apartment: fruit-filled pastries, cinnamon rolls, and even waffles. With butter and maple syrup, no less.

"Morning," Matt said softly, sitting on the bed next to Hooch. "How do you feel?" Fingertips on the side of his face, lightly heading downwards, just touching the edge of the collar.

Hooch blinked himself awake, it took him two seconds from sleep-drowsy to wakefulness. Revived and with his energy returned. "Good." He'd needed the sleep after the ten hard days and nights, and the sense of being owned and taken care of the collar provided him, had helped him relax completely. "I'm not dreaming the unhealthy, sugar-laden, butter-dripping goods?"

"Special occasion," Matt smiled. He pulled back, fingers lingering before he picked up one of the coffee mugs and gently placed it into Hooch's waiting hands.

"What's the special occasion?" Hooch scooted up to sit, taking the first sip with a look of pleasure on his face.

"I'll tell you after breakfast, I have an idea." Matt's fingertips returned to the collar, moving slowly downwards, lingering momentarily on Hooch's left nipple, before leaving the skin. Selecting one of the cinnamon rolls and putting it on a plate, he handed it to Hooch, exchanging it for the cup.

Hooch tilted his head, but he knew better than to ask. He bit into the pastry when offered, allowing a small sound of pleasure at the burst of flavors. During the last ten days, as grueling for the Delta Force trainer as for the recruits, he'd lost weight despite eating as much as he could, but he was burning it quicker than he could keep it on. He made his way through the first pastry in record time, then went onto the waffles dripping with syrup.

Matt watched him with satisfaction, his own coffee cup in hand, and indulging in a raspberry Danish. Waiting until Hooch had demolished the pile of sugary, sticky treats—he didn't dignify them with any other name—before sitting next to Hooch on the bed, on top of the covers, hand on Hooch's chest, fingers lightly resting on the left nipple again. "I think," he said, with just the smallest hint of a caress, "that a ring here would look amazingly hot," he paused, "and leave no doubt whatsoever that you were mine." Hoping he hadn't overdone it.

Hooch's eyes widened a fraction. He swallowed down the last bite, dark eyes on Matt's face. "What about the right?"

"Hmmm," a low sound in Matt's throat, "we'll see how one goes first. Wouldn't want to rush things."

"Okay." Hooch agreed without hesitation. "When?"

"This afternoon." Matt tilted his head to one side, "so you're healed up a bit before we go to the club."

Hooch drew in an audible breath. The duvet hid his almost instant arousal, but Matt knew him well, he could tell from other signs such as dilation of his pupils. "That's unexpected."

The mysterious smile, so unlike Matt. "I wouldn't like you to be bored with me." Matt leaned forward to breathe into Hooch's ear, hands undoing the buckle, removing the collar. "You're all sticky, and not in a good way. Shower."

Hooch nodded, surprised, but that quickly changed to calm acceptance that was so unlike the turmoil and storm that was Hooch. When he got up, there was no hiding any longer of his full erection.

Matt quickly coiled the collar and laid it aside before tugging Hooch towards the bathroom, turning on the shower and making sure the water was a comfortable temperature before urging Hooch inside. Quickly getting out of his clothes, Matt joined him, glad the cubicle was large enough for the two of them with room to spare.

Matt's closeness and the warm water certainly didn't diminish Hooch's erection, but he ignored it, because Matt was ignoring it. Hooch's mind, right now, he was doing nothing he wasn't told to do—he didn't even want anything he wasn't given. Decompressing in the secure knowledge of not having to give any orders, not having to make any decisions, and not having to be the tough Delta Force instructor that he was. It was a new experience for Hooch, to be washed by Matt and to be taken care of, for there was no other word for how Matt treated him, and it did something to him that he couldn't name yet.

Matt shut the water off, guided Hooch out of the shower and dried him thoroughly. "I have a class to take," Matt said, matter-of-factly as he helped Hooch into loose, comfortable clothes, which did nothing to hide his hard-on. "Why don't you chill and keep Rex company?" He looked down at Hooch's erection. "I'll take care of that later this afternoon."

Hooch sucked in a breath, then nodded. Matt Donahue did seem to have it in him, after all. Or maybe he'd just grown up while growing accustomed to Hooch and his special brand of crazy. "Yeah, will do. I just get my netbook."

"Okay," Matt gave him a lingering kiss, and left the bathroom.

The sound of paws in the corridor, as Rex looked first at Matt's retreating back, then stuck his head around the bathroom door to see Hooch standing perfectly still, before apparently deciding that he had clearly been adopted by two lunatics, and returning to the living room in a huff.

When Matt returned around lunchtime, Hooch was on the couch, fast asleep, the netbook slipped off his lap and open on the floor. Rex laid out in all his long-legged glory along Hooch, wedged between couch and body, Hooch's arm on the snoozing dog. Hooch was wearing the collar again, and his face looked younger and softer than Matt had seen it in a long time.

Matt picked up the netbook from the floor, closing it quietly and putting it in the middle of the dining table, to prevent any accidents. He sat down on the only unoccupied spot on the couch, putting a hand on Hooch's arm to wake him up.

Unlike himself, Hooch didn't wake immediately, but swatted at the hand on his arm, mumbling something about Rex and stop and to go to sleep the fuck already.

"Hey, don't blame the dog, it's me," Matt chuckled. "Do you want some lunch?" The chuckling grew as both Hooch and Rex sat up at the last word, turning dark eyes on him.

Hooch shook his head to clear the cobwebs off. "Fuck, did I conk out again?" He eyed the dog beside him, who looked first at him, then at Matt with expectation and a little dribble. "He's more desperate." Hooch pointed at Rex.

The dog looked at Matt, who shook his head. "Come on then, both of you." He got up off the couch and went into the kitchen, filling the bowl with dry food for Rex, and back to healthy food for Hooch and himself.

Hooch sat at the table, watching Matt. He'd never tried to help with any cooking, as it was safer for both of them if he never did. "I checked out after care for piercings."

Matt turned to look at him. "Is it going to interfere with work?" he asked, always aware that Hooch's work involved some fairly dangerous shit at times. Make that most of the time.

"Not if I'm careful. Salt baths every day, barbell first not a ring, and I can always tape it up if necessary." Hooch flashed a grin. "Even Delta are not naked most of the time."

Matt couldn't hold back a snort at that, thinking of all the impressive shiny equipment, fancy uniform and toys that Delta had (and seemed to break, lose, or otherwise render useless all the time). "It should be alright in a couple of weeks, then. Or I can just tell everyone else to keep their paws off you."

"The healing takes several weeks, sometimes months." Hooch tilted his head, focused on Matt. "Can I make a request?"

Matt made a noise of agreement and looked at Hooch, turning off the heat from the stir-frying vegetables.

"Because of my job, would you consider having them put both in at the same time? Would cut the healing stage down to once."

Matt's eyebrows went up. "Sure." He blinked. "Wow. If I thought you'd be like this about them..."

"Matt, you told me you want me to be pierced. There is nothing I wouldn't do if you ordered me to, because I know you'd never demand anything unreasonable." The hyper focus on Matt increased. "If you tell me to get my cock pierced, I will. If you tell me to get my ass tattooed, or my chest, or my arms, or anything else that isn't visible when in uniform, I will. If you tell me to wax my body hair, I will. Do you understand?" The intensity was almost palpable. "That's what ownership means, and I've always been aware of that."

There was an audible click of teeth, even though Matt had managed to stop his jaw from dropping. Seeming to collect himself, he stepped closer, but then stopped. This wasn't about physical touch, or even physical symbols, even though Hooch was wearing the collar. "Yes," he swallowed, once more reminded—though he'd always been aware—of the power, the *trust*, that Hooch had placed in his hands. The growing heat when Hooch had mentioned all the other possibilities, strangely appealing. Things to file away and consider for another day. "Yes," he repeated.

He turned back to the food, as though he could somehow distract himself with the more mundane tasks, but even they were about how Hooch was under his control when they were under the same roof: Matt deciding what they ate, when they ate it. Matt dished out the lunch, putting Hooch's plate in front of him with the bottle of chili sauce, but eating his own plain. Quiet, deep in thought, both about the plans for the afternoon and what he had seemingly agreed to do and be—for many more years to come.

After lunch, Matt was the one who led the way down to the garage and drove to the tattoo parlor - he'd made the appointment at a place recommended by several of the regulars at the gym, known for its meticulous standards and adherence to hygiene, and the complete unflappability of its staff in the face of any and every request.

Their request, however, was very much on the tame side for the business. After the usual warnings and advice about proper care, the deed was done with remarkable efficiency and speed.

Hooch, the crazy masochistic bastard that he was, enjoyed the pain of the piercings far too much. He stoically watched the needle being pushed through the nub of flesh without the any flinch, with his hard-on uncomfortably trapped in the tight black denims, but neither did the staff bat an eyelid, nor did Matt acknowledge his predicament. The fresh wounds were lightly bandaged, and they were sent on their way with information on aftercare.

Matt snuck a glance over at Hooch in the passenger seat, bulge still obvious though his face remained impassive, looking straight ahead, eyes half-closed. "Nearly home," Matt said, though he wasn't sure whether this was to Hooch or himself.

"This feels…" strange, painful, sore, different, over-sensitive, "good."

"Good," Matt echoed, exhaling. A risk, though one that had paid off. "I can't wait until I can put the rings in," he said. The plain, polished steel rings he'd bought to put in, once the wounds had healed. How they would gleam against the tanned skin. Watching Hooch's reaction, which was a tiny, hardly visible tremor, as they pulled into the secure parking under the gym and got out of the car. Matt was thankful that Hooch's obedience extended to not objecting to Matt driving, for once. This seemed the only time Hooch could let go and not need to control every aspect of his life including the driving 'in case his combat driver training skills were needed'.

Hooch hurried past the reception area with a cursory greeting to Mandy, eager to hide the very visible erection, which had no place in a respectable gym. He didn't even stop for Rex's obligatory petting.

Matt had to force himself to slow down, to behave normally, greet Mandy and a couple of the regulars who were hanging around, and soothe the upset Rex, before heading upstairs.

The short time it had taken Matt, it had been long enough for Hooch to get out of his clothes. He stood in the middle of the room, naked, the collar snugly back around his throat, the white of the taped bandages over his nipples bright against his tanned skin.

Checking that both doors were firmly locked, Matt walked up to Hooch slowly, shedding his clothes as he went, knowing that Hooch's eyes were on him every step of the way. Standing right in front of Hooch, his hand brushed against the taped bandages, gently at first, and then just enough pressure to sting, before stroking Hooch's weeping cock. "I told you this morning I'd take care of this," Matt told him, strokes firm. "I keep my promises." He took his hands off Hooch and took a step back. "Turn around. Bend over the couch."

Hooch suppressed a shudder, his cock so hard for so long, he was that desperate, he had to force himself not to make a sound as he turned as ordered and bent down low, spreading his legs far apart. Dipping even lower until his arms were outstretched, hands gripping the top of the couch, head lower than his ass. Spread as wide open as it was possible. He felt his breath come in short gasps, straining for control.

Matt counted slowly in his head to ten, drawing out the tension, before stepping closer, hands on Hooch's ass to spread him further apart. Nudging forward, he went slowly because he was without any lube except for his pre-cum; going slowly, so that Hooch could feel the gradual burn and stretch as he pressed forward; going slowly, so that Hooch could feel every inch of him as he entered and claimed. Possessing. Owning. His.

The groan that forced itself out of Hooch's chest told Matt how very much Hooch was his indeed, right now, with fraying control. Hooch's long, strong legs trembled, his knuckles turned white in an ever more desperate grip on the couch, and his muscular back shuddered with tremors.

Hands on Hooch's hips holding him still as Matt moved, once he had buried himself deep inside. Long strokes, knowing that Hooch was so aroused from the piercing and the long anticipation that it would not take much for him to come apart. Besides, Matt's own control was rapidly disappearing as his thrusts grew more erratic, Hooch bucking under him with increasing desperation.

Losing every last fragile remain of his control, Hooch cried out, forced himself backwards and onto Matt's cock, meeting his powerful thrusts to increase the onslaught of sensations. It was too much, far too much to take, and he came with an intensity that made his knees buckle.

Matt collapsed into him, Hooch's spasms drawing out his own orgasm as he emptied himself into Hooch. Only barely remembering not put his full weight on the body beneath him, for fear of abrading the newly pierced nipples further, but pulling him up and to the side, they fell onto the other half of the couch together, Hooch cradled in Matt's arms.

"You..." Hooch murmured, still shuddering through the last remaining tremors, "are quite something, Matt Donahue."

"As are you, Hubert Bozic," Matt held him close, nuzzling Hooch's neck, just above the collar. "As are you."

After a few more moments resting, waiting until their heartbeats returned to normal, Matt reluctantly eased away from Hooch and padded to the bathroom to quickly clean up, before returning with a wet cloth do the same for the boneless Hooch. Satisfied with his work, he went to the kitchen to prepare the salt solution for the new piercings, feeling Hooch's eyes on him as he moved around the living area.

"What, you're not falling asleep?" Hooch's amused and sated voice came from the couch.

"Hmmm, no, not yet." Matt was back as he removed the dressings and started to wash the wounds in the salt solution. "That's later. When you fuck my brains out."

Hooch hissed at the salt solution on the wounds, then ignored it. "I'm ten years older than you, you have to give me some time." He looked down onto his nipples, and damned if he didn't love the metal against his skin.

Matt smirked as he continued to tend to the tender flesh. "We have all the time in the world, old man, all the time in the world."

"Who are you calling an old man? You do realize I could kill you with one hand and very little effort, kid?"

"Who're you calling a kid?" Matt grinned as he finished with the salt water and moved back to properly admire the metal shining against Hooch's tanned skin. "Who'd look after you then, huh?" He stood up and reached down to pull up the boneless Hooch. "Now, you still haven't caught up on your sleep from the training exercise. Back to bed with you and I might even join you for a bit of a snooze."

Hooch grinned sleepily and followed Matt into the bedroom. He couldn't help the yawn. "Got to make sure I don't bleed onto the bedding."

"It's stopped, mainly," Matt said, pulling back the covers, "but what's a go through the washing machine? They need to breathe a bit, and I like the look of that metal on you. So much so, I'm going to take a lot of photos, trust me on that."

Hooch grinned then yawned again and slipped under the covers. "Anything else you want me to get pierced, just say so." He let the words stay in the room, turned onto his side, relishing the ache in his ass as he closed his eyes. He was beat. Again.

Matt got in next to him, holding him close and enjoying the feeling of Hooch in his arms. Relaxed, rested, at ease. Touching the collar with his lips thoughtfully, he thought of the next fortnight until the club, pondering a few more ideas before he, too drifted off to sleep.

Hooch was back at work after his long weekend off. Pierced nipples carefully taped to avoid irritation of the still fresh wounds, and with renewed energy after the first weekend of what felt like a new chapter for Matt and himself. He wasn't expected back home before his usual time in the evening, but at mid-afternoon there was a small commotion outside the front door, which made Mandy look up and listen.

It was clearly Hooch's voice that she heard outside over the sound of an idling vehicle.

"No, I am fine."

She couldn't understand the reply, probably muffled by coming from inside the car.

"I said," Hooch's voice again, carefully pronouncing his words in the sharp way he had when he was getting annoyed, "that I am fine. Get back to base and make sure my truck's here by tomorrow."

The other voice again, and then Hooch's, louder this time and clearly pissed off. "Get your ass back to base, Corporal. I said I am fine, now fuck off!"

His outburst was followed by the sound of the engine revving and the vehicle taking off, probably faster than it should.

A few seconds later the frosted glass door opened and Hooch stepped through. He held his pack in his left hand by its straps, while the right was secured in an elevated sling with a plastic cast around the wrist and most of the hand. His right eye was swollen, butterfly strips holding a gash above it together, and most of the right side of his face was bruised.

Hooch, battered and so pissed off, he was positively steaming with anger.

Mandy's jaw dropped. "What happened?" she asked in shock.

"Don't. Just don't." Hooch fumed, dropping the pack beside the reception desk. "The fucking idiot should be thankful I could only hit him with my left and merely broke his nose."

Still staring, Mandy swallowed. "Do you want me to get Matt?"

"Not if he's busy taking a class." Hooch walked over to the vending machine and fumbled for coins in his uniform's back pocket, but utterly failing. Too unused to using his left hand, which only pissed him off even more.

Sufficiently accustomed to military men to know that any attempt to assist would just make things worse, Mandy shook the shoulder of the equally gaping Danni at the reception desk, motioning her to go off and get Matt who was due to finish a class in five minutes, and to intercept him before he headed off to the showers. She stayed and kept an eye on Hooch.

Rex crept out from behind her legs and stared at Hooch warily, figuring that it was a bad idea to get too near to large, angry men wearing combat boots.

"Goddammit!" Hooch hit the vending machine with his left fist, before whirling round to vent his anger somewhere else, but his gaze fell on Rex who whined at his outburst and slunk back, cowering. "Sorry." Some of Hooch's anger deflated at the frightened look of the dog. "Wasn't aimed at you." He held out his good hand but didn't crouch down as he usually would.

Rex looked up at him, still wondering who this large, angry man was who had taken the place of the comfy, mellow human of the weekend. He hunched down and slinked closer, before cautiously touching a nervous, trembling nose to Hooch's outstretched hand.

"Hey, sorry, Rex." Hooch petted the dog's head, controlling his anger in the face of Rex's fear, who gradually gained confidence. Hooch was still petting Rex, albeit awkwardly, when Matt came through from the gym, towel round his neck and sweaty.

"Shit," Matt's voice was barely audible. He'd been warned by Danni, but the reality was somewhat more than he expected. "What happened, man?" All-buddy like in public.

"What happened? Some fucking idiot thought he was Rambo and didn't need combat driver training and would show off his 'skills' to me. That's what happened." Hooch growled, but gave another pat on Rex's head nevertheless.

"Hey, let's get you upstairs for a change of clothes." Matt reached for Hooch's pack. "Come on."

Hooch followed Matt onto the stairs. "Do we have coke? Full fat? I couldn't get the motherfucking machine to work." Despite all the good work Rex had done in controlling his anger, it was flaring up again.

"Just the emergency stash," Matt told him. A couple of glass bottles they kept at the back of the fridge. The stuff with sugar, not corn syrup, that was a pain to track down but that Hooch preferred and craved when his body was depleted.

"Thank fuck." Hooch went to the couch and slowly sat down, preferring the left side. "What a fucking mess," he groaned with his head back and eyes closed. "I'm signed off for the next seven days."

Matt was rummaging at the back of the fridge for the coke, before retrieving a single precious bottle and bringing it to the couch to put it into

Hooch's grateful hand. If Hooch noticed that the cap had already been removed, he didn't say anything.

He emptied the bottle almost in one go, before opening his eyes again. "They had to pull me off that idiot."

"Delta?" Matt frowned. If so, standards were slipping. But they wouldn't waste Hooch on anyone else.

"Candidate. Thought he didn't need training, was already hard as nails." Hooch gingerly touched his swollen eye and tried to frown, but quickly gave up on that. "He fucked up his chances, might be kicked out altogether. Crashed the vehicle and me in it. Doesn't look good on his record." He pointed to his elevated hand. "No fracture, just sprained, or I would have stuffed his balls down his throat."

Matt snorted, perfectly aware that Hooch probably had come very close to doing just that before he was pulled off the idiot. "Anything else apart from the obvious?" meaning the injuries.

"See for yourself." Hooch indicated his uniform and then wiggled his left hand with a look of frustration on his face. "I'm shit with my left."

"Come on then, to bed, so you can lie down properly." Pulling Hooch up and urging him the short distance. Stripping Hooch was awkward with the sling. When he lay down, naked, Matt inspected the damage, which consisted mainly of bruising down the right side. More discoloration than damage. He noticed the tape over his pierced nipples had been removed and at his questioning look Hooch rolled his eyes. "I had to get checked over. Medics had a field day."

Matt's eyebrows went up. "What did they say?"

"That I should know better."

A smile tugged at the edges of Matt's mouth as he traced a fingertip over the left nipple. "So what's new?" playing with the tender nubs and then going to the right, to make things even. "Do you want me to change the dressing on the cuts yet?"

Hooch drew in a sharp breath, watching the progress of Matt's finger with his intense focus. "No, I'm fine. They told me the butterfly strips should stay on, the rest is surface damage." He looked up, "I've had worse."

Matt snorted, knowing full well, then the expression on his face turned thoughtful. "Any plans for the next seven days, then?" he asked, deliberately casual.

"Other than equally getting bored to death and being pissed off that I can't train Lucifer, while looking like a painter's palette gone wrong? No."

Fingertips dancing over skin, stopping at the second half of Hooch's sentence. "Funny you should say that." Matt's fingers flattened, pressing into an unbruised section of Hooch's abdomen, sliding around and resting on his hip. "I've been thinking about what you said on the weekend, about doing anything I asked if it wasn't visible when you were in uniform."

"Hm?" Hooch made a distracted sound, then focused at Matt's last words. "Yes." Not a question.

"I find that I do like these," he bent down and brushed a kiss on each nipple, "very much." He straightened. "But I was thinking that when we go to the club, I should make it a little more obvious that you are mine. My mark, right here." The hand that had been on his hip, gently but firmly moving under Hooch on his uninjured side, until fingertips pressed into Hooch's back, just at his waist.

Hooch's eyes widened. "What were you thinking of?" Full acceptance, without knowing what Matt had in mind.

Matt leaned closer, almost nose to nose. "Ink. Permanent. My mark tattooed on you, where everyone there can see."

Hooch's lips parted, stunned for a moment, his heart racing as adrenaline spiked within seconds. "Yeah. I'd..." he swallowed, "like that."

Matt's smile grew. "Good." He drew back. "Should probably wait a few days until the worst of this goes down first, though." Indicating the mess that was Hooch.

"My back's fine," Hooch protested, "and I'm only bruised, nothing major."

"That means I can book you in." Matt replied. "But first," he stood up and rummaged in the wardrobe for the comfy, loose clothes that Hooch normally hated to wear, "you're going to get some clothes on and settle on the couch and watch that stack of DVDs that you bought in Edinburgh. With the dog, because I have to get back downstairs."

"Bully." Hooch groused, but didn't complain when Matt helped him into the clothes. Even putting socks on one-handed was awkward, and navigating anything but drawstring waistbands seemed nearly impossible. They opted for a shirt, easier to pull on with his arm in a sling. "I'd feel a lot better if I could use the idiot as a punching ball."

"I'd imagine by the time the guys on base are through with him, he'd prefer it if you had," Matt said dryly, imagining what a guy who'd probably be thrown out because of his own idiocy would be going through. Not feeling a shred of sympathy, not when the idiot had been responsible for Hooch's injuries.

Hooch followed Matt back out into the living room, where he settled down on the couch, the remote in his hand, and a space left free for Rex. Having evidently forgiven him, Rex rested his chin on Hooch's uninjured thigh, staring at the television, barely acknowledging Matt's departure with a lazy twitch of an ear.

When Matt returned later that evening, he found Hooch asleep on the couch on his good side. TV on mute but running, a blanket over himself and Rex, who had curled up in his customary spot at Hooch's stomach. A few remnants of dog food in the bowl showed Matt that Hooch had fed Rex, and a bottle of pain killers right beside Hooch's cell phone gave Matt a good indication that someone, probably the doctor herself, had called Hooch to bully him into taking the pain killers as instructed, since the man hated taking them because they made him drowsy. Hooch didn't even stir when Matt stepped closer. Only Rex looked lazily up and twitched his ears.

"Hey, Rex," Matt gently smoothed a hand over the dog's ears. "He been OK?" Rex laid his head back on Hooch's stomach as though saying 'yes, calm at last, and he has rotten taste in movies.'

Matt smiled and turned to Hooch, reaching out to touch his shoulder, but deciding against it, before heading to the kitchen, knowing that the sound and smell of food being prepared would wake Hooch anyway.

Matt was well into cooking dinner before Hooch stirred, woken by the combination of smells from the kitchen area, his rumbling stomach, and Rex getting off the couch—where he'd become a regular thanks to Hooch's bad influence. He was bleary-eyed, unlike his usual instant waking, and several hours after the accident he was stiff and sore, and not in the good way.

"You want to use the table, or stay on the couch?" Matt asked, guessing that Hooch was in considerably more pain than he would ever show.

"Table." Hooch groaned and stretched carefully. Sleep had been forced onto him from the painkillers, but it had made every muscle and bruised part of him seize up and protest the movement. Eventually he got up and to the table. "I hate those goddamned pills."

Watching Hooch carefully, Matt set the food on the table, a casserole that was easy for Hooch to eat with one hand. "How often are you meant to be taking them?"

"Every four hours." Hooch yawned, awkwardly covering his mouth with his left. "Not going to. They knock me out."

"That's the point." Matt was adamant. "You need a chance to heal up." He paused, not knowing how close to tread. "You're not supposed to be that knocked up before you go to the club."

"Yeah, damn. That's one reason I was so pissed off." Hooch glared down at his hand still elevated. "I haven't been for months."

"I know." Not since September, one of the longest stretches yet. "So you'll need time, and rest." A small smile as Matt speared a cube of chicken. "Plenty of time to think what you might want to do, and to wonder about what I've got planned before then."

Hooch's brows rose, but then he remembered Matt's mention of a tattoo from earlier. "I'm not knocked up everywhere." Looking at Matt over his fork, dark lashes shadowing even darker eyes.

"Knocked up enough," Matt was firm. "Besides, you get some of your best ideas when you're bored." That mysterious smile again, so unlike Matt, "and the bruising needs to go down a bit before some of the other things I have in mind."

"I also get seriously annoying and a right pain in the ass when I'm bored." Hooch countered, then gave up trying to eat with the fork, reaching for the spoon instead.

Matt's eyes flashed as though he was enjoying some private joke. "Oh, there'll be pain, though I don't know if you'll enjoy it or not." Ignoring Hooch's accurate prediction that after a week of boredom, he would be well-nigh unbearable. "Do you need to tell the club that I'm coming or anything? Do I have to fill out a new form?" Remembering the plethora of forms when Hooch had joined.

"I'll tell them. Wouldn't be surprised if they let you come for free."

A quizzical look. "Why?"

"I think I'm…" Hooch let the spoon move slowly on the half empty plate, looking for the right words. "I think I'm quite popular." He shrugged.

"But you…" but you're always blindfolded and never speak to anyone there, Matt was about to say, but stopped, when he realized just what Hooch was trying to say. "Do they know about me?" he asked, genuinely curious.

"All they know is that I'm yours." Hooch put the spoon down to wrap his hand around the back of his neck, rolling his head. "They know you own me and they know what I'm like, so I guess they figure you're superman or something."

Matt only barely restrained a snort. "I see, plenty of advance publicity I'll have to live up to, then." Echoing what he'd said in the airport lounge when they'd started talking of this. It seemed half a lifetime ago, and he was surprised to remember it had only been a couple of weeks. A very enlightening couple of weeks.

Hooch grinned. "You won't have to do anything, just be there. Kiss me, if you want, because I never allow anyone there to kiss me. I don't care about them, they are just tools to deliver what I need to function." Hooch pushed the unfinished plate away. "But you, you're different."

Matt realized he'd just been playing with his food, and put down his fork. "How?" though he suspected the answer, Hooch, honest to goodness talking, was a rare enough thing that he didn't want to discourage it.

"They are the tools so I can be with you." Hooch trailed off as he tried to find words once again. The eternal struggle. "I want to be your partner, and the only way I can be that without going off the rails is by them being the tools to keep me in check." He frowned lopsidedly. "You're different because you're never a tool, you're the goal."

Fuck. Just when he thought he had a grasp of Hooch, he went and pulled this sort of shit. But it made a strange, bizarre sense, it really did, in its fucked-up way. "Do you," Matt swallowed, "do you think you're there?"

"Do you?" Hooch countered.

So easy to say 'yes', the answer he wanted to be true. "I don't know," barely audible. "Sometimes. Most of the time." Taking control of himself, Matt took a deep breath, placed a hand on Hooch's uninjured wrist.

Hooch looked at Matt's hand on his, and there was no denying, a fleeting expression of hurt had crossed his face. "It's been how long?" He asked quietly. "You think I ever get there?"

"I do." Two words. Unknown when, or how, but somehow, sometime, they would.

✱ ✱ ✱

A few days later, when Hooch's injuries had healed somewhat, and he was so antsy and twitchy from the forced inactivity that even Rex refused to sit on the couch with him, he and Matt returned to the studio where he'd had the piercings done.

Matt had clearly been having discussions with the artist about the actual design, because there was no more than an introduction, a shake of the hand, and then a talk on the particular technique to be used and aftercare before the obligatory forms and disclaimers were signed and explained, before Hooch was motioned to a chair. He was asked to take his top off and his denims, to straddle the chair and lean forward, and he did so almost gratefully.

Matt was looking at him steadily, as though wanting to ask him whether he was sure, but also holding back from asking, because that was not what Hooch wanted.

The sound of the artist putting on rubber gloves in Hooch's back, then a hand on him, motioning him to bend a little further, and steadying him in readiness.

The first time the tattooist's needle pierced his flesh was like a scratch to his skin. A short, intense sensation, immediately followed by the next and the next once more. Relentless, as long as the tattooist worked on the design. Hooch tensed his muscles, but there was little on his lower back except for smooth skin over sinews and bones.

He began to sweat and lowered his head, his breathing shallow as he sank into the buzz the endless 'scratch' of the needle gave him. Through all the time it took, far longer than he'd expected, Hooch was hard while lost in the physical sensation, coupled with the knowledge that now, for the first time in his life, he was truly marked.

* * *

The drive home was silent. Hooch sat in the passenger seat with his eyes closed, the expression on his face thoughtful. Matt pulled into the secure parking at the gym and got out, going around to the other side, ready in case Hooch needed a hand out, but not offering it unless it was needed. As he'd expected, Hooch didn't ask for any help, getting out of the truck with slightly stiff movements.

"Crap, can we take the elevator?" Matt asked, watching Hooch's stiff movements but knowing that Hooch wouldn't ever admit weakness. "Forgot I promised Mandy I'd bring up a box of brochures. Just wait a minute." He disappeared into the storeroom and emerged with the bulky package and pressed the button.

If Hooch was grateful he didn't let it on. He waited until they stepped inside the lift before he spoke. "You're a shit liar, you know that, Donahue?"

A snort as Matt leaned against the lift walls. "I wouldn't have to if you didn't always have to be the big scary Delta in public."

"Only in public?" Hooch grinned.

The doors opened and Matt went to put the brochures under the reception desk, saying hello to Mandy, and greeting Rex from his new place sprawled on a rug in the reception area, heading to the door up to the apartment. Rex lazily stayed where he was, enjoying the winter sunshine, and the compliments and company of the clients.

Hooch followed up the stairs, slower than usual, but clearly upholding the 'big bad Delta' image. "How long has it been?" Hooch went straight to the kitchen area, starting to make coffee in their fancy machine.

Matt glanced at the clock, as though he didn't already know. "Nearly four,." he told him, standing on the other side of the kitchen bench. "How does it feel?"

"Sore." Hooch craned his neck to look at Matt. "Translated to: good." He was a lot calmer than before, and the antsiness born out of boredom had disappeared for now.

A steady look, before Matt was satisfied that Hooch wasn't being stoic and invincible. He accepted the coffee with a nod, and took a sip. "Do you want to have a look?" he asked.

"Contrary to what you might think," Hooch added a lot of cold milk to his double espresso, "I'm damned well dying of curiosity."

"I'll go get the mirror from the bathroom if you go to the bedroom?" Matt asked, already heading in that direction.

Hooch nodded, went off to the bedroom where he sat down to take his boots off. Bending over was tricky with the gauze taped over his lower back, which felt as if all of his back had been covered up. He'd pulled off his shirt and denims and was working on his briefs, when Matt returned.

"I'll do it," Matt put the mirror down on the bed. "Close your eyes."

Hooch's brows rose a fraction at the command, but he did as Matt told him to. He stood up when he was naked, eyes closed. Matt positioned him in front of the mirror, before carefully removing the gauze, holding his breath as he did so. He exhaled audibly when Hooch's back was bared, before picking up the mirror and taking a step back. "Open," he said softly, holding the mirror so that Hooch could see the artistry.

Hooch opened his eyes, stared at the vast expanse of ink all across his lower back. "Holy shit!"

Matt nearly dropped the mirror. "You don't like it?" He blinked.

"Wrong question. You wanted me to have this, there's no way I wouldn't like it." Hooch turned from left to right, best he could, to look at the tribal design from all angles. Black ink against his tanned skin, spanning all across his lower back and dipping down in the middle, pointing downwards to his ass crack. "It's a lot bigger than I thought. Shit, Matt, it's amazing." He squinted his eyes and stilled. "Wait…is that…" trying to see clearer, "is that an 'M' and a 'D' in the design?."

Still too early, too sore for Matt to put a hand there, to trace over his initials on Hooch's back, the curves and the lines cunningly hidden in the design. He stepped closer, touching Hooch not on the tattoo, but his unbruised shoulder, leaning close. "Mine," he said simply, "and anyone who gets close enough to see you will know."

Hooch held Matt's gaze in the mirror. "Yours." His next breath was shaky, and he could feel his cock getting half hard. "Your piercings, your tattoo, your mark." Getting more aroused by the second. "This is the goddamned motherfucking hottest thing in my life."

Watching Hooch's arousal through the mirror, the eyes so dark they looked all pupil, his hardening cock was one of the most erotic things that Matt had seen. His hand slid around to Hooch's chest, lingering on the pierced nipples before slowly trailing down his stomach, fingers brushing on the light dusting of hair.

Matt's fingers slipped off as he stepped back, around, dropping to his knees in front of Hooch. "Keep your eyes on the mirror." He ordered, before swallowing Hooch whole.

Hooch's knees buckled at the sudden onslaught, but he braced himself, set his feet apart and kept his eyes firmly on the mirror. The back of Matt's head, the way his neck moved, his shoulders, the broad back, and how the sensations of Matt's tight lips, pressing tongue, light scrape of teeth, and constricting throat, contrasted with only being able to see his back, and nothing more.

As always, the little convulsion and shudder just before Hooch came, and Matt sucked down harder, increasing the pressure, feeling the warm rush of liquid, swallowing every drop and lapping Hooch clean before sitting back on his heels.

"Fuck me." Hooch murmured. His voice thick and rough with lingering arousal.

A look of disbelief as Matt took in the fresh tattoo, the bruises faded to mottled yellow, the strapped wrist, the other injuries. "Ah, no. Not right now. Not when you're injured front and back."

"My face." Hooch urged, lowering himself to sit on the edge of the bed and spreading his knees apart for Matt to stand between them.

Lust warred with doubt on Matt's face, wary that this was another one of Hooch's moods that would be too far in his condition. He stepped closer, between Hooch's legs, then brushed his cock against Hooch's lips.

The bruising on Hooch's face had gone down, and the cut was healing well. There was nothing that could and would hold him back right now, and when he parted his lips to let Matt's cock slide between them, he immediately opened his mouth wide, grabbed hold of Matt's hips, forcing him closer and Matt's cock deep down his throat. The sound Hooch made was choked-off and needy.

Matt bit back a sob as Hooch sucked him greedily, pulling him in, the grip on his hips almost painful as he fought to keep his hands away from Hooch's head. Touching Hooch lightly on the shoulder, letting him know he was about to come, before it felt like he was coming apart. Anchored only by the strong hands on his hips and his cock down Hooch's throat. He was kept close and down, Hooch's throat convulsively flexing around Matt's cock as he came. Hooch fought his gagging reflex, wanted and needed to, punishing himself with his eyes watering, but wanting Matt's cock to cut off his air, more than he wanted anything else.

Gasping, panting, Matt felt himself slowly come back into his body, and withdrawing from Hooch. "That," he said when he had his breath back, "was amazing."

Hooch wiped his lips with the back of his hand. "Yeah." His rough voice the only indication of what he had just done. "Just as your mark on my body."

A smile, as Matt flopped on the bed next to Hooch, eyes on the tattoo, before meeting Hooch's eyes again. "Mine," he repeated, wanting to trace the lines but knowing that he shouldn't. He sighed. "I guess I should cover these up again, at least until tonight."

Hooch huffed. "Right now I come with a maintenance manual. Bathe and disinfect the nipples, moisturize and disinfect the tattoo. What next?"

He hadn't expected the gleam in Matt's eyes, a contrast to the sated expression. "Nothing until next week," he told Hooch, "that should be the last thing, and it's not permanent. And there's less aftercare." With that, he got up off the bed and padded off to the bathroom for the first aid kit.

Hooch stared after him, thinking how wrong he had been. Matt did have it in him, after all.

* * *

Hooch had to continue moving carefully for the next few days, as his injuries from the training accident continued to heal, but he was much less restless. He submitted mock-grouchily to Matt's tending of the tattoo, but the feel of those callused fingers on his skin was better as it had always been, as they now traced the swirls and lines that marked him as Matt's.

* * *

When Hooch went back to work, confined to his desk and administration, he was grateful that his slightly stiff movements were accepted by everyone as remnants of the accident. The medics, however, who had to check him over, shook their heads and told him off at the discovery of the tattoo—they expected it of soldiers in their twenties, not instructors in their forties who should know better.

* * *

The week before the President's Day long weekend, Hooch had been working late, putting in place plans for an Exercises in spring. He often didn't make it home until Matt had gone to bed in readiness for his early morning class, and Wednesday night was no exception. Hooch returned to a largely dark gym and apartment, but Matt was sitting up in bed as Hooch entered the bedroom after his shower. When he got into the bed, Matt wrapped his warm body around Hooch's chilled one, skin to skin, not a hair between them, because Matt had none left below his neck, not even the groomed patch of pubic hair he usually kept.

"If I'm going to be showing myself off this weekend, I might as well make sure I'm presentable," he said in response to Hooch's silent query. Hooch's hands remained where they were on Matt's newly-denuded skin, as Matt continued. "I've made an appointment for you tomorrow evening on your way back from base. I've told Pam you lost a bet," he added, meaning the beauty therapist who usually took charge of Matt's vanity. "With one of the instructors from Camp Lejeune," the flash of his teeth visible in the darkness, knowing it would rile Hooch.

"You fucking bastard," Hooch growled, but he didn't quite hide the grin. The feel of Matt's perfectly smooth skin under his hands silenced any objection he might have had. "Is that an order?" Nuzzling Matt's neck.

Matt smiled and titled his head back to allow Hooch more access. "Yes, it is. After two piercings and a tattoo, it should be a breeze."

Hooch grumbled, "I'll do it, but it's close to telling me to get my root canals done."

"Who knows, you might turn out to like it. You seem to like it on me," Matt chuckled.

"I had my legs waxed once, when I did lose an actual bet. There's good pain and there's bad pain. Waxing doesn't fit into the first category. I don't understand how you keep having it done." To prove the opposite of his point, he caressed the smooth skin of Matt's back, down to his ass and back up again.

Matt wriggled under the firm movements. "I like being smooth and you've certainly never objected." He gasped as Hooch's fingers slid between his ass cheeks, checking that he was, indeed, completely bare. "Are you trying to tell me something?" he asked, pushing back on the fingers.

"One way of warming up, huh?" Hooch leaned in closer, nipping at the sensitive skin below Matt's jaw.

"Hmmm, you're a better source of heat than anything I know," Matt shifted slightly so that he was lying on his back, legs parted, "but that doesn't mean you can get away with not warming up the lube first."

Hooch laughed, leaned over to the bedside drawer, and proceeded to do just that.

* * *

Pam, Matt's beautician, was as efficient as she was amused at Hooch's 'lost bet', and even more so at the string of profanities that accompanied each and every one of her expertly swift movements; ripping off body hair that had never received to such torture before.

The crescendo of his swearing, when she got to his pubes, made her laugh out loud and she had to stop in her administrations of the hot wax. "I suppose this will teach you to tangle with the Marines," she teased. "Come on, the faster we get this done, the less it'll sting."

Hooch wiped the sweat from his forehead. "You're lying. It'll sting just the damned same."

"Stings more when you draw it out," she countered. "I've been doing this for a lot longer than you. Now hold still."

Hooch's eyes followed her movements to the little pot of hot goo and back with an expression of absolute misery on his face.

"This will probably be the bit that hurts most," she warned him, picking up a cloth strip from the pile on the trolley.

"Yeah, no shit." Hooch spread his legs so she could get access to every little nook and cranny. "Are you going to say the same about my ass crack?"

"Probably," she said cheerfully. Ripping away before Hooch could do more than give a strangled yelp in answer, and continuing with quick, sure movements. Making sure every bit of skin was bare, pausing only to get a set of tweezers for a few stubborn hairs.

"Holy motherfucking shit!" Hooch shouted. "Why don't you flay me while you're at it?"

"Tut tut," Pam admonished him, enjoying the process entirely too much. For men who put their bodies through unimaginable pain, it seemed that her military and sports clients were such babies about this simple procedure. "All done at the front now. Besides, this can't possibly hurt anywhere near as much as those," she indicated the pierced nipples, "or the tattoo on your back did."

"No way." Hooch grumped, but obeyed and turned onto his front, spreading his legs as far as the surface allowed. "This is different, it's agony of a very special kind. Hell, it even tops a cigarette burn."

Pam knew better than to tease about the cigarette burns, noting the pattern of small round scars on his skin, and even though she knew that he couldn't see her, she hid her smile behind her hand as she stirred the goo again. Matt had said that his roommate would be a bit cranky about losing the bet to the Marines instructor, but this passed even her expectations. "My mother says," she told him, holding him still while spreading the wax, "that you shouldn't wager anything it won't hurt you to lose." Getting a cloth, pressing it down, pulling it away, mentally steeling herself for the expected shouting.

"Fuck!" Hooch yelled and bucked up. "That's fucking worse than the front!" He craned his neck backwards to look at her. "Did your mother mean literal pain?"

"Probably," she chuckled, "but this is the last bit. So, the less you complain, the quicker this will be over."

"Go on, I can see you can hardly wait. You're enjoying this too much, you should have been a member of the KGB." Hooch braced himself one last time.

She didn't answer, because he was completely right. Admiring the perfect curves of his ass she spread the warm mixture, pressed, ripped. "Just a few more seconds," she told him as he started to relax. "I'll do a tidy up with the tweezers."

And people thought she was joking when she said that sometimes she really did love her work.

"Seconds," Hooch got out between clenched teeth, "you liar." But he stayed still and tried to think when was the last time anyone had inspected his ass crack with quite so much concentration.

Pam suppressed her laughter as she completed the task quickly and neatly, with just the last few stubborn short hairs pulled out. "Do you want a mirror?" she asked, dropping the tweezers in the container of disinfectant.

"No, I'll wait." Hooch didn't want to tell her for what. "I've had enough of it for now." He moved to sit, legs dangling down and only his toes touching the floor. Completely un-self-conscious, forgetting that officially, he was supposed to probably feel self-conscious around a woman. Looking down at himself, he was about to touch the slightly reddened but perfectly smooth skin of his groin, when she swatted his hand away.

"Nuh-huh. No touching and no sex for twenty-four hours. No hot baths either. You don't want to get bumps and spots, do you?" Hooch looked vaguely horrified at the prospect and she smiled. "It's only the first time the waxing is quite so uncomfortable. The hair is coarse and deep-rooted." She turned to look into her bag and pulled out a dark blue bottle. "Here, it's special skin care, use this all over your body, it'll help prevent skin irritation. Don't use body lotion for a day, but have a gentle body scrub in two days."

Hooch stared at the bottle, then her. "Do I look like someone who owns body scrub and uses lotion?"

"You look like someone who eats nails on toast for breakfast and burps fire," she replied cheerfully, "but appearances are deceiving, I'm told." She paused, then picked up a printed piece of card that had been on the shelf. "Here are the instructions. Don't forget. But I'm sure Matt will tell you if you do. He's a complete pro at this. Hardly screams at all, these days."

Hooch raised his brows. "He doesn't, does he?" took the card and the bottle, before pulling on a pair of boxers, because he wasn't supposed to wear tight underwear. "And I get to pay for this 'pleasure'."

A grin. "Well, that's what happens if you mess with the Marines." Pam picked up the dirty towels and left the room so that Hooch could get dressed.

Hooch shook his fist at her. "Army above all." He grinned as she left and put on his clothes. His skin felt strange, hyper-sensitive, and he'd never been so naked before in his life. Naked and defenseless, and that he liked. Exposed to the very last bit.

* * *

The daypack in the living room and the faint sound of typing was evidence that Hooch was already back by the time Matt had finished his last class and climbed up to the apartment. He walked to Hooch's study to find him hunched over his netbook, Rex sprawled on the floor next to him, looking bored.

"So," Hooch said without looking up from the screen, "you hardly ever scream anymore?"

"Ah, she told you," Matt groused, but with a grin. "Didn't want you to think that all this," a hand down his body, "came without effort."

"I know that a lot of effort goes into your body." Hooch looked up with an exaggerated leer. He half-spun round on his desk chair, sprawling and looking up at Matt. "No sex, she said."

"Why do you think I booked it for today and not tomorrow?" Matt grinned back. "How was it?"

"Awful. A motherfucking nightmare. Tweezers in my ass crack? Your beautician should star in a horror flick."

Matt couldn't hold back his laughter. "She does do a thorough job, doesn't she?" He tilted his head to the side. "Come on then, let's have a look."

"But no touching." Hooch mimicked Pam, holding up his finger. "No sex for twenty-four hours, no touching, you don't want any bumps, do you? No body lotion, body scrub in two days, and use this to prevent skin irritation." He pointed at a blue bottle on the desk, then stood up. "What the fuck was she talking about?"

"You'll need that unless you want ingrowns," Matt told him. "Just put it on after your shower. The only thing that makes it any better is keeping it up and just getting used to it."

Hooch looked with increasing focus at Matt. He didn't say anything for longer than was comfortable. "Take a look," at last, "then answer me a question." He pulled the shirt over his head and opened his belt buckle, to make quick work of trousers, boxers and socks.

Hooch, bare and smooth, skin reddened. Not that he'd had much hair to begin with, but the effect was quite...different. Matt was dimly aware he was staring, and dragged his eyes up to Hooch's face. "What's the question?"

"Do you want me to keep it up?" Straight to the point.

Matt blinked. "Not if you don't want to. Seriously, so long as I don't get hair in my teeth, I don't mind."

Hooch shook his head slowly. "No, you didn't answer my question. I rephrase: do you prefer me like this? Do you want me like this?"

Realizing what Hooch was asking, what he needed, Matt bit his lip. "Yes," he said truthfully. The perfectly honed lines of Hooch's body, shown off without the light covering of hair; the groin bared, completely vulnerable, completely exposed. Dimly remembering one of the many websites he'd been scouring in the last few weeks, discussing why most subs and slaves were shaved, to emphasize that they had no control over what happened to their bodies, that they had nowhere to hide.

Hooch considered his answer carefully. "Then I will." He took a step closer to Matt, nude body almost touching the clothed one, and lowered his voice. "I don't want to be given choices when it comes to my body."

"Alright." Matt hesitation, "I'm still getting used to this," he confessed.

"So am I." Hooch said quietly.

A few breaths of silence.

"Coming for a shower? I'll put that stuff on you afterwards."

"Yeah, I still have the stench of hot wax in my nose." Hooch made his way to the bathroom to get the shower started.

Rex watched them go, and then crawled under Hooch's desk for a nap. They wouldn't be paying him any attention for a while.

* * *

On Saturday morning, Matt left Hooch still sleeping in their bed to go downstairs to take the early morning class. After bidding farewell to the smaller numbers than usual, because of the long weekend, he went to his office to retrieve the box that he'd kept there since it had arrived the previous week. He'd only tried on the items once, to make sure they fitted, but now was the real deal. He carried it back up to the apartment.

Hooch had woken up in the meantime, showered, shaved, caffeinated and breakfasted, and was doing some work on a large map spread out on the dining table. "Morning."

"Morning," Matt answered, putting the box down. "What'cha doing?"

"Planning the next exercise trail run." Hooch pointed to Matt's box with his pencil. "What's that?"

"Ah, well, it's what I'm wearing tonight," Matt answered. "Do you want to see or should that be a surprise?" He stopped. "There are change rooms at the club, aren't there?"

"Of course. I don't drive there naked with just a collar. It costs shit loads of money, they got everything you could want." Hooch looked at Matt. "It is up to you if you want me to see it or not."

He should have known. "Just let me know if it's ludicrously inappropriate." Matt opened the lid and lifted out an armful of soft black leather. "What do you think?"

"It's black leather." Hooch deadpanned.

"You suggested it." Matt smoothed out the leather trousers, and something with straps. "I'm not sure about the harness," he said, "but it looked good on the model."

"You are aware that no model is as good looking as you are, right?"

Matt snorted at Hooch's teasing, but started to pull his T shirt over his head anyway. Stripping off the rest of his clothes, he had to sit to wriggle into the tight leather. Knowing his exact measurements from the tux he'd had made for the wedding had helped him get the closest size, which meant that when he stood up, it clung to him like a second skin.

"What do you think?" he asked, looking at Hooch.

"Holy fuck." Hooch breathed out with obvious approval. "Yeah, those fit. And the harness?"

Matt picked up the tangle of straps and, after working out the arrangements, slipped it over his head. "Help me with the buckles?" he asked, stepping closer to Hooch.

Hooch's fingers were remarkably gentle as he stroked over Matt's perfectly smooth and perfectly tanned skin, contrasting with the black of the leather and the metal buckles. Once he'd tightened the harness in all places, he guided Matt with his hands on Matt's shoulders to turn round and face him. Taking a step back, Hooch looked at him for a long time. "You, Matt Donahue, are motherfucking hot. You look fucking amazing."

"I have a reputation to uphold, you said," Matt reminded Hooch. "I thought I'd make an effort." He looked down at himself, the inevitable result of Hooch's touch and proximity and the tactile warmth of the leather having the inevitable effect. "What time do you think we should get there? I've blocked out all of today in case there's any prep you want…" he cut himself off, and then corrected "…any prep that needs to be done."

Hooch acknowledged the correction with an upwards tilt of the corners of his lips. "I usually just shave again and clean myself out, that's it. Twenty-hundred hours is a good time, leaves plenty of space for scenes." His hand almost touched Matt's hard-on, but stopped short a millimeter before the leather. "May I?"

Matt nodded, mouth suddenly dry. He swallowed, then confirmed. "Touch me."

Hooch did, palming Matt's erection as he stepped closer. "Tonight," his voice had dropped, "you can order me to do anything to anyone, and can allow anyone to do anything to me."

Matt's nostrils flared as he tried to stop his knees from buckling. "Yes," he breathed, "and tonight you're leaving the collar at home."

Hooch sucked in a breath. Everything would be different this time. Better.

* * *

They took advantage of a lazy Saturday morning to just chill after Hooch had sucked Matt off, but didn't get to come in return. Matt spent a lot of time thinking about the night, especially when he started packing his overnight bag for the hotel, which he did with care. A change from his usual method of efficiently throwing a few items into a bag in a few seconds, habits learned in the Marines never leaving him completely.

Hooch didn't show any signs of preoccupation with the night's plans, except for retreating to the bathroom for a while, to get cleaned thoroughly. Going commando under a less tight fitting pair of denims than usual, he chose to wear a loose black flannel shirt.

"Ready?" Matt had their bags by the door, keys in hand. Trying not to betray his nervousness. No matter what happened, everything would be different after tonight, though better or worse he had no idea.

Hooch seemed calmer than he usually was when he went to the club. "Yeah, ready. I usually check into the hotel first. You got a twin room?"

Matt nodded. "Yep," as usual when they were in the States—and especially within this state. "Mandy came and got Rex while you were in the shower, so we're good to go."

Hooch picked up the truck keys. "Let's go." He seemed relaxed where he usually appeared tense before a visit to the club. All the way on the drive to Raleigh he projected a calm that eventually rubbed off on Matt.

They checked into the hotel, a large, soulless one where they were no more than numbers on a vast database, and went upstairs. "So, what now?" Matt asked, after making sure that the heavy door was securely locked.

"We go to the club." Hooch smiled. "If you're ready."

Matt swallowed and met Hooch's eyes directly, a calm he didn't quite feel, but tried to pretend. "I am." Yes. He'd made the decision to step down this path with Hooch, and now, after putting the markings on Hooch, now was when he would finally find out whether he could go all the way down this road.

Hooch touched Matt's face. "If you want to leave, or if things get too much too quickly, just call me Hooch. I don't use safe words for myself, but this is not about safety." He let his fingertips run down Matt's face. "No one knows my name. The people there only know me as 'H', so if you call me by my name, it'll get through to me, in whatever situation."

Leaning into the caress, Matt made a movement that was close enough to a nod. "Let's go, then." He said, voice level.

Hooch let Matt through the door first, then slipped the key card into his back pocket as he followed him to the elevator. The ride to the club was short and silent. They were greeted by staff in reception, in the same perfectly efficient and discreet manner as always, handing a brand new members' card to Matt, explaining how it functioned simultaneously as key card and as purchasing card at the bar and restaurant. A young man, dressed in a tailored suit that showed off every line and angle of his body, and with a narrow black leather collar around his neck, led them through the changing area, which was as scrupulously clean and as well-furnished as the rest of the place. Instead of lockers there were personalized wardrobe spaces, accessible via the members' card, and comfortable changing rooms to provide privacy for those who wished it. Hooch pointed to one of the doors with a questioning look on his face.

Matt, who had been silent all the way through, comparing the memories of his only visit to the club four years ago and the new areas he was seeing now, looked in the direction that Hooch was pointing. "Is there anything I need to keep in mind before I get changed?" he asked, feeling strangely calm even though he could feel his heartbeat up to his ears.

Hooch opened the changing room door with his card. "I suggest you observe in the beginning. You get a lot of clues from how the other people react to our arrival."

Matt gave him a quizzical look as they entered, but remembered Hooch's prediction that he'd be 'a celebrity.' He put his bag on one of the benches as Hooch closed the door and started to undress.

When he was naked, Hooch turned to look at the full-length mirror with a sense of fascination, before focusing on Matt. "Need help with the buckles?"

Matt had been admiring Hooch in the mirror too, the metal and the ink on the smooth body. He had managed the trousers on his own, but still held the straps of the harness in his hands. "Yes,"

Hooch slipped the harness onto Matt, calloused fingers caressing the smooth skin as he went along. His touches seemed almost reverent, as he closed the buckles and adjusted the leather until it sat perfectly. Their eyes met in the mirror, and the contrast between the nude body with its metal and ink, and the body in black skin tight leather and combat boots was stunning. "I have never been that naked." Hooch murmured.

Matt turned, hands touching first the barbells in Hooch's nipples and then trailing behind to the tattoo, over the bare flesh. *His* marks, all fresh and still healing. His marks, on Hooch. Their eyes met, in person and not in the mirror. "No, you're not naked. You wear my marks. You'll never be rid of them. Or me."

The effect of Matt's words on Hooch were evident, his cock half-hard. "Does that mean I've reached the goal yet?"

Remembering back to the talk in the kitchen. "When I said that I didn't know, that was the truth." Matt began, "but I think the reason why I didn't know whether you had got there was because you've always been there. From the start. From the day you didn't walk out of that mud hut in Saudi, and the day you turned up at my door after we'd both left the Gulf. We're in this together, no matter what happens."

Hooch smiled, his emotions showing on his face, usually bottled up and locked away. "Thank you." Just that. "Ready?"

Matt took a deep breath and nodded. "Ready."

Hooch unlocked the door then handed the card to Matt to keep it. "It's a first for me as well," he said, as he waited for Matt to step out first. "I've never seen the place nor anyone in it."

Matt slipped the card into a pocket cleverly hidden in the low waistband of the trousers, before raising an eyebrow at Hooch, and remembering that Hooch had said he was blindfolded at the club. "Let's go, then. I wonder if they've redecorated since we got the tour the first time round."

The door closed behind them with a soft sound, and so did the next one, as they exited the main changing area. As they stepped out into the hallway towards the theatre, Hooch slotted himself a step behind and to the side of Matt. It surprised him how easy it was, and how he didn't have to watch his steps nor think about his speed, perfectly in sync with Matt. He should have known, after all these years, but this was new territory. Some people they encountered openly stared at them, as if trying to figure out who they were, while others kept their eyes down, yet others again appraising Hooch's entirely nude body, and Matt's perfectly sculpted one.

When they reached the main room, it took only a few seconds, before a male voice called out in disbelief "H?"

Remembering what Hooch had said earlier, Matt turned around to face Hooch who kept his gaze straight ahead, but focused on Matt the moment he looked at him. Only Hooch, with his attuned senses and knowing Matt so well, could see how he steadied himself. "Onto the stage and kneel."

Hooch obeyed immediately, moved the few steps to the raised platform in the middle of the crowd, and sank down to his knees. Hands behind his back, staring straight ahead and into the distance once more. Kneeling in full view of everyone.

Matt raised his voice to cut through the sound of the people around them. "Is that who you call H?"

"Yes." The male voice that had called out earlier was heard again, as the man stepped closer. In his late thirties, the disbelief on his face, but not his voice. "You wouldn't be..." he trailed off, "of course you are, you're his Master."

"Owner." Matt corrected and a murmur rose across the crowd. Like waves of amazement and respect rippling through subs and doms, males and females alike.

Another man stepped out of the crowd. Tall, broad, bearded, thick dark hair over even thicker muscles. "Allow me to touch?" he asked Matt.

If Hooch recognized either of the voices, he showed no reaction.

Matt held the other man's eye for a fraction longer than was comfortable, then nodded, inclining his head towards Hooch.

The man went across and took Hooch's chin in his hand, tilting the head up to inspect the face. Only Matt could read Hooch so well, he saw the minuscule jump in his muscles, as if controlling the urge to attack the man. "Dark brown," the man commented. He checked the smoothness of Hooch's skin, tweaked the freshly pierced nipples, which made Hooch's nostrils flare. One large hand took hold of Hooch's half-hard cock, the other gripped his smooth balls, giving both a brutal squeeze. Hooch's cock reacted instantly. The man looked up with an approving look, but before he could say anything, Matt called out: "Turn round."

Hooch immediately obeyed the command, moving on his knees without the use of his hands, presenting his tattooed lower back to the crowd.

After a long inspection, the dom straightened up and looked at Matt. "He bears your mark," he stated, his voice full of awe.

"Of course." It felt so strange, at once detached and possessive, wanting to tear the man's arms off for touching Hooch, and yet feeling removed from it all. Matt couldn't deny the surge of power at the respect and awe in the eyes of the others.

The first man joined Hooch. "Will you be using H tonight?" he addressed Matt. The eagerness that this might not be what Matt had planned, was written across his elegant face and audible in his New England accent. "Or do you want him to be used for your viewing pleasure?"

Sensing Hooch's reassurance rather than seeing it, Matt considered for a moment. Much as the thought of others touching Hooch made him stew, this time—at least at first—he wanted observe, as Hooch had suggested, to get a sense of what it was that Hooch needed. One thing to imagine it from the half-sentences and the aftermath, quite another to see it. "I shall watch," keeping his voice cool, "you may use him."

"How many?" A third voice asked from the crowd. A black guy stepped through, with shaved head and fit body, the unmistakable look of a someone who was still or had been in the military. "There are several of us who are H's regulars."

Matt gave an appreciative look at the guy's muscles, pretending to consider, as if he didn't know the answer Hooch craved. "You may," the same level tone, "I'll let you know when he's had enough."

Not quite answering the question, but allowing him to stop at any time.

"We all had scenes with H," the tall and elegant guy said, identifying himself as 'Eagle', "and each of us realized we had a hard time breaking him on our own."

'Breaking him'. Matt knew this was what Hooch craved and needed, but it still felt like a gut punch.

"We've been having extended scenes here on stage with several of us together for the last two years." The black guy added, who called himself 'MC', the moniker telling Matt all he needed to know about the man's military background.

"I see," Matt nodded, trying to pretend a calm he didn't feel. "And now?"

Looking at the men, each of them so different. Wondering, at the back of his mind, what it was that each of them did to try and break Hooch.

"You most of all know how unbreakable H is." The hairy biker-type guy drawled, the name 'Skull' tattooed on his neck.

"Yeah," a forth man stepped forward. Short but broad built, identifying himself as 'Tank'. "You're his owner."

"Do you want us to give you a scenario?" Eagle asked.

Not looking at Hooch, but continuing to keep his eyes on the men, Matt inclined his head slightly. "Yes." Feeling the eyes of the men on him, on Hooch, who was still kneeling with his back to most of the room.

Tank spoke up first. "Ropes. I'm a shibari master." He didn't elaborate any further, clearly expecting Matt to know what he was talking about. "H is a tough bastard, can withstand the worst positions for the longest of periods." He was in awe of Hooch's stamina, that was obvious. "I want to try a new technique, hang him from a beam."

"I like to deliver pain." MC said lazily with a slow, almost predatory smile. "H takes a lot of whipping, beating and flogging before he screams. You must be a damned genius to manage on your own." He nodded towards Matt.

Eagle raised an amused eyebrow at MC. "Wandplay. I got H to be able to take the second to largest one the last time he was here. You've been training him, haven't you?" He flicked his wrist, "and electricity. H got a special scream for that."

Skull only raised his right arm and made a fist, smirking. "Guess."

Matt wasn't sure how he managed to keep a straight face through the introductions, and the assumption that he knew what they were talking about, and that he did them to Hooch. Each sounding worse than the other. He wanted to run out of there, dragging Hooch with him, but this was what he had promised to do. He knew that Hooch needed this, needed what these men gave him, and he would never understand it if he did not see it through. He hoped that his audible voice didn't sound as shaky as his internal one, as he nodded at Tank. "You can start."

All of the four men stepped onto the stage, and turned Hooch round to face the rapidly gathering crowd of spectators. Hooch kept staring straight ahead at nothing. This was 'H', and the scene was going to be extreme. Everyone who'd ever been to the club knew of Hooch, and most had seen him on stage. The fact that 'H' was there for the first time with his owner; not wearing the collar, not blindfolded, but bearing new and permanent marks of ownership on his body, was enough to bring a buzz into the whole theatre and raise anticipation. Staff seemed aware, too, looking more ready to serve than ever. This night was going to be something special, and no one wanted to miss it.

Eagle talked to a member of staff who vanished behind the scenes, MC conferred with one of the bartenders, and Tank motioned to staff to bring his kit. While waiting for the natural ropes to arrive, all cut to the same lengths, he laced his fingers into Hooch's short hair and pulled his head far back. He held out his hand and Skull handed him a broad metal posture collar with rolled edges, but no padding, and secure locks. Tank placed it around Hooch's neck and snapped it shut, forcing him to keep his head up and back, so high Hooch struggled to swallow. He couldn't look down, couldn't see what was happening to him, and while not blindfolded, he was effectively blind. The effect of the discomfort was immediately obvious on his cock, now fully hard.

Matt looked on, trying to keep his face impassive; trying to ignore the buzz behind him in the crowd. Watching Hooch, the way his cock hardened as he was manhandled into the collar, unable to make eye contact with him now. Matt fought to remain still at the sound of machinery above them, as a heavy metal beam, perhaps eight feet long, was lowered on long steel chains.

The murmuring in the room grew as a male staff member, wearing a collar, latex hot pants and nothing else, returned with his arms full of ropes.

He placed them down at Tank's feet before walking away backwards, never turning his back on the stage. Tank picked up the first length of rope just as Skull and MC took hold of Hooch's wrists. They were obviously used to working as a team. Matt kept his eyes on them steadily, careful to observe Hooch's reactions, oblivious to anything else.

Skull and MC pulled on Hooch's arms, stretching them out as far as they could, while Tank positioned the beam behind Hoch's shoulder blades and outstretched arms. Eagle stepped behind the other two men and held the beam in place, to stop it from swinging on its chains. Tank took the first length of sisal rope, wrapping and knotting it around Hooch's biceps. Tightly binding his arms upper arms to the beam, meticulously and alternately, trying the immaculately placed rope artful knots. Rope binding deeply into flesh and smooth skin, but never cutting Hooch's circulation off. A true shibari master, slowly and confidently creating a piece of art, as he bound Hooch's wrists to the beam as well, then proceeding to fix the hands and each finger, leaving him crucified to the physical extremes.

Eagle fixed a tight cockring and ball spreader onto Hooch's hard cock, ensuring he would stay erect without being able to come. Hooch, spread out, muscles and tendons tensed and clearly displayed, the faint gleam of metal in his nipples only serving to emphasize the power and the strength of his body, bound and trapped by the ropes. Cock weeping and reddened against the leather straps and metal.

Matt's mouth was dry long before Tank completed his complicated dance with rope and knots, which now crossed and bound Hooch's chest and abs. Sisal pressing tightly into strained muscles, to emphasize the strength of the helpless body.

Satisfied with his work, Tank nodded to someone at the back of the room, and the bar started to rise, pulling Hooch off his knees and onto his feet, until he was stretched out, displayed for all the room to see, and yet the beam rose higher.

MC and Skull remained at Hooch's side, and when Tank finally gave the order to stop the lift, Hooch hung free, unable to touch the ground with his feet, the full weight of his body supported by his outstretched arms and strained shoulders.

Matt couldn't see his face, upturned to the ceiling as it was, but he saw Hooch's breath come shallow and fast, the barbells in his nipples catching the light as his chest moved rapidly.

Each of the two men took hold of one of Hooch's legs, and at Tank's nod they spread them impossibly far apart, holding them in place while Tank bound Hooch's ankles, as securely and as artfully as his arms and upper body.

Fixing the ankles to metal rings in the stage floor, he kept the body suspended and open, and under an incredible strain. Tank went on to bind Hooch's legs, displaying bunching muscles and cutting into delicate flesh at his groin.

When Tank was done, he had created a work of art made from rope and body: intricate twists and elegant knots. A masterpiece of pain and discomfort as Hooch's body hung suspended and stretched to the extremes, but kept accessible at the most sensitive areas. His smooth skin was covered in a thin sheen of sweat, making Hooch's tanned body gleam in the light of the theatre. Caged and framed in rope. Muscles, tendons and extended veins straining against the bonds.

Matt thought it was just as well he'd kept his words to a minimum so far; there was no way he'd be able to say anything when it felt like there was an enormous lump in his throat. Watching Hooch, undoubtedly in agony, but knowing this was what he needed, craved, and that he had promised to watch tonight.

Tank looked at Matt, before he stepped back to join Skull and Eagle, letting MC take centre stage. The muscular man had ordered one of the ever present staff to bring an array of tools of corporal punishment, such as a heavy yet flexible black leather paddle, adorned with blunt metal studs that delivered the maximum damage without breaking skin. Several floggers and whips, and even switches. MC turned to Matt as he picked up a sturdy flogger with an abundance of long, thin round leather cords, and a whip with several strands of thin braided lead-tipped leather.

"H's owner," he addressed Matt, "which one to start with?"

It was then that Matt realized he hadn't given his name, nor a pseudonym. No matter, though, because that wasn't important here, all he was was H's owner. Matt hoped that the gulp he took as he tried to force the lump down his throat wasn't visible. One thing to watch Hooch strain against the cruel ropes, muscles painfully constricted and his own weight pulling him down—quite another to see the collection of tools, all for the purpose of inflicting more pain. He repressed the shudder that ran down his spine at the thought of any of them striking Hooch, and looked MC straight in the eye. "The whip, first," he said, hoping that it would be the slightly less painful. "Careful of the piercings and the tattoo. They're still fresh."

MC nodded in agreement and put the flogger down, before testing the whip. The sound stark in the room, despite the murmur of the crowd. Hooch strained against the ropes, hearing the sound but unable to see what MC was doing. He visibly braced himself for the inevitable first strike, but nothing happened as MC waited, not giving a clue, rendering him unable to anticipate what was coming next. The moment the tension in Hooch's bound body eased a fraction, MC raised the whip, and hit the helpless body with a powerful strike. Hooch jerked in the bonds that hardly allowed him any movement, a groan escaping, suppressing a much more tortured sound.

The next lashings came down with no rhythm to brace for, and no less strength. MC hit the middle of Hooch's chest, avoiding the fresh piercings, then concentrated on his abs, until deep red welts appeared wherever the skin was exposed. Suddenly moving around, an almighty strike hit Hooch's back and he almost screamed, the groan reverberating in the room that had become quiet.

Hooch's body jerked and shuddered, sweat running down the rapidly discoloring skin, but he didn't scream. Not yet. Not enough yet. Holding onto his inhuman control.

Matt had to force himself to remain still through the whipping, stoic. This was what Hooch needed, craved, what he had sought here, a facsimile of the real thing. The wounds were real and painful, the whip was, but in the end this was the safest place for such things. Each of the men on the stage, no matter what they did to Hooch, knew the boundaries. At the end of the night, Hooch would be bruised and covered in welts and scratches and grazes, but he was always in good enough shape to get home. Matt clung to that. He had to. Even as he fought to stop himself from rushing up on the stage and unbinding Hooch and dragging him away. Back home, safe, away from chains and whips and bizarre toys.

MC stopped abruptly, turned to Skull who had appeared behind Hooch, and nodded at him. Skull grabbed Hooch's hip with one large hand, digging into the welts until Hooch hissed in pain, the other positioning a thick butt plug, its lubed-up black silicone glistening in the light on the stage. He pushed slowly but relentlessly, forcing Hooch's ass cheeks apart, driving the oversized plug through the ring of muscle and deep inside. Hooch involuntarily tried to jerk away, but the ropes held his strained body so securely, nothing stopped the merciless intrusion that left him gasping and whimpering. Visibly fighting for breath while forcing down groans, when the plug finally had been pushed fully into his body, securely held in place by the widened ring-muscle, stretching around the silicone ring.

Matt inwardly winced when the plug was forced in, sternly telling his mind not to be so cowardly when it scuttled away from the realization of what Skull was doing to Hooch. Hooch, who had not made a sound beyond a few groans, drenched in sweat and struggling against his bonds. Hooch, who needed this so that he would not fall prey to a darkness that Matt still did not understand, and had long realized that he never would. It was part of Hooch, regardless, and something he needed to come to terms with. Still not knowing what was harder, to watch things being done to him Matt's presence, or to see him go once a month, and come back bruised and worn, but strangely calm and leveled.

Hooch was trembling, instinctive shudders running through his body, as he was left alone for a while. Displayed for the audience, and unable to expect what would happening next.

The moment of peace didn't last long. A knowing glance went between Eagle and MC, who had taken the metal studded paddle from the tray and positioned himself where Skull had stood earlier. The first almighty strike of the paddle hit Hooch's ass and he almost screamed—barely suppressing the desperate sound with ever increasing groans. The paddle struck again and again, driving the plug deeper inside with every assault. No rhythm, no pattern to anticipate the beatings, and a speed that made it impossible for him to ever brace or gather himself.

Hooch's ass turned raw and deep red, with angry welts and visible imprints of the metal studs, his skin broken in places. His cock, though, harder than Matt had ever seen it. Nearly deep purple and leaking continuously.

Eagle was readying his toys at the side of the stage. A tray with gleaming metal and a small piece of machinery with cables trailing from its front Spreading lube on a thick metal wand, Eagle stood patiently until MC, as sweat drenched as Hooch's wrecked body, stopped the paddling. Eagle stepped close, took Hooch's metal-ringed cock into his hand, positioned the wand at the slit, and as slowly and relentlessly as Skull had fucked Hooch's ass, he forced the rod inside by letting its weight pull it down the urethra and guiding it deep into Hooch's cock.

Hooch, seemed close to breaking. The noises he made were mindless and animalistic, his whole body straining and fighting, trying to get away from this most extreme of intrusions.

Matt stared at the metal rod as it entered Hooch's cock, hoping that his disbelief was not noticeable, as all eyes were on Hooch and the stage. Hooch, trapped and unable to move, writhing in the bonds as Eagle slowly twisted and moved the wand.

A movement out of the corner of his eye brought Matt's attention back to Tank, who had been standing aside, observing the others with Hooch, watching the effect of his art in action.

When the wand was finally deeply embedded in Hooch's cock, Eagle reached for a couple of cables from the machine, and secured them onto the metal rod, right below the insulated tip that protruded out of Hooch's cock. He clipped a different set of cables onto the barbells in Hooch's nipples, then nodded at Tank who stepped away. Eagle set two dials to different strengths on the machine, held onto the insulation to keep the metal rod inside Hooch's cock, then flicked two switches.

That very instant Hooch's body tensed then thrashed in convulsions but held in place by the ropes, an inhuman scream ripped from the very depths of his self. The scream cut through the mounting buzz of the audience, his wailing climbing higher, louder, and ever more insane, the further Eagle increased the intensity of the electric current that tortured Hooch inside and out.

MC reappeared, pushing a hip-height padded examination table in front of Hooch, and with a rattling of chains, Hooch's upper body was lowered onto the table, until his ass was raised and his upper body crushed down by the weight of the steel beam across his shoulder blades and outstretched arms. He never got the chance for his knees to buckle, because Skull stood right behind him, grabbing hold of his hips once more, and with a latex-gloved hand he swiftly twisted and pulled the over-sized plug out of his ass.

Hooch howled, one scream bleeding into the other, until Eagle turned the dials down. With the decreased electricity at a steady pulse, Hooch's screams turned to raw sobs. His face was soaked with sweat and wet with tears. Nearly black eyes focused on nothing. Far away in himself with only his body there. A body that jerked violently when Skull pushed all five fingers of his large hand into Hooch's ass, loosened from the plug, the muscles without resistance after the vicious paddling.

When Hooch opened his mouth to cry out, Tank stood in front of him, forcing his cock with one thrust down Hooch's throat, all the way to the root. Fucking the helplessly upturned face with as much ferocity as Skull was fisting the ass.

Matt realized that his breaths were coming fast and shallow, and he took a step forward without thinking. Catching a glimpse of Hooch's face around Tank's cock, pressed hard against the man's abs with every thrust, eyes black and wild. Matt's gaze was fixed on Hooch, taken at both ends by Tank and Skull, while Eagle detached the cables from the nipple piercings and the wand to slowly glide out of Hooch's cock, which was an almost dark purple, straining against its rings and straps.

MC had laid down his punishing tools, looking on the final act. He snapped his fingers and a young man without collar, dressed in skin tight leather chaps that left his ass and cock free, scurried up the stage and immediately sunk to his knees in front of the big man, freeing his cock and sucking him with greed.

Hooch bucked against Skull's fist, deeply embedded within his body, and Tank's cock that was thrusting erratically into him. Trying to squirm away from both of them, but unable to move, until Tank came with a shudder and abruptly withdrew, cum splattering Hooch's face.

Eagle was about to swap places with Tank, when Matt found himself walking up on the stage, focusing on Hooch's face: his expression was mindless and detached, in agony and yet removed. Not knowing what compelled him, Matt stopped in front of Hooch, taking Eagle's place.

"That's enough." Matt ordered, as he fumbled with his zip.

With his hand steadying Hooch's jaw in a gentle grip, Matt slid his painfully hard cock in between Hooch's lips. Hooch was too exhausted to do much more than let Matt move in, unresisting as he made his way down Hooch's throat, constricting, contracting as Matt moved down.

Skull withdrew his fist slowly, standing to the side, allowing a slave to crawl towards him and free his cock to suck him off.

Matt's hand other hand touched Hooch's face, brushing away sweat and tears. He continued to hold in place and simultaneously caress him as he neared completion, feeling his breaths and his thrusts become erratic, the closer he got to release. Never taking his eyes off Hooch's face: lips stretched around his cock and dark, wild eyes blown wide and diluted, until he came down Hooch's throat. Matt quickly withdrew so that Hooch wouldn't choke, his cum dripping out of Hooch's slack mouth.

"Cut him loose." Matt's voice was surprisingly firm and clear above the hum of the crowd. Several staff members hurried to cut ropes and free Hooch, while Matt quickly zipped himself back up.

He didn't wait for Hooch to be cut lose, but got down on one knee, and motioned for staff to pull the table away. The moment the support was gone, the full weight of Hooch's body rested against Matt's chest. All the while staff continued to work on the tough ropes and the chains.

Matt steadied Hooch's helpless body and fumbled for the cock ring, undoing it and letting Hooch's cock free. A few firm strokes were all it took for Hooch to finally orgasm with a raw, broken cry, and he collapsed. Matt unclasped the metal posture collar and flung it to the side, as the last ropes were cut off and the heavy steel beam moved aside.

Matt lifted Hooch's head and looked straight into his eyes, which weren't able to focus, but he saw peace and repletion in them. Covering Hooch's mouth with his own, not heeding the remains of cum nor the sweat and tears, and the kiss was deep but tender, a kiss that was rarely seen at the club. No hunger or lust or possession, because Matt did not need any of that. No need to claim Hooch, because Hooch was his.

The staff helped them both up and off the stage, carrying Hooch between them, and guided them through the crowd. They were lead down another corridor, with doors on either side, and the nearest one opened to a decent-sized room bathed in a golden light and with a bed, couch, comfortable chairs, and adjacent bath. A selection of drinks, candy, ice, salves, sterile wipes, wet cloths, painkillers and gauze was arranged on a low table beside the bed. The two staff helped Hooch lie down on the crisp white sheets of the softly padded bed, where he immediately curled up on his side.

As the door closed behind the staff, Matt went and sat on the bed, next to Hooch who had not moved a muscle since he had been laid there. Stretching to lie beside him, facing Hooch whose eyes were closed, he brushed the wet hair away from his face—an affectionate gesture rather than one that had any use whatsoever, before he reached for a wet cloth to clean Hooch's face. The body could wait, Matt decided, pulling a warm blanket over them both, heedless that he still had his combat boots on.

Hoch kept his eyes closed, breathing slowly, while Matt kept gently stroking his sweat-damp hair, not sure where else to touch. Every part of Hooch's body had been tortured, and every touch would bring more pain: the last thing in the world Matt was willing to do.

They lay like that for half an hour, during which Matt reached for a bottle of lucozade with a straw close by, helping Hooch take slow sips until he had emptied it.

Finally, Hooch opened his eyes. Matt had never seen them like that: dark and soft, nothing but calm and utter peace in them. Hooch's voice was raspy and broken as he whispered: "thank you."

Matt leaned over and pressed another kiss to Hooch's lips. No words, because they didn't need words. Putting the empty bottle on the bedside table, he eased out of the bed and went to the bathroom to start filling the tub, before pressing the call-button that would summon a staff member. The woman was there as Matt opened the door, and asked for their bags to be brought to the room.

Turning back to the bed, Matt stripped under Hooch's half-lidded gaze, before pouring a glass of water and offering a couple of painkillers. "Take these." An order, despite his gentle voice, and Hooch obeyed without hesitation. All of his movements were sluggish and revealed the pain he had to be in, but he lifted his head and swallowed the pills with a few mouthfuls of water. Matt smiled and reached for Hooch. "Bath, then nap." An instruction this time. "I'll let you know when it's time to head back to the hotel."

Hooch let himself be helped up, heavily relying on Matt's support, and accepting it for once. More sated and more safe than he'd ever been before.

* * *

The next morning, after a light breakfast because neither of them really feeling like eating, despite the hotel's sumptuous spread, Matt drove back to Fayetteville with Hooch half-asleep in the passenger seat. The road was nearly deserted on a long weekend's Sunday morning, giving Matt plenty of time to think.

The gym was quiet when they returned just after lunch, with only a few die-hards working out. Mandy was not due to come back until the Tuesday morning, bringing Rex back with her. Still quiet, they hadn't spoken more than a dozen words to each other since the club, they went upstairs to the apartment, where Matt decided to get a load of washing going.

Hooch had sat himself down on the sofa, but soon slid down to lie on his side, putting weight onto his badly bruised and abused ass was too much, and the car ride had already tested his stoicism to the limits. Each and every of his movements was stiff and slow, but he had a deep calm about him he'd never displayed before. His eyes tracked Matt as he went to and fro with the laundry basket, lying still and silent, he kept watching.

With the washing machine started, Matt went and got a bottle of water out of the fridge and two glasses, and walked to the sofa. Instead of sitting on it and jostling Hooch, he sat on the floor, and poured two glasses, handing one over. "Was that…" Matt began, "how you thought it would be?" Not sure what he had expected before going to the club, even less sure what Hooch had been expecting.

"Better." Hooch took a sip of water, studying Matt's face with quiet focus. "You?"

"Knowing is still different to actually *knowing*, if you get what I mean." Matt paused and put his full glass of water down on the coffee table with a little clunk. "Do you…" he knew the answer, but wanted the comfort of the confirmation. "Do you want me to go with you again?"

"Yes." Hooch's reply was firm and came without hesitation. "I want you to go with me every time, but the decision is not mine." He smiled slightly. "What do you want?"

As he thought. As he had known. "I want…" Matt stopped. "I want to think about it a bit. I wouldn't be able to see you do *that* every month," 'that' such an inadequate word, "but I don't know whether that means I don't go every time, or that we don't do that every time." He leant down, still on the floor, but head and one shoulder on the sofa, close to Hooch. "I'd like to go again," he said truthfully, "but let me think about the details for a bit."

"Of course." Hooch's smile deepened. "Maybe I won't crave *that* so much if you come with me all the time." Crave, not need. He was beginning to understand the difference.

Matt closed his eyes. The words unvoiced, but understood all the same: I hope so too.

The rest of the long weekend was quiet, with Matt doing all the little domestic odd-jobs that were part of life: the bits and pieces that needed to be done around the apartment, the detested preparation of tax returns, and the equally dreaded cleaning out of the fridge and freezer.

Hooch spent the two days mostly sleeping, letting his body recover as much as possible before returning to work. The expertise of Tank, Skull, Eagle and MC had ensured that except for some lingering stiffness and a few marks and fading bruises, which could be explained by some roughhousing or an overenthusiastic football game, Hooch would almost be back to his usual self come Tuesday.

Matt, meanwhile, had used the time that Hooch was asleep productively, doing some research from the privacy of the apartment, where there was no chance a stray staff member or gym customer catching a glimpse of what he was doing. It seemed easier now than it had been when he had been browsing before his trip to the club, having a better idea of what he was looking for, and being able to better process what he found. Some he still found incomprehensible, but he realized that it had nothing to do with whether he would ever understand that arcane world of rules and rituals and sheer weirdness, but everything to do with Hooch.

The evening before going back to work, Hooch was standing at the ironing board, meticulously pressing his uniform. A task he'd never let anyone else do for him. He'd just finished the last tunic, and was walking past Matt who was surfing the net on the dining table.

When came back from the guest room he used for hanging his kit, he stopped at Matt's chair and quietly put his special credit card on the table beside Matt's laptop. The one that was linked to his investment accounts.

Matt looked at Hooch, at the credit card, at what he was browsing on screen and back at Hooch again. "Are you serious?" he asked, redundantly, because Hooch was never anything but serious.

"Sure I am. Nothing gives me greater satisfaction than spending my goddamned inheritance on kinky shit." He flashed a sharp grin. "Go on. You're on the card anyway."

Matt blinked at the deliberately casual tone. "I'm what?" he asked. As far as he knew, Hooch hadn't ever mentioned him to any part of his old life, their relationship, nor the little detail that Hooch happened to exclusively fuck men these days.

"You're my partner, aren't you?" Hooch shrugged, still a little stiff.

That he was. But nevertheless this was a surprise. There had always been two Hooches, as though there was a wall between what had happened before he enlisted and after. His past was a different world, and it rarely encroached on the present. Now and then he would fly back to Texas for a few days, summoned for something or other he rarely spoke about, and then there were Christmas cards, and a call on his birthday from his sister but that was all.

"Yes, yes I am." Matt looked at the screen. "Do you want me to tell you what I'm doing with it or do you want to be surprised?"

"Surprise me." Hooch squeezed Matt's shoulder before he went to put the ironing board away. "Whatever you choose, I will do it, wear it, have it done, accept it, and want it." He walked past again, carrying the folded-up board. "Never forget," he stopped at Matt's chair, "you own me."

Matt swallowed, his mouth suddenly dry, looking up at Hooch. "I know."

"Yes." Hooch stated. The one word holding everything. He smiled as he walked into the spare room.

In bed that night—no sex, because Hooch was still not up to it—and neither, if he was being completely honest, was he, Matt shifted so that he was on his side, waiting until Hooch turned as well, to be eye to eye. "I will go with you to the club," Matt said, "every time. But I decide when you go on the stage," that seemed a good enough euphemism, "and it won't be every time we go. Sometimes we'll just…play."

"Play?" Hooch's brows rose in a mix of surprise and intrigue.

"Play." Matt said. His fingers lightly went to caress Hooch's throat, where a collar would lie. "No whipping, no flogging, no electricity, only a little pain. But while we're there, you'll do as I say. Sometimes I might choose to restrain you with leather, or rope, or chains. Sometimes all you'll wear is my collar and a leash, like some enormous big cat, purring at my feet."

Hooch swallowed so hard, Matt's finger moved with the Adam's apple. "That sounds like a great plan." His voice had become instantly huskier. "What about others?"

"Not much point going to the club if it's just you and me, is there? We could just get a drawer full of toys and surf the internet for ideas and have some fun right here, no need to drive all the way to Raleigh, book a hotel overnight, and get Mandy to take the dog. We can still play with others, but I decide who gets to have you, and how."

"That's the hottest thing I've ever heard in my life. You," Hooch poked his finger into Matt's chest, "are quite a lot more than 'something', Matt Donahue."

His raised eyebrows were barely visible in the darkness of the room, as Matt moved even closer. "I know."

"And I'm a damned lucky bastard." Hooch's hand went southwards towards Matt's cock. "So lucky, in fact, that I have to suck you off now."

Matt wasn't going to argue with that, and he wriggled into a more comfortable position as he felt Hooch shift under the duvet.

From the moment Matt felt Hooch's lips close around his cock and Hooch's hands on his ass, until after he had come and Hooch pulled him into a tight embrace for Matt to drift off, there was only Hooch. As always.

* * *

They went to Hooch's club together every month or so, as Hooch had done on his for the past four years. It never seemed necessary for Matt to acquire a name at the club. He was always simply "H's owner," which amused him when he found out that it was the reverse of the usual order of things, but it suited them. As Matt had decided, Hooch did not always go up on stage when they went. More often than not he and Matt stayed in the main area of the theatre, still the focus of attention. Matt made an effort to take part in a little of the more social side of the club, making the odd posting on the secure forum on the club's members-only website, and going through the club's impressive directory of purveyors of specialist toys and artisans who made items to order and to measure.

At home, Hooch's 'kinky shit' credit card, as they called it, got a strenuous workout as Matt went shopping on the internet, and the collection of well-edited toys soon overflowed from the bottom drawer of the bedside table, and into a securely locked metal chest at the foot of the bed. When Matt soon after started to amass a collection of made-to-measure black leather to wear at the club, a heavy wardrobe with built-in rails, drawers and shelves appeared, so that everything could be neatly organized, including the newly acquired spreader bars.

In early December, after they'd been and gone to Matt's family for Thanksgiving—a tradition they'd manage to uphold almost every year—Hooch was cooking steak at Sunday lunchtime.

"Matt?" he called out from the kitchenette, cutting above the sizzling of meat and through the smoke of hot oil.

"Yeah?" Matt replied from the spare bedroom, where he'd been changing the sheets.

"Do you have anything planned for the holidays?"

Hooch noticing such trivialities was remarkable enough that Matt padded out of the room. "No, not especially. Why?"

"Anne asked me again if we were coming for Christmas." As she had every year. Matt's mom was nothing short of persistent. Hooch switched off the hob and laid the steaks onto plates to rest.

"We've just been there." Matt frowned. Much as he would have liked to have Hooch experience a Donahue family Christmas, he knew that crowds, sociability, small children and Hooch didn't mix. Particularly not twice in two months.

"Yeah," Hooch pulled the tray with fries out of the oven and shook them onto the plates, "but I think we should go. It means a lot to your mom."

Matt stared at him. Blinked hard. Hooch never failed to surprise him. Just when he was starting to feel he was really getting a handle on the kink, Hooch had to go the other way. "You want to go to Michigan, ten feet deep in snow, to get trapped in a house with my family, complete with screaming toddlers and sulky teenagers, sleep in the room next to my parents, and get stuffed full of turkey for the second time in two months?"

"Yeah, well," Hooch shrugged, then carried the plates to the dining table. "I figure if it means so much to Anne I suck up and get myself through it somehow." He fetched the ketchup, pepper grinder and salt, then sat down.

Matt stumbled to his chair, feeling numb. "Why now?" he asked.

"Because," Hooch vigorously shook the ketchup bottle, "you gave me a new way to cope."

Strangely enough, that made sense, as much as anything about Hooch ever made sense. There had been a new stillness, almost a contentment about Hooch, as Matt had ventured more and more into their own particular form of ownership. As if for Hooch, allowing someone else to take control, enabled him to settle, calm down and let go. Matt nodded, and picked up his knife and fork. "I'll book the plane tickets. Do you want to tell her we're coming, or shall I?"

"I leave that to you." Hooch smiled briefly, before tucking into his steak and chips. "I plan to go to the club the weekend before the holidays. You good with that?"

The weekend before Christmas was what passed as the themed 'holiday party' at the club, which would be full of members. From what Matt had been reading on the club's private online forum, the night would be even wilder than usual. Hooch had never gone that particular weekend before, and it was going to be a new experience. "Sure," Matt replied, "but not on the stage. We're not explaining any injuries to my nieces and nephews. Or even worse, my parents."

Hooch didn't try to hide his amused grin. "I didn't expect to, but I saw you buying that high leather collar and leash set." He took another bite, chewing carefully. "I didn't snoop, by the way, you left the page up." He paused, "also, I have a Christmas present for you that requires work beforehand to be in time for the club."

Matt put down his flatware and looked at Hooch, wondering what he was up to now. Rex, by now sensing that for some unknown reason, his humans were distracted from their steak, came and sat down next to Matt: perfectly straight, nose trembling, quietly hopeful eyes staring at Hooch.

"You've been talking about wanting to put more piercings on me. I booked an appointment tomorrow for a cock piercing." Hooch tilted his head ever so slightly.

Matt swallowed as he imagined it, then nodded. Approval granted.

"The appointment is in the evening. I was told I should go for a Prince Albert. You agree?" Hooch cut off a piece of steak, sneaking it under the table for Rex. As if he ever failed to do that.

"Yes." Matt picked up his knife and fork again, ignoring the delighted sounds of a greyhound chewing his favorite treat. Despite the fact that Rex was meant to be his birthday present, the dog was well and truly Hooch's. "Yes," he repeated. "I agree and I will come with you."

"Good." Hooch smiled once more, going back to his favorite meal. He and Rex, they had too much in common.

* * *

A couple of weeks later, Matt stepped out of the changing room at the club, dressed in his usual black leather. No concession to the season, despite the subtle decorations in gold and silver and crystal at the club, and the seasonal refreshments and snacks. He wrapped the new leash around his hand; long enough for Hooch to crouch at Matt's feet when Matt was standing, but not much more. Hooch moved his neck, trying to get the high collar to settle. Though it was covered in soft doeskin, and carefully fitted so as not to restrict breathing, it was still high enough that it was uncomfortable for long periods of time.

Matt had added new adornments to Hooch's body in the form of weights hanging from the nipple rings, made from the same darkly gleaming metal as the new piercing in his cock and the cock ring and ball spreader.

Hooch had never had weights attached to his nipple rings before, because Matt had insisted on a thorough healing, and the new sensation added to keeping his ring-bound cock hard, which ensured that his erection remained proudly displayed by Matt, his owner. He had to concentrate on walking properly on the leash, to keep in step while not able to look down, but then the whole thought behind this new broad collar was so that his face was there for all to see, and especially his eyes. Matt had commented that Hooch's looks had always attracted him and that hiding his features and dark eyes from the club was criminal.

They headed towards the theatre, sure of their steps. They had tried a few of the smaller themed rooms but they kept coming back to the theatre, to the crowd, even when Hooch did not go on stage. Matt enjoyed showing him off too much; enjoyed the admiration that Hooch attracted. The doors opened in front of them, attended, as always, by the silent, collared staff.

Inside, the theatre had more of the gold and silver decorations, augmented by heavy, dark purple drapes. There were bodies on the stage, at once more artistic and less real than the usual participants, and Matt remembered there were meant to be organized shows tonight from invited professionals.

Hooch kept his eyes straight ahead, learning quickly how to keep pace on the leash. He didn't seem to notice the admiring glances towards the two of them, both from men and from women. Matt was stopped soon by other regulars who greeted him and pulled him into a conversation, surprised and glad he was there, what with H never having attended the Christmas ball before. No one addressed Hooch, because here, at the club, he was nothing but Matt's possession.

A gentle tug on the leash caught Hooch's attention. "Sit," said Matt softly, into owner-mode. Matt lowered himself into a low sofa, indicating the soft carpet at his feet.

Hooch obeyed immediately and went down to kneel at Matt's feet, shoulder touching a leather-clad leg. Kneeling like a large, dangerous cat, tamed by its owner.

Matt reached out a leather gloved hand, stroking the side of Hooch's head with light fingers, a gentle tug on the leash drawing Hooch even closer. Matt looked up as a pair of legs appeared in front of him.

"Merry Christmas." Matt recognized MC's voice. He hadn't been at the club for a few months, and Matt knew better than to ask. Hooch was far from the only club member who needed discretion above all else. "Is H for use tonight?"

"Not on the stage," Matt told him. He lifted a glass from a tray. "We'll see what we do down here later in the evening." His voice was firm, no promises, and yet all promise, his hand still stroking Hooch's face and hair. MC nodded and departed.

The club was buzzing, with a lighter, more festive mood than was usual, and Matt put it down to more of the less hard-core members attending for the holidays party. The staff wore red collars, a departure from the usual black, as they circulated with food and drink. There wasn't a great deal of play going on yet, mainly people arriving and greeting others. Robertson mingled amongst them all, like he very rarely did. Immaculately dressed, his slave demurely at his side, eyes down.

He caught Matt's eye, nodding acknowledgement, and spared a glance at Hooch, before returning to his conversation, but not before Matt caught a strange, satisfied look on the owner's face: the triumph of being correct. Odd.

"What a surprise to see you here," another voice, just off to Matt's side. It was Tank, a naked but hooded slave on all fours on a very short leash, with whom he had been attending the club in the last three months. The slave was always bound by ropes, every time in different but equally artistic and decidedly painful ways. The elegantly-limbed and smoothly waxed man had a well kept body of indeterminate age, manicured nails, a gym-fit body, and never attended without a full black leather hood that was fixed to the tight locked collar he wore, and which covered his entire face including his eyes. With only holes at the nostrils and a thin breathing tube that indicated the gag he was wearing unless his mouth was in use, no one had ever seen the slave's face, ensuring utmost discretion. Tank gave the leash a tug and the man knelt down with remarkable grace.

"Good you're here, I have a gift for you." Tank made a gesture towards one of the staff, who hurried off.

Matt barely flicked a glance towards the hooded slave, and kept his eyes on Tank. "I'm intrigued." Leaning back slightly to get a better angle, but not taking away the hand that had been absently caressing Hooch.

Tank watched the caress and his mouth quirked up in a half-smile, but he said nothing. The staff member re-appeared with some lengths of Tank's shibari ropes, before disappearing once more, never turning his back to either of the men, while not paying any attention to the kneeling bodies.

"May I?" Tank indicated Hooch. "H needs to stand, back to me."

Matt inclined his head, not even a full nod, as he tugged on the leash. "Up," he commanded. Hooch rose smoothly to his feet, presenting his back to Tank, cock jutting out at the level of Matt's face, but he knew better than to hope for relief.

Tank took Hooch's wrists and began to loop, then pull and knot the wrists tightly together in Hooch's back. He continued up his lower arms, forcing the elbows together, so that Hooch's shoulders were forced back, his sculpted chest with its nipple adornments thrust out, and his shoulder blades stayed uncomfortably close together. When Tank finished, he had tied Hooch's arms together in his back, as if in a sleeve, all the way up to his biceps, making it impossible for him to move or to give himself any relief from the strain.

Hooch hadn't made a sound throughout the binding, but his cock was now weeping and his chest expanded with his shallow breaths. The knotting was intricate, creating patterns on skin and muscles.

"Does it meet with your approval?" Tank slowly turned Hooch round, three-hundred-and-sixty degrees.

Art in rope and flesh, Hooch's muscles straining and his body's honed, hard edges shown off to devastating effect, Matt could do nothing but nod. Tank's skills and keen eye had never failed to impress Matt in the months that he had been a regular at the club. "Very much so," Matt said after a pause. "So much so that I think H should thank you for it. Down." The last word to Hooch, accompanied by a tug on the leash.

Hooch lowered to his knees, then turned to face Tank, shuffling closer to nuzzle his leather clad groin indicating how he knew he was supposed to thank the man.

Tank unzipped and took out his cock, guiding it to Hooch's lips. He stood with his legs braced, keeping his hand on his own slave's head, who appeared to be extremely concentrated, as if listening to every sound, lost in his hooded darkness.

Matt flicked a glance at the slave. He'd considered, and then discarded the notion of hoods and such restrictions on Hooch—he wanted Hooch to see, to hear, to sense all that was going on, and, if he wanted to be honest, he wanted to show Hooch off. Hooch; Hooch was his, not some anonymous, shadowy figure.

Hooch applied every skill he'd ever acquired, having only the use of his lips, tongue and throat, he quickly got Tank hard. He proceeded to force himself mercilessly down and open, taking him deep down his throat, as he fucked himself on the cock.

Matt noticed Tank's reactions, saw how the man was getting closer to the edge. Hooch's skills never failing, Tank suddenly laced his fingers hard into Hooch's hair and abruptly pulled him off. Cock dark and hard, glistening in the dim light from saliva and precum.

"Stop." He snapped his fingers and his own slave immediately reacted, faster than Hooch could move out of the way. Scrabbling to try and blindly find his master's cock, with his arms bound, painfully bent and up his back, Tank helped guide his hooded slave, before unclipping the mouth shield and pulling out the gag. The greed with which the slave sucked down on Tank's hard cock surpassed anything Matt had ever seen, and within a few seconds, hands clamped down on the leather-clad head to hold it still while thrusting deeply into his slave, Tank came with a groan. The slave greedily swallowed, his tongue swirling and lapping with obscenely wet noises, as Tank pulled back a little to allow him to clean up the cock he so very obviously craved.

When Tank pulled the slave off, the man spoke, his voice hardly ever heard at any of their outings at the club. A voice that was deep and smooth, a beautiful baritone. "Thank you, Master." No more, before Tank pushed the gag back in and clipped it securely to the hood, petting the slave's head.

Hooch had returned to Matt's feet, kneeling once more, and Matt lifted a glass of water with a straw off a tray that appeared at his elbow, holding it in place for Hooch, who took sips as long as Matt encouraged him to. Matt surveyed the room, before returning to Tank.

"Merry Christmas." With that Tank turned, tugging sharply on the leash and his slave crawled on all fours, closely at his feet.

Hooch rubbed his face against Matt's knee, when the water was taken away, then looked at him for a moment, dark eyes full of his peculiar mix of lust and calm. The room was filling up, and there was more than one long look that came their way, but Matt stayed where he was. A gentle hand on Hooch's shoulder, feeling the tension in the muscles bound in their awkward position. Strained, yes, but Hooch could stand to be restrained for a lot longer.

"Tank told me you are here." Matt heard the New England accented voice before Eagle stepped into his vision. "I had hoped so, I got you a present." He was without his personal slave, who was 'being performed on' centre stage.

"Present?" Matt asked, surprised to receive a second gift.

"A thank you for all the times I played with H." Eagle produced a slim, leather bound box, then looked down at Hooch's cock, and his smile grew.

"Perfect. Thought you'd go for a PA sooner or later. Metal and ink suit him."
He opened the box and showed the contents to Matt. A shiny metal wand,
medium thickness compared to the heavy ones Eagle had been using on
Hooch in the last months, with a short 90-degrees rod screwed on, and
screw-on rings on top and side bar. Exquisitely made and certainly expensive.
"May I?"

Accustomed enough to Eagle and his preferred game to know what was
coming, Matt nodded his permission as Eagle took the wand out of the box.

"He has to stand up."

Matt gave another tug of the leash, which was all it took to order Hooch
to stand up. Unable to look down at himself, due the high collar, Hooch's
breath quickened with anticipation, making his exposed chest visibly expand.

Eagle snapped on latex gloves, positioned himself so that Matt could
watch the proceedings, before he bent towards Hooch's cock and carefully
removed the piercing. He unscrewed the side rod, then produced a small,
sealed tube of petroleum jelly. He not only lubed the wand itself, but squirted
a generous amount straight into Hooch's slit, and the cool lubricant suddenly
inside his cock made Hooch gasp and his body tense. He had a good idea of
what was going to come, but his thighs showed a visible tremor, as he braced
himself.

"The wand is hollow," Eagle explained while allowing the weight of the
metal rod to slide into the opening and down the urethra. "It can be worn for
several days and nights. H can piss through it, and come, if you allow him to."
Eagle held Hooch's cock in place without forcing the object inside. Always
careful, he was known in the club for his skills that avoided damage. Hooch
shuddered, his breath speeding up, the deeper the wand slid down. Eagle gave
it a few gentle twists to encourage it further, and all the times before that he
had played with Hooch's cock, using his largest wands, made it easier for
Hooch to accept this one. Eventually it was all the way inside, and Eagle
carefully pushed the side bar through the piercing hole and screwed it in
tightly. By the time he was done the wand sat securely inside Hooch's cock,
with metal rings protruding out of the tip of his cock and the piercing hole.

"I think it suits him." Eagle said to Matt as he stepped back and pulled his
gloves off. A female member of staff appeared at his side, took the discarded
gloves and handed him a wipe, with which he cleaned the superfluous lube
from Hooch's cock. "Beautiful." He stated with satisfaction.

Matt couldn't help but agree with him. "It is indeed," was all Matt said to
Eagle. Hooch was now visibly shuddering with the intrusion, sweat breaking
out across his shoulders, but there was nothing he could do, bound as he was.

Matt waited a second more, a smile curling at the corner of his mouth as he stood up. "Very nice indeed," he commented, standing in front of Hooch. "Bend over," he ordered, taking a step back so Hooch had sufficient room. "I think we'll have a special treat." He took Hooch firmly by his shoulders to keep his face level with his own cock. "Make it slow," he told Eagle, as the other man realized what Matt intended. "Draw it out. I want him to enjoy it properly, but unable to come."

Eagle gave a grin, not sparing a glance at his own slave being used up on the stage, as he concentrated on Hooch's ass instead. He pushed Hooch's legs apart as far as possible without losing balance completely. Taking his rapidly hardening cock out, he gave himself a couple of strokes to fully harden, then rolled a condom onto his cock and lubed himself up. Discomfort for slaves was one thing, discomfort for himself unacceptable.

Hooch shuddered as he bent low and opened up, feeling the wand deep inside his cock, stimulating with every movement, and the weights in his nipples hanging free, adding to the sensations. He groaned and opened his mouth when Matt pushed his gloved thumb between his lips, sucking and licking at the digit.

Matt unbuttoned his fly with one hand and freed himself, then nudged at Hooch's lips, to feed him his cock. Sparing a glance at Eagle, meeting the other man's eye, they both pushed into Hooch at the same time at both ends.

Hooch's body alternated between trembling and tension, desperate sounds vibrating against Matt's cock, as he tried to push back to gain more sensations from the cock that was filling his ass, or to push forwards to create greater suction and to take Matt deeper, but he could do neither, held between the two men as if in a vice.

An audience began to gather around the tableaux, but Hooch didn't care about anyone but the two men, the two cocks, that were filling him front and back, speared between them and whimpering with increasing desperation, as they sped up their strokes, and increased the strengths of their thrusts. His sweat-glistening body could never get enough, and the combination of cock ring and Prince's Wand made it impossible to come.

Eagle was losing his rhythm, but he caught Matt's eye, a matter of good manners, guest to host, and waited until Matt's barely perceptible nod. Only then did he speed up his thrusts until they became erratic, and when he came, it caused Hooch to whine with need, but his cry was muffled by Matt's cock. Eagle waited barely a second, before withdrawing from Hooch, keeping hold of the condom. A silent staff member appeared at his side to take the used condom and hand a damp cloth to him to clean himself up. Eagle gave him a "Merry Christmas", before he went back to the stage to take care of his own slave, which Matt barely took notice of.

With Eagle gone Matt held tightly onto Hooch and thrust harder, rougher, deeper, as if boring down his throat before feeling like he had exploded down Hooch's throat. Barely managing to keep their balance, they only narrowly avoided collapsing on the floor. Both sprawling down once Matt had withdrawn, and Matt moved to Hooch's side for a deep kiss, like they usually ended such things. Tasting, licking himself from Hooch's lips, while Hooch whimpered against his own. Matt eventually broke the kiss and looked down at Hooch's cock—weeping, red and desperate—and touched the protruding rings from the wand, giving it a few gentle tugs.

Hooch hoarsely cried out against the side of Matt's neck, trying to thrust into his hand, but Matt hushed him softly. "Not yet." He let go and petted Hooch's sweaty face, before kissing him deeply once more, ignoring the desperation.

Matt tucked himself away and sat back down. The leash had been wound around his wrist all that time, and he tugged at it, as he opened his knees for Hooch to move between. "Kneel." He quietly commanded it, and Hooch, despite the pain he was in and the raging lust and need, did immediately as he was told. Kneeling between Matt's legs, facing the crowd that was slowly dispersing. His cock a deep purple, straining against the metal rings that bound it and the wand that was inside it, but he forced himself to sit still as ordered.

Matt requested a double whisky and soda from one of the staff, then dug his thumbs and knuckles into Hooch's overly stretched and twisted shoulders, massaging the strain, making Hooch moan softly.

Fingers firm against Hooch's burning muscles, Matt stopped when the drink arrived. With a hand on Hooch's chin, he gently pushed Hooch's head back, and tipped the glass against his lips. Hooch obeyed the unspoken order and took a sip, but the glass remained and kept nudging against his lips, until Hooch had finished all of the whisky. Matt held up the glass and ordered another, before going back to firmly massaging Hooch's shoulders.

After the second whisky, which Matt made Hooch drink in one go once more, he felt Hooch lean heavier against him, like a large, dangerous cat that had been tamed to be petted. The alcohol was clearly doing its work.

Matt brushed his gloved hand against Hooch's skin, long strokes down head and neck, bound arms and back, over the ropes. Light, affectionate, and Hooch came closer, as always more tactile under the influence. Moving his hand under Hooch's chin once more, he pulled his head back even further than before, and brought his mouth close for a deep kiss, thoroughly tasting Hooch and whisky and his own cum. One hand holding Hooch's chin still, so that Hooch was unable to move away from the assault, the other gently smoothing his head and neck, before moving across to the front, to stroke his chest and play with his pierced nipples.

Hooch's breathing increased, quietly moaning into Matt's mouth. At first trying to strain and gain more, but he had no leverage whatsoever, and he soon fell into utter passivity, as he let his mouth be plundered. It only served to increase his discomfort and need, but he didn't care. Not now, that in his mind and his world there were only Matt and himself, and Matt was giving him more than he had ever known he needed: the absolute control that allowed him to give up his own.

When Matt broke the kiss and took his hand off Hooch's hard and reddened nipples, Hooch whispered hoarsely, "please..."

Matt paused. Hooch, begging, when he never did under the lash or the most brutal beating. He would scream, thrash, and moan but never beg. "Hmmmm..." a rumble, as he nuzzled Hooch's neck. "Please what? Please let you go?" He touched the ropes so beautifully binding Hooch's arms, but Hooch shook his head. "Please let you come?" a light touch on Hooch's straining cock, the touch of leather on the sensitized flesh bringing a shudder, and yet Hooch shook his head. "Or is that a please for more?" His hand went back to the nipples, twisting one of the gleaming rings.

Hooch let out a hissing breath and nodded. He arched further back, ignoring the impossible strain on his shoulders, arms and back, until he was bent across Matt's thighs, presenting his taut chest while looking at Matt, dark eyes blown wide.

Matt trailed a single finger down from Hooch's jaw, gliding over the collar until he reached the left nipple, circling it, pinching it, rolling it, meeting Hooch's eyes, who gasped and moaned. Usually silent, this time he didn't hold back, not when the pleasure outweighed the pain, and his brain was intoxicated. Matt put his lips on the left nipple, while his hand moved to his right, nibbling, moving the heavy ring around with his teeth, lathing the hard buds with laps and kisses, nips and tugs of the ring, alternating between the nipples with mouth and fingers.

Hooch moaned loudly, bending even further backwards to breaking point, and his whole body shuddered as suddenly, unexpectedly, every muscle in his body tensed and he let out a deep, hoarse cry, shaking violently as orgasm hit him. Despite the restraining cock ring, he ejaculated into the hollow of the wand deep inside his cock, his cum held back by the screwed-on top. The orgasm was so sudden and intense, Hooch slumped against Matt's legs and slid down, out cold.

Matt was beside Hooch in barely a fraction of a second, removing the collar first to ensure that Hooch could breath comfortably, then turning him on his side to carefully remove the wand and cockring while two staff members appeared as soon as they realized he had lost consciousness, and swiftly cut the ropes from Hooch, freeing his arms.

Matt didn't notice the small crowd that had gathered curiously, polite enough to disperse once they realized what had happened. Another staff member brought a tall glass of cold water and a cool damp cloth, but by then Hooch had jerked awake, blinking stupidly around himself. "Matt?" His voice was softer and more disoriented than Matt had ever heard it.

Matt had taken his gloves off and was gently stroking Hooch's face, skin to skin. "You came without permission," he said softly. "Normally, I wouldn't like that but it was hot." Lips on Hooch's again, coaxing and then devouring.

When Matt broke the kiss, Hooch had recovered enough to have his wits about, albeit still mellow from the whisky.

Matt chuckled, used the cloth to wipe the sweat off Hooch's face, then cleaned his cock that still had cum dripping out after the wand removal. At last he tipped the water to Hooch's lips, encouraging him to take small sips. Hooch's arms were useless right after being freed, and so he sat on his hip, leaning into Matt's solid presence as he drank.

After a while Matt took the glass away, waved a member of staff closer and gave her some directions before she left quickly.

"Let's get this back in." Matt took Hooch's cock piercing jewelry when it was offered to him and bent down to carefully thread it through the piercing hole. Hooch winced slightly, his urethra sore from the PA wand, but Matt knew Hooch would cherish the discomfort.

Satisfied that Hooch had recovered somewhat, Matt stood and moved back to the chaise where he had been sitting, stretching out. Hooch followed more slowly, settling to once more kneel between Matt's legs. Matt kept the weights in Hooch's nipple rings, but deliberately left the collar and leash off.

The show on the stage had moved to acrobatic contortions, though they were the still the sanitized, artistic moves that were miles away from what Hooch craved. Hooch watched too, for once the observer and not the observed, relaxed and half-dozing, accepting food from Matt's hand in the form of the tiny canapés that were circulating around the room, miniature treats that were barely more than half a nibble, works of art in and of themselves. Contrasting tastes and textures, chosen by Matt, from the saltiness of smoked salmon and caviar, the spiciness of tostaditas topped with chili and pork, to the sweetness of the macaroons.

No games, no playing, nothing else for the rest of the evening, until it was time to go to the hotel. Sitting and watching the others, while Matt exchanged pleasantries with the doms, masters and mistresses, while caressing Hooch's face, kneading his shoulder muscles, or carding his fingers through the dark hair, now peppered with grey at the temples.

Power, control and ownership had nothing to do with collars or chains, floggings or fucking, ink or metal, but everything to do with Hooch and Matt.

CHRISTMAS 2006, FLINT, MICHIGAN

The 23rd of December was hell for any traveler, by road, rails or air, but Matt had booked first class tickets, and their checking in was less painful than for most. They were settled in their seats as the plane took off, when Hooch craned his neck to look at Matt. "I don't have presents for your family."

Matt met his eyes as he accepted a glass from the hovering stewardess, ignoring the batted eyelashes. "All taken care of," he told Hooch, "and already delivered. You can buy more than just kinky shit off the internet, you know."

Hooch grinned with relief. "Thanks, buddy." The latter added for the benefit of the far too nosy stewardess. "What did you get?"

Matt scratched the side of his nose. "iPods for everyone over the age of 12, whatever the site suggested for everyone under. DVDs and stuffed toys, mainly."

"And your mom and dad? I should have got something special for Anne." Hooch frowned.

Matt looked around, but the cabin crew were busy preparing for handing out meals, and the other passengers occupied with their own concerns. "Taken care of. From both of us. Mom thinks it's special enough that we're coming at all."

"Okay, but what did you get for her?" Hooch insisted.

"A new camera, and I got dad a laptop." Matt studied Hooch with curiosity. "Why the sudden interest?"

Hooch shrugged, but his nonchalance wasn't entirely genuine. "Because we're there for the first time for Christmas?"

The look Matt returned was skeptical. "Nothing at all to do with how she sees right through you?"

Hooch sighed deeply. "You bastard," but the corners of his lips quirked, "I like her, okay? And I'm a fucking idiot for not getting her something personal, but damned if I even knew where to look and what to get."

Such thoughts, let alone words, were remarkable enough from Hooch that Matt thought for a few seconds before replying. "Just having you—us—there is going to be weird enough for her this year, I think," trying to calm Hooch down. "Next year," he paused, letting Hooch get used to the possibility, "bring her something from home, a book or something on the history of the place. She likes that sort of thing."

"Really?" Hooch managed to raise only one brow. "Sounds damned boring to me." He fell silent once more, but he moved his arm beside Matt's on the arm rest between their seats, and ever so slightly pressed their arms together. He closed his eyes, indicating to Matt that as usual, he'd be the silent travelling companion.

Matt gave an amused snort, but put his headphones on, ready for the boring flight north into the snow.

* * *

They were met by Anne at arrival, as it had proved all but impossible to rent a car, and she greeted them both with a hug. "I'm so glad you could make it. Everyone's arrived and looking forward to seeing you, and thanking you for all your presents. You really shouldn't have."

Hooch hugged her tightly, the only other grown-up person in the world he did that for. "You have to thank Matt, if it had been up to me you wouldn't have anything because I forgot."

She just laughed, reaching up to pat his shoulder. Hoisting the luggage into her car they were soon on the road.

Anne updated them on the past month as they made their familiar way back to the house. Hooch listened intently to the normality of their lives, while Matt stared out at the snow-covered landscape, his childhood hidden under thick blankets of white. Arriving at the house, greeting Matt's father and brother who were clearing the driveway, before going upstairs to put their bags down. In Matt's childhood room again, with the double bed that had been bought so many years ago for the first visit at Thanksgiving. Almost the only bed, apart from their own, that they could share.

With Hooch and Matt's help the driveway was cleared quickly, and when they returned into the house, warming drinks were waiting for them.

They promised to help clear the driveway, and Hooch went upstairs to gear up. He had planned ahead and had packed his military winter gear, the urban version. He didn't have clue, when he came back down, what he looked like: all in black, and so very much the dangerous motherfucker he really was.

Anne struggled not to let on how taken aback she was, but Matt understood. The moment he saw Hooch geared up, he knew the impression he gave to everyone: the veneer of civility was off and he showed how deadly he really was. A glance at Hooch confirmed what he already knew, that

Hooch was oblivious to the effect he had on most people. Not even when Hooch's eldest nephew, a grumpy teenager, came into the kitchen for a drink, took one look Hooch, and slowly backed out again.

"Is something the matter?" Hooch asked, taking a sip of the hot cider as the teenager fled the room, watching Matt's silent parents and brother. "I look like a complete idiot in winter gear inside the house," he grinned, "is that it?"

Whether it was the smile, or that Hooch had come up with an acceptable alternative explanation, there was a visible lightening of the mood in the room. Anne laughed. "I've just never seen you in it before, even though it's sometimes a bit chilly at Thanksgiving. Black suits you." In a sort of dangerous, I-shall-kill-you-if-you-do-not-do-as-I-say way, she didn't add.

"Didn't think camo was appropriate for Christmas." Hooch pointed his gloved hand at the window. "Anything else that needs doing outside while I'm geared up?"

"No, all done," John huffed. Matt's dad was a man of few words but undoubted warmth. "Just got to watch the driveway the next few days."

"Okay." Hooch put the empty mug down. "I get changed, then. Let me know when it needs doing, I got the gear."

Matt laughed at his dad's surprised expression. "Delta." He shrugged with a grin.

"Ah, yes," John said at Hooch's retreating back, listening to the footsteps on the stairs. "Just goes to show they are a breed apart."

Matt almost choked. "Hooch is a breed apart alright." He didn't add anything despite his mother's quizzical look.

The rest of the day went quickly, until it was time for early dinner, where everyone—as was traditional—ate too much, before putting on their winter overcoats and piling out to the cars to drive to Midnight Mass. Matt had somehow managed to persuade Hooch to mix up his military winter gear with civilian clothes, so as not to look like he was there to put a bullet in someone. His greatest achievement in that persuasion was that Hooch still had no idea how menacing he could be to a civilian, even when he didn't try at all.

Hooch had become increasingly silent, but refused to tell Matt what was the matter. Instead pretending to be fine, with an expression meant to resemble a smile pasted on his face. With the cars filled with talking relatives, fidgeting children, and the various bits and pieces that were being taken to church, there wasn't any opportunity for Matt to ask what was wrong. They soon arrived in the parking lot, everyone decanting from the cars, and Matt's family was being swallowed up by the crowd.

Matt knew that Hooch would need a moment to prepare himself for the onslaught of the mass of unfamiliar people, and they waited for a few minutes on the far side of the car. "You look like you're about to implode. What's wrong?"

Hooch clamped down on his control so tightly, his teeth ground as he shook his head. "I'm fine. Just not big on churches, especially not the Catholic ones with all their sin bullshit. I heard enough of that for a lifetime."

Matt blinked at the tone and the words. Hooch was an iceberg in more than just the obvious, but also in what was usually so deep below the surface: the gaping holes in his past, that not even the increased contact with his sister over the last few months had come close to filling in. Something was seriously wrong. "Do you want to go back?" Matt asked, "say one of us is coming down with a chill?"

"I'm not disappointing your mom." Hooch's jaw set into a determined line. "No bastard of a motherfucking priest from a lifetime ago is going to make me do that. I only regret I didn't kill the fucker myself." Hooch forced himself to take a deep breath and went into pokerfaced mission-mode. "Let's go."

Taken aback when Hooch moved off suddenly, Matt almost scrambled to catch up, hoping with all his might that he hadn't just jumped to horrific conclusions from two simple sentences. He walked a reassuring half step behind Hooch as they joined the milling, friendly crowd in the parking lot, so wrapped up and muffled in their winter coats and hats and scarves it was difficult to tell who anyone was.

Matt stayed close to Hooch at all times, always an eye on him, making sure he knew where he was, but he didn't need to rescue him. Hooch was doing a remarkably good job at pretending to be a normal socialized human being. When they moved into the church, aglow with hundreds of candles and beautifully adorned with an abundance of traditional Christmas decorations, Matt shepherded Hooch into a pew, so that he sat between Anne and himself. His mom looked at him with a carefully guarded question in his eyes, as she glanced at the tense man beside her, and Matt mouthed 'help him' at her, behind Hooch's back. Anne nodded slightly, smiled, patted Hooch's hand and sat back, waiting for the choir to start and mass to begin.

Matt sat close, legs touching, trying to be reassuring but feeling the tension in Hooch as he went through the motions. Obviously familiar to Hooch, even if, as he said, it was from a lifetime ago.

Hooch never knelt, stood instead when the majority of the congregation knelt at the appropriate times, and never opened his mouth to join in any 'amen' let alone the Lord's prayer, nor did he sing any of the hymns. He remained tense throughout the rituals, staring straight ahead. To Matt it seemed as if he had retreated into his military mission headspace. Hooch's tension increased during the sermon, his whole body strumming with what Matt was convinced was his urge to fight or flight. Not giving a damn that they might be observed, he placed his hand onto the rock hard muscle of Hooch's thigh, trying to ground him with his presence. He noticed from the corner of his eyes that his mom gently patted Hooch's hand again, then simply left hers on his, so that Hooch found himself sandwiched between two solid, warm presences, and Matt loved his mom for that more than ever.

At last the mass was over, and Hooch seemed to almost slump with relief. He took a moment before getting up, still safely between Matt and Anne, with Matt's dad a step behind, who had clearly sensed that something wasn't quite right. Walking down the aisle slowly, Matt tried to shield Hooch as much as he could as faces from the past came to greet him and to look curiously at Hooch.

Now that the organized part of the mass was over, Hooch managed to get back into his social-dealing mode, and while he left all the talking to Matt and his family, he did shake hands and didn't look as if he was going to bite them off any second. Eventually, the crowds gathered outside at the snow covered and twinkling Christmas tree, to enjoy mince pies and mulled wine in the cold night.

Hooch slipped away at the first opportunity and was standing at the side, in the darkness. His hands in his pockets, he was gazing up into the clear black sky.

"Hey," Matt's voice behind him was soft. "Drink? You look like you need it." Mulled wine in a Styrofoam cup. Practicality for a night when nobody wanted to be left with washing-up that could be avoided. The wine had been barely drinkable even before it had been boiled with sugar and spices in bulk and then ladled out into foam cups in a parking lot, but it was still warm, and alcoholic. Hooch looked rather in need of both.

"Thanks." Hooch took the cup and sipped on it. Steam curling around his face. "Now I know why you are quite the something that you are."

"Oh?" Matt took a step closer, but not touching Hooch. Too exposed out here, even though they were some distance away from the main crowd.

"Yeah, you have a great family. How a family should be." Hooch drained the last of the wine in his cup, not giving a sign how it tasted to him. "Thank you for…" he hesitated, "for letting me be part of it."

"You're welcome," Matt said, "in both senses."

They stayed there, in the quiet and the dark, until they could hear the sounds of the crowd starting to disperse, and returned to the cars and the rest of Matt's family. Anne and John gave Hooch a concerned look, but when it appeared that there was nothing to worry about, they returned to the task of rounding up sleepy children for the car ride back to the house.

They ended up one vehicle short, because the latest newborn had been taken home earlier, and both Hooch and Matt squeezed into the back seat with a couple of kids, between a child seat and a booster pad, refusing to let any of the older folks cram themselves in there. The younger one, a toddler of two, was so tired, she immediately drooped, snuggled up to the man beside her, and took hold of his large hand, which happened to be Hooch's. His look of quiet panic was priceless, but Matt just shrugged with a 'can't do anything about it, buddy' gesture and John and Anne in the front appeared to be oblivious. Hooch had no other option than to sit still, keep his hand where it was, and let the kid sleep. Only Matt noticed how Hooch gradually relaxed, his breathing evening out in sync with the kid's. Who would have known.

Matt barely hid a smile on the way back to the house, and as he unbuckled his little niece and carried her to bed, more thoughts burned through his mind. He had no time to ask Hooch that night, because by the time he got to their room, Hooch was already in bed and fast asleep. Crawling in beside Hooch, spooning behind him, Matt tried to get some sleep, knowing that it would not be long before the morning, anticipating to be woken by the sounds of shrieking children at dawn.

* * *

A few short hours later, Hooch jolted awake at a blood curdling scream that had him jump out of the bed, ready to attack and defend, before the next high-pitched squeals and screams stopped him in his one-man mission. "What the fuck?" He stood in his boxers in the dark, chilly room, blearily scrubbing his face.

"I guess they liked the iPods," Matt muttered sleepily, reaching for a pillow and crawling under it, to muffle the sounds. "Come back to bed, it's cold, and they won't be done for a while yet."

"Whatever nice things I said about your family last night, scratch that. Today they are out to give me a heart attack." Hooch grumped but slid back under the duvet. Glad he wore shorts when at Matt's parents. The thought of racing downstairs stark naked and in full warrior-mode, made him shudder first, then chuckle against Matt's skin.

Matt shifted backwards, craving the contact even as he grumbled at the chill. "Kids, Christmas, damage to ear drums. It's traditional. I suppose at least we can be thankful that that's one worry we'll never have."

"I would never have produced a kid anyway." Hooch imitated an octopus as he wrapped himself around Matt to soak up his heat. "I got myself a vasectomy when I joined up."

Matt started, and tried to turn around but was prevented by Hooch's firm grip. "You couldn't have been more than a kid yourself. Wasn't that a bit drastic?"

"Was it?" Hooch would have shrugged, had he been in a different position. "I wasn't going to fuck up anyone's life, so I made sure."

Several minutes passed while Matt thought of, and discarded, a dozen different things to say, and settled for leaning back further into the embrace. "I see." Not that he particularly wanted to, but between what little he did know of Hooch's family, Hooch's amusement in spending his inheritance on his club membership and their collection of increasingly kinky sex toys, and an 18-year-old's vehemence that he would not have children of his own, the picture was emerging, and it was not a pleasant one. "We'll have at least until 8 before any of the adults go downstairs to calm them down," Matt changed the subject, "unless you want to be subjected to endless showing off of presents, I advise we don't go down before 8.30. Anything you want to do before then?" The tone suggestive, as was the pointed shove into Hooch's groin.

"You sure the little monsters of your family won't come storming up here demanding to show off their presents instead?" Hooch chuckled, pushing his groin back against Matt's ass.

"Door's locked, and they know that everyone will be down soon anyway." He paused, grinned. "I'm quite sure we're not the only ones thinking what we're thinking this morning."

Hooch scrunched up his face. "Don't make me imagine sex amongst your family members." He shuddered for good measure, "but I have heard that orgasms are the best way to start Christmas."

"That it is," Matt laughed, "Merry Christmas." With that he wriggled onto his back, waiting for Hooch, who pulled off his boxers and joined Matt back on the bed, but upside down and on his side. In one swift motion he rolled Matt onto his side to face him, and sucked down on Matt's cock while his own nudged against Matt's lips.

Matt never saw Hooch's grin, but he could hear the contented purr.

✳ ✳ ✳

When they got downstairs, the living room was awash with wrapping paper, sticky tape, and excited children. There were lots of hugs and thankyous from the children (and the adults) for the presents. Hooch found himself sitting on the floor with two of the five-year-olds, watching one of their new DVDs with infinite patience and quite a lot of entertainment, while Matt was shocked to see his far-too-cool-for-this teenage nephew regress to childhood—or became a polite adult—and actually was enthusiastic about his new iPod.

Hooch looked up from watching the Pixar cartoon, as Anne pushed a second mug of hot, steaming coffee into his face. He smiled his thanks, and went back to watching, while sipping his coffee. "Uncle Hooch?" One of the kids piped up.

It took Hooch a moment to catch on. 'Uncle Hooch' was a new one. It sounded strange to his ears, because his nephews had never called him that. "Yeah?" He balanced the half empty mug on his knee.

"We want to go and have a snowball fight later. You coming?" The kid looked so hopeful, Hooch couldn't do anything but agree. "Yeah, will do."

"Uncle Matt, too?"

Hooch glanced across at Matt who was chatting to one of his sisters. "I'm sure I can persuade him."

The boy whooped and announced to the whole room that Uncle Hooch and Uncle Matt would take all of the kids out to a snowball fight later. Hooch's expression of sudden panic was back once more, because 'all of the kids' had not been in his plan, but it was too late to protest.

After making sure that everyone was wrapped up warmly, Hooch in the all-black tactical gear that made the kids stare open-mouthed, Matt lead the way out to the large park in the next street that had been the site of many a snowball fight. As soon as they arrived, Hooch sorted the kids into two teams, more or less evenly matched in age and size. He put Matt in charge of one, himself of the other, and declared that this was going to be a proper, snowball war-game, before he spirited his team out of hearing distance for a 'strategy meeting'.

Matt stared after him, then shook his head with a grin, and went to do the same for his own team. While he had keen memories of his time as a USMC, he knew that if Hooch pulled out all the way, he wasn't going to have a chance, and thus he had to try and out-guess his Delta partner.

He had the advantage of some familiarity of the park, if vague, and at least there hadn't been the funds to change the park much in the years since he left. He guided his team to a part of the grounds near the play equipment that gave them easy maneuverability and plenty of snow to stockpile ammunition.

Keeping an eye on Hooch, visible in black, he set his team to snowball making, and waited.

Hooch ushered his troop into the lightly forested area, where they first made stacks of snowballs, which Hooch distributed in small piles along the area, strategically planning attack, defense and—if must be—retreat. He sent out a few of his team, three older kids armed with snowballs, to draw the other team closer by taunting them while pelting them with snowballs. Retreating into the trees, he waited until his scouts were engaged in a fight, before guiding his remaining troops in an arch along the side of the park, flanking the opposing team. The smallest kid held tightly onto his hand as they walked quietly, using the trees as visual shelter as best as they could. When his faction was close enough to belly-crawl through the snow, he placed the kid on his back, where she held on tightly, securing a stack of snowballs as ready ammunition for the moment of sneak-attack.

Matt's team, realizing they were being drawn out into the open, had retreated to the play equipment, where they had the advantage of height, raining snowballs down on Hooch's scouts. Matt kept a keen eye on the park, knowing that Hooch had held half his team in reserve, and he cursed himself that he had lost sight of them.

The older kids of Hooch's team were holding out well. He'd briefed them that it would be hard, they were the decoys, after all, and he'd fired them up, just like he had done when he'd led his team into dangerous missions. The kids had lapped it up, bursting with pride to have been chosen and raring to go. Now they held their own, even though pelted with snow they still kept fighting back.

Suddenly a battle cry from the bushes surrounding the play area, immediately joined by a cacophony of kids' voices that yelled as they attacked Matt's team, that screamed in surprise, having been taken in a pincer movement. Hooch himself came running, the girl holding onto the hood of his tight fitting parka, and Hooch secured the kid with one hand, with the other aiming at Matt, snow balls flying in a crazy mayhem.

It was chaos of running and screaming kids, melting snowballs, white powder and lumps everywhere, slush and absolute fun. It was clear that Hooch's team had 'won', though that was largely moot when everyone was drenched, chilled, laughing and exhausted, more than ready to head back to the house for lunch. Emily clung to Hooch like a limpet, refusing to let go until they were safely back and she was handed over to her mother, protesting all the way that she wanted to stay with "Unca Hooch".

Hooch was still grinning like a loon by the time he'd stomped off the snow on his boots and had shaken off his clothes and hair. When Matt turned to tell him good humouredly he was a bastard for getting snow down his neck and chest, he stopped in his tracks and said nothing, just ruffling the snow out of Hooch's damp hair with a sudden big lump in his throat.

Everyone went to their rooms to get changed, kids and grown-ups alike, before lunch was ready. Hooch stood in the room in his briefs, toweling his hair, when Matt came inside from the bathroom.

Matt closed the door firmly, took the towel and gently helped with the job, the awkward bits where his extra inch of height helped. "I think my mother and sisters are about to nominate you for sainthood for keeping the kids out of the house." He put the towel down. "Thank you," he turned to take Hooch in his arms. Even though he hated himself for deflating the mood, he asked because he had to: "what did that priest do to you?"

Hooch tensed and stepped out of the embrace. His face was closed off. "I'm not talking about this."

Matt's eyes fixed on him in worry, glad that he was between Hooch and the door. "Ok, fine, not now, but at least let me know if…well, I had no idea until last night when we got there and I would have come up with something else if…well…" who would have thought that there was one thing more awkward to talk about with Hooch apart from his need for 'time out'.

"Let it go, Matt." Hooch's facial expression softened, as he kept his gaze on Matt. "Let it go, okay?" His voice gentled, reaching out to gather Matt back into the embrace. His lips moved against Matt's neck as he murmured, "the past is the past. Let it stay there."

Matt nodded into Hooch's shoulder, knowing when to leave something. He'd left it well alone for fifteen years already, hadn't he? "Should get dressed. They'll be calling us down soon."

"I'm starving." Hooch smiled as he let go of Matt once more. If the smile was a little forced, it wasn't the worst of his attempts at it, not by a long shot. "Taking the kids out was probably a ploy by your mom to get me to eat even more than usual."

"You should know that by now." Matt stepped back and headed for the door, leaving Hooch a few precious minutes of privacy before he had to come down and face the horde again.

When Hooch appeared downstairs, he was dressed in a tailored button down shirt that Matt had never seen on him, and which must have cost shitloads, judging by the fabric and the way it fit perfectly. Clearly Hooch's concession to the holidays. He was carrying a large manila envelope, which he placed onto the bedecked mantelpiece. Everyone else was already at the table, inviting him to sit at his customary place, right beside Matt.

For whatever reason, they skipped saying grace, and if Matt suspected that something was up, he didn't let on, but sent his mother a grateful look all the same. If at all possible, the table was even more loaded with food than it had been at Thanksgiving, so much so that the sturdy solid hardwood table was groaning under the weight. As predicted, Hooch was the recipient of all over gratitude from his in-laws for keeping the children occupied so that the adults could get on with the task of getting the meal under way without having overly excited children and their new toys getting in the way.

The children kept chattering away about the 'awesome battle' they had had, and if Hooch received an occasional not-wholly-approving look from one of the parents, it was quickly tampered by the relief and the knowledge that this man, no matter what Matt's family might sometimes think about the quiet Texan officer, was probably the most reliable and safest choice to have around their kids. Besides, there was Matt, and everyone around the table knew without the shadow of a doubt that Hooch Bozic was devoted to Matt.

Hooch was more relaxed now, comfortable with Matt's family through the repeated exposure over the years. The loud, happy, loving family with its perceptive matriarch who had taken him in without a question or a murmur. It was when he moved to reach for another serving of the mashed potatoes, that Matt realized that the fabric of Hooch's shirt, though not exactly thin, was of such fine weave that the shape of his nipple rings was just barely visible when he moved. Matt swallowed his bite of ham with difficulty, wondering if anyone else could see, or whether it was because he knew what Hooch was wearing underneath.

No one else gave any clues if they'd noticed or not, but they might simply be polite. Hooch, turned his head as he reached for the salt, and gave Matt one quick, sharp grin. For once, clearly not oblivious.

Matt shot him a look and looked down at his plate, listening to his brother talk about his upcoming ice-fishing trip to Alaska, nodding at all the appropriate places, because that was all Paul really wanted when he spoke about his beloved fish.

Stuffed to the gills, as usual at his parents' house—Matt was amazed that nobody in the family was fat, given the amount of food that everyone down to the smallest child seemed to enjoy. Dessert, however, was where his sisters had always concentrated their efforts, and it seemed that after the table had been cleared from the main meal, it was just as full of pies, cakes, home-made ice-cream and other sweets.

Hooch sat in his chair as if he was never going to be able to get up again, after Anne had ladled a third helping onto his plate, which he'd been too polite to refuse,. He groaned, trying to resist any of the desserts, but in the end he agreed to ice cream, hoping it would somehow fit. The strong coffee afterwards, followed by whisky or brandy for the adults, was much appreciated.

It wasn't before they'd all retired to the collection of sofas, chairs, and cushions on the floor, with all of the kids engrossed once more in their toys and gadgets, that Hooch retrieved the thick manila envelope, and handed it to Matt with a simple, "Merry Christmas."

Matt looked at him quizzically, because Hooch never really took the usual suggested timelines for presents, and bought things when he felt it appropriate, such as Rex coming several months before Matt's actual birthday being fairly par for the course. He opened it, eyes wide, and dropped the entire pile of papers in shock once he read the heading on the first one.

Matt picked up the stack papers, all neatly ordered, and the little plastic card that had fallen out, before the rest of the family noticed what was happening. He flipped through the documents: will, powers of attorney, insurance documentation, pension documentation, bank accounts, investment accounts. Neatly set out in typeface, all the formalities that they could do to make their partnership official, everything short of what their state and Hooch's job would permit. Matt looked across at his partner, stunned.

"Some of those you have to sign in front of witnesses who aren't related to you," Hooch said. Sounding casual to anyone but Matt, who knew him better than Hooch probably knew himself.

Matt nodded, still in disbelief. "I…" he swallowed. "Thank you." He'd think of possible witnesses later, but for now still amazed at the thought behind Hooch's actions. "I guess I should go and see your attorney too," he said, knowing Hooch would understand that he'd reciprocate formally.

"It was all I could do." A hint of insecurity in Hooch's voice, very much unlike him.

"It's more than…" Matt stopped again—what was it with him being unable to think things through, "it is all that we can do." Quite literally. Nothing else that could possibly be done, considering who they were and where they lived. "Thank you." He looked down and carefully placed the precious documents back in the envelope before anyone else in the room noticed the quiet in their part of the room.

For the first time ever in front of Matt's family, Hooch reached for Matt's hand and squeezed it tightly. It was clear to Matt what Hooch would have rather done but didn't dare to.

Matt squeezed back, then let go as Emily toddled up, large stuffed bear held close, completely smitten with Uncle Hooch, who smiled ruefully at Matt before picking up the little girl to sit on his lap.

2011

SEPTEMBER 2011, FAYETTEVILLE

It had been a pleasant summer away in Europe, first to Kisa's wedding in Budapest—that had been a lot more enjoyable than they had envisaged—followed by a relaxed, sunny trip down the Adriatic coast. A respite from all the gloom and the doom, a reminder that there were still plenty of happy things going on in the world, and just how lucky they were. They returned home in early September, and settled back into life as it had been. The gym ran smoothly, still as popular as ever, and Matt was able to take more time off to indulge in his photography, which had turned out to be quite successful. Male nudes remained his specialty, with one particular body appearing more often than others, though he was very careful about publicizing his art, using a pseudonym.

He had been paying attention to the achingly slow progress of the repeal of DADT but hadn't been involved as much as he would have like. One thing for him and Hooch to be an open secret at the base, quite another to be seen to be actively interested.

Hooch didn't appear as if he had been interested at all, never mentioning the a potential repeal of DADT. He did his job like he'd always done, lived his life with Matt like he'd always lived it. He'd made Major a couple of years previous, increasingly working on a strategic level, which he'd learned to accept, because at fifty-one his body had begun to make him feel the extremes of his life.

Everything was as it had been, until Tuesday, 20th of September.

Hooch had gone to work early, leaving Matt in bed with a cup of coffee beside him. With the top news of the day firmly embedded in his mind, he dumped his pack on his desk first, before walking straight to his CO's office.

"Major Bozic, what a surprise." The man looked up. It had been three COs since Hooch had taken the instructor post, three men who could have been clones of each other.

"Good morning, Sir." Hooch saluted, then sat down when indicated. "About the Ball at the end of the month…"

"Yes, Major?" The man looked slightly harried. He hadn't been in his post long, and Hooch doubted that he knew very much about anything that wasn't plainly in front of his face.

"I feel it necessary to inform you that I will bring my long-term partner for the first time." Hooch looked at the man with an unreadable expression.

A glance look in his direction as the Colonel focused on him. "I fail to see…" he began, before it registered what Hooch was saying. The man blinked, as he remembered the news of the day, even though it felt like he'd been spending months at endless committee meetings on the topic. Another blink. "Ah. I see. That's…" he swallowed, and a look of disbelief crossed his face before it was forcibly schooled back to neutrality. "Forgive me' Major, this is somewhat unexpected."

"With all due respect, Sir, but from what I understand, you must be one of the very few personnel on base for whom this will be unexpected." Hooch's face was still in neutral.

The Colonel opened and closed his mouth several times as though discarding the first few responses before settling rather feebly for: "I appreciate that you are telling me in advance, Major." Treading water while trying to get his lagging brain into order, to process both new pieces of intelligence. "I presume," he hesitated just a fraction on the pronoun, "your partner is aware of the etiquette?"

"Etiquette?" Hooch tried very hard to keep his poker face, but a grin was threatening to break out. "I assure you that he does. He is a former US Marine and first Gulf War veteran where, incidentally," Hooch's blasé air was spoiled by his grin, "we met."

"I see," the Colonel said faintly, and it was clear that he was trying very hard not to see. "Twenty years," he said, almost to himself. "I…" he stopped, "that was a remarkable exercise in discretion."

Hooch settled back in his chair. "The first seven were easy, we didn't live together. The second thirteen were trickier, but I had help on base. Seems that ignoring anything and everything has been a specialty of my boys." Hooch sat up straight once more. "Are you familiar with my military record, Sir?"

The Colonel had given up trying to hide his shock and simply stared and nodded. "Yes, I am very aware of it, Major."

"Would you say I served my country well?"

"Of course." Not quite knowing but suspecting where the conversation was going, but without a way to avoid answering the simple truth to the simple question.

"So, you wouldn't think I have been a bad influence on the morale of my men in any way."

A look, unreadable. "No, of course not." The words almost forced out.

"Just checking." Hooch stood up. "If you don't need me for anything else, Sir, I'd better get to work."

"Yes," the Colonel echoed faintly, still not quite believing his ears. "Thank you for telling me, Major. I...ummmmm," he blinked, and tried to finish the sentence. "I look forward to meeting...uhm...Mr..." he trailed off.

"Donahue, Sir. Matt Donahue." Hooch saluted and strode out of the office with a shit eating grin on his face.

The Colonel watched him go, paused for a second, and then opened the bottom drawer of his desk filing cabinet for his hidden bottle of bourbon.

Hooch didn't realize he was whistling as he strode along to the cafeteria to grab his morning coffee. Nor did he notice the dumbfounded looks from the other personnel as he passed them. Major Bozic, cheerful, was a sight rarely seen.

"Sir?" a voice somewhere to the left of Hooch called out.

"Yeah?" Hooch turned his head, about to step into the canteen.

"Is everything alright, Sir?" there was a look of disbelief on the speaker's face.

"Fuck, yeah." Hooch grinned, "didn't you hear the news?"

"News?" the Captain parroted. Major Bozic grinning was news in itself.

"DADT got repealed." Hooch turned and walked through the open door, leaving the Captain standing.

"Sir?" the Captain called after him, then followed, lengthening his stride. "Sir?" he called again coming up to Hooch. "Yes...but?"

Hooch huffed a laugh. "I'm gay, Captain." He grinned as he turned into the self-service lane.

The Captain's jaw dropped momentarily at the pronouncement, before closing with a click. He wasn't the only one who had heard Hooch's proclamation, and a buzz began to spread through the room. Hooch silently grinned to himself as he filled his cup. He was fifty-one years old, he'd served his country all his life, and for many years he'd even laid it on the line. He deserved some fun on account of others.

* * *

The day continued as it had begun, with Hooch amusing himself with the same bluntness. He might be a desk jockey these days, but he still managed to get all of Fort Bragg talking, and wasn't it ironic that all it took was saying out loud his partner was a man.

He remained in excellent spirits on the drive home. When he got back to the gym, Matt was in the reception area, leaning over the desk, talking to Mandy.

He looked up at Hooch's entrance, noting the rare grin. "What's up?"

"This." Hooch dropped his pack on the floor, stepped towards Matt, took his face into his hands, then proceeded to kiss him deeply. In the middle of reception, right in front of staff and customers.

The cheering, hooting and hollering was deafening by the time Matt recovered from his shock and pushed Hooch away. "I take it that means we're now out." He said, rather redundantly.

"It would look more convincing if you didn't push me away." Hooch grinned as he crossed his arms in front of his chest, ignoring Mandy's delighted giggle that would have otherwise scraped his nerves raw.

"You think?" Matt raised an eyebrow before reaching for Hooch and plastering himself against the leaner man, returning the kiss with equal enthusiasm.

The noise crescendo started up once more, Mandy's voice cutting through it all as she delivered a cheerleader-worthy encouragement. Hooch was breathless and laughing when they broke the kiss, only now noticing how the training rooms had emptied and a crowd was filling the reception area. There wasn't a single person that didn't show approval. The gym attracted loyal members. "Twenty years with that kid, how did I survive that?" Hooch smirked.

Matt laughed. "Come on, old man, I think this calls for a more private celebration. Clear the way, guys." Taking Hooch by the arm and pulling him towards the door to the apartment.

One of the regulars shouted: "DADT repealed, huh?" Others clapped as Hooch raised a thumb, the last bit of him that was still visible before Matt had pulled him through the door and up the stairs.

Bursting into the door at the top of the stairs, Matt preceded Hooch into the room by barely a step. "What brought all that on?"

"The guy downstairs got it right." Hooch flashed a grin. "You didn't think I was following the whole thing, did you?"

Matt blinked. "Oh God, you told everyone on base today, didn't you?" barely a question.

"Yeah." Hooch grinned, smug from head to toe. "I started with my CO."

"And went all the way down to the janitor." Matt groaned. "How did they take it?"

"It didn't seem to be a surprise to many. Worst secret of Fort Bragg." Hooch shrugged.

Matt shook his head, but a smile was beginning to emerge. "Just when I thought you couldn't pull any more crazy stunts." He stepped closer and put his arms around Hooch's neck. "I believe I promised a private celebration," the smile was full-blown now.

"I believe you did." Hooch placed his hands onto Matt's hips. He really should tell Matt about the Mess dinner, but he wasn't going to spoil the sex he was about to get.

"Bedroom?" Matt disengaged from Hooch and headed in that direction without waiting for a reply, shedding his clothes along the way.

Hooch followed suit, chuckling as he worked his way out of his uniform. "Guess I'm getting too old for carpet burn."

* * *

Matt was half-asleep, in a sated post-coital haze, playing with one of Hooch's nipple rings. "You've got something on your mind," a statement as Hooch stared at the ceiling.

Arms behind his head, Hooch lay stretched out in all his smooth and tattooed glory, a feast for Matt's eyes. "Yeah, I told my CO I'll bring my partner to the next Ball." Hooch let the words stand in the room, sounding casual, but there was minute tensing of his muscles beneath Matt's fingers.

The fingers stilled. "Did you now?" Matt's eyes snapped open, instantly wide awake. "And what did your CO say to that?"

"He's looking forward to meet you in a couple of weeks." Hooch replied with a straight face.

"Oh, I'm sure he does," Matt replied drily. "So, I'm the 'plus one' now, am I?"

"Haven't you always been for the last thirteen years?"

"I guess I have." Matt smiled, his fingers started moving again. "When is it?"

"Last Saturday this month." Hooch craned his head to look at Matt. "You OK with that?"

An affectionate snort. "I suppose I am." he paused. "Be weird, actually, Officer's Mess and all."

"Is that weirder than being there as my partner?"

"Each as weird as the other, actually." Matt replied, before turning over to his belly so he could look Hooch in the eye. "I'll come, with one condition: I get to choose what you wear—under your uniform."

Hooch's brows rose. He didn't say anything for a moment, then replied with a firm: "yes."

"Good," Matt nodded, "I might just come up with something special."

Hooch huffed. "I'm sure you will. My body is proof of that."

Matt grinned smugly and shifted onto his side. "And now I really need a nap after all that."

Hooch leaned across to kiss Matt's shoulder. "I go feed Rex."

"Huummph" Matt murmured sleepily in agreement, dropping off.

OCTOBER 2011, FAYETTEVILLE

Ten days later, the afternoon of the Ball, Matt was looking through their toy cabinet, while Hooch had an appointment with Pam for his regular full body wax. Hooch's well-edited toy collection had long since outgrown the bottom drawer of the bedside table, and had expanded to a wide selection that took up the space of a double-door wardrobe.

Matt touched the collection of leashes, all black leather, from when he'd have Hooch curl at his feet at the club, like some enormous pet panther, obedient and yet patently dangerous. The drawer of neatly arranged collars, though the first one from the pet store, its leather supple and worn, still had pride of place. The polished metal cock cages and chastity devices, made to measure. The collection of piercing rings and bars, and the weights to go with them. The containers of dildos and butt plugs in various sizes and materials. The wands, metal rods and hollow tubes in differing lengths and thickness, some of them to be secured via the piercing holes, others to fuck his cock. Going through them all, pondering what he might put on Hooch that night.

He could choose a collar, but the risk of glimpses of the collar being seen was small but there, so he abandoned it in favor of pondering things placed further down: he could choose nipple rings with weights that would pull on Hooch all night, which would have him in definite discomfort. His gaze fell on the brand new chastity device that looked like something out of sci-fi movie in polished chrome, which would mean that Hooch's cock was kept under control all night.

He was just pulling open the drawer that held the butt plugs when he heard a noise at the front door, as Hooch returned from his appointment. "Matt?"

"In here," Matt called out.

"I'm going to get cleaned up."

"Sure." Matt smiled to himself when he heard the familiar sounds of Hooch moving about the apartment, and then the shower starting.

He returned his attention to the toy cupboard to considered the rest. Not all that much that could feasibly go under Hooch's uniform—in addition to the collars and leashes, the wrist and ankle cuffs were out, as was the rest of the collection of butter-soft black leather. The chains would jingle too much fastened to the nipple rings, as fantastic as they looked against the black ink on Hooch's chest, and the ball spreaders and parachute weights were equally impossible in uniform. He pondered a wand, but it would be the first time for Hooch to wear a metal rod inside his cock anywhere other than the safety of home or the club. They were out at an official function tonight, he wasn't going to risk for Hooch to get into any potential problems.

He was that concentrated on evaluating all the possibilities, that he almost missed Hooch's arrival, but a sound at the bedroom door made him look up.

It was Hooch, naked and with damp hair, leaning against the door jamb, with a part amused and part curious expression on his face.

Hooch was perfect: beautiful, wild and dangerous as he stood with his legs braced and his arms behind his back. Almost all of his body permanently adorned with tribal tattoos in black ink, which incorporated Matt's initials several times, and was carefully designed to minimize the visual impact of Hooch's scars. The stunning design formed a coherent and artistic whole, running across his shoulder in back and front, winding around his biceps, down his pecs and chest, contrasting with the metal of the heavy gauge rings in his nipples, along his abs and down his thighs, to snake around to the back, meeting the first tattoo across the lower back, where it united with a design up his back, that flared all the way across his strong deltoids. His cock, which began to harden under Matt's scrutiny, with its Prince Albert piercing, and the gleaming metal rings of the scrotal ladder beneath. Last but not least the piercing that wasn't visible when Hooch was standing like this, the guiche ring, Matt's favorite of them all.

Hooch was perfect as he was, and in that moment Matt realized that it was all about what he *could* do, what he *could* make Hooch wear, how he *could* make him suffer; there were no limits. Hooch was well and truly his, in every sense of the word.

Tamed by Matt, and the ownership manifested itself on and in Hooch's body; on his skin, and through his flesh.

Matt didn't say anything as he picked up some metal, stepping close to Hooch. He brushed a hand from shoulder to nipple, lingering, caressing, before removing one, then the other of Hooch's usual rings. Teasing them alternately before putting in the heavier rings with weighted beads.

He stepped back to admire his handiwork. "Now get into uniform."

Hoch looked taken aback, but if the lack of any other adornments surprised or even disappointed him, he didn't voice it. Instead he just nodded and started to dress in his uniform. He could feel the weight pull and tug at his nipples with each movement, causing sensations that shot straight to his cock.

Matt smiled at Hooch's discomfort and brushed a kiss against his cheek as he stood up. "You'll have to learn to control your cock unless you want to spend the night with a hard-on." He watched Hooch for a moment, before making a slow gesture across the assortment of gleaming metal, black silicone and leather, laid out on the bed. "Then again, you might want to think about what I'm going to do to you once we get back here."

Hooch swallowed as he carefully slipped into the starched shirt. The touch of fabric against his over-sensitized nipples made him want to hiss. "I think in that case I'll be spending the night with a hard-on."

"We'll see." There was a gleam in Matt's eye as he turned to the wardrobe for his own clothes. "It depends how it goes tonight."

* * *

By the time they returned to the gym late at night, Hooch was desperate after Matt had told him at they left the function, that he wanted him to undress the moment they stepped through the door. Careless of his dress uniform, Hooch obeyed the order, leaving pieces of clothing strewn across the living room for a miffed Rex to ignore as he was woken from a sound sleep on the couch.

"Stop." Matt's voice was deceptively soft as he kept Hooch from turning into the bedroom. "Brace yourself on the dinner table." He knew he didn't have to explain anything else, and true to his knowledge of things unspoken and years spent together, Hooch immediately went across, hands far apart on the table, bending over until the metal of the weighted nipple rings touched the cool surface, and spread his legs as wide as he could.

The sound of a tube being flicked open in Hooch's back, and the rustle of clothes, before a hand too hold of his hips and he was nudged further down.

"Don't make a sound," Matt ordered, and the next moment he entered, not allowing Hooch to accommodate to his cock. It took only a few thrusts before he came, while Hooch fought to remain silent, his body entirely ignored by Matt.

After recovering for a few seconds, Matt withdrew with a kiss to the back of Hooch's neck. Not having been given permission to move, Hooch remained bent over the table.

"I think," Matt said against Hooch's ear, "I'll put you into the new device tonight. Consider it the first stage of your chastity training." He ran his hands over and down Hooch's tattooed back, all the way to his ass, which he cupped in both hands. Pulling Hooch's ass checks apart, Matt bent down and swiped his tongue along the crack, catching some of his own cum that had been leaking.

Hooch trembled, and the tension in his body told Matt how much Hooch had to control himself to remain silent.

"But first," Matt stood back up, "you're going to hold my cum inside you, stretched and ready for me in the morning."

Hooch nodded silently, swallowing hard.

"Don't move." With that order, Matt went into the bedroom to the toy cabinet, where he'd laid out what he'd chosen earlier.

He returned with a butt plug that was not the largest in the collection by far, but made of cold, unforgiving metal, and designed to be locked to the new device. He didn't prepare Hooch, using the cum in Hooch's ass as the only lube to take the worst off the burn, as he pushed the plug slowly into Hooch, letting him feel every movement as he twisted the cool metal inside, until it was embedded deeply in Hooch, held inside by Hooch's own body.

He was rewarded with an instant quickening of Hooch's breath, and another tremor, more pronounced this time.

"Remember the first time I tied you to the bed?" Matt asked.

Hooch nodded.

"You asked for twelve hours, then." Matt reached down and ran a hand across Hooch's tattooed pecs, twisting and flicking each heavy nipple ring in turn, while Hooch fought to remain silent. "You get twelve hours now." Matt suddenly pulled Hooch up to stand. "Go take a cold shower, make sure the plug stays inside you, and don't touch yourself. You're not going to come, but I want your cock to be soft when you return."

"You bastard." Hooch groaned out, the order to remain silent forgotten. His voice was hoarse with arousal and unfulfilled need. "You're a fucking bastard and I fucking love you."

"And I love you." Matt's smirk didn't disappear as he lightly slapped Hooch's shoulder to get him going. "I give you five minutes."

Matt was satisfied that Hooch's movements weren't completely sure when he watched him go to the bathroom to force the arousal down. In the few minutes it took for the cold water to work, Matt went to the bedroom to take hold of the chastity device, which had cost more to manufacture to their exact specifications, than many cars.

He looked up when Hooch returned, stepping through the door and close to the bed, still damp, and his black-inked skin covered in goose bumps, but his cock was soft, as ordered.

Hooch's dark eyes tracked Matt's finger over the metal. Brand new, immaculate craftsmanship, and fashioned perfectly to Hooch's body with a few special features: the cage for his cock had studs inside that would make any hard-on more uncomfortable than most other devices; the rear opening was large enough to fuck and even fist-fuck him while he wore the device, and it sported secure fastenings for butt plugs of varying sizes. It was expertly created to be worn for extended periods of time, making it possible for Hooch to piss and get cleaned out, but never to come, unless Matt—his owner—allowed him to.

Matt's smile grew as he picked up the device. Hooch widened his stance for easier access, and stood eye to eye before Matt slowly moved to kneel down, so that he could look at what he was doing. Carefully fitting the device on at the front, moving with gentle fingers so as not to touch Hooch's cock unnecessarily while locking the cage around it. He avoided the heavy gauge Prince Albert piercing until the very last moment, when he fit a small bar through the piercing's ring, fixing Hooch's cock to the cage even more securely, before pointing the cage down and snapping it to the chrome base. Moving his hands between Hooch's legs, Matt brushed against the guiche ring while pushing the base plate snugly back, then arranged all three rings of Hooch's scrotal ladder piercing until they lined up perfectly to the bar-fitted slots that had been worked into the device. He snapped each bar shut through each ring, then closed the two halves of the device at Hooch's hips, which locked securely, with only Matt having the key to open it.

Matt stepped back to admire the view of the polished, gleaming chrome against Hooch's smooth and tattooed skin. "Now lie down and sleep." He pulled the covers back to emphasize his order.

Hooch shuddered when he tried to obey, because every movement caused sensations that shot straight to his cock, which instantly swelled against the confines of the cage but the metal studs dug painfully into the hardening flesh, tormenting between arousal and pain. He tried to will his breathing back down to normal to have any chance of sleep, but utterly failed. A cacophony of counteracting sensation threatened to drive him insane: his cock was hard and yet unable to fully be, with the studs digging painfully into the aching flesh, the piercings in his cock and balls being manipulated with the tiniest of movement.

A sheen of sweat appeared on his forehead, as he forced himself to get onto the bed. Lying down nearly made him gasp, but he bit his lower lip to stay silent, feeling the rapidly warming metal plug move inside his ass, which was still overly sensitive from the far-too quick fuck. With all of the hardware locked securely into place, there was nothing he could do but bear the sensations that simultaneously made him want to beg for more, and plead for less.

Hooch lay on his back to at least avoid any more movements to his tortured nipples, figuring that he wasn't going to get any sleep for the rest of the night.

Matt lay down next to Hooch pulling the covers over them both. "Wouldn't do for you to get bored with me."

"No danger of that." Hooch answered hoarsely, breaking the silence once more.

Matt grinned and reached out a hand to play with the heavy nipple rings.

"If you want me to sleep…" Hooch gasped, "this is not the best way."

Matt's grin grew, if possible, ever wider. "Oh," he rumbled, not taking his hand off Hooch's chest, "maybe not, but we're not going to know unless we try." Matt's hand crept southward over the metal of the locked device, warm from Hooch's body heat, and settled between his legs. Flicking the guiche, he was rewarded with a suppressed groan from Hooch, whose whole body trembled. "Next time, I'll keep you in for twenty-four hours." He mused, "and then I'll show you off at the club and I'll let you get fucked by anyone who wants to, all night, while you wear this." He saw the effect his words had on Hooch, whose struggles increased. "And after that…" Matt murmured into Hooch's ear, lips touching while he spoke, "I'll keep you in it for a whole weekend, not allowing you to come, or even an entire week, while you're off duty."

Matt smiled when Hooch whimpered.

"Let me see," Matt contemplated, while his fingers kept moving over metal and lightly touching the trembling skin beneath. "I spent the evening with you, in a roomful of officers and their wives, ten days after the repeal of DADT, a CO who still can't quite believe that his most senior Delta instructor came out of the closet, and, of course, the food was shit. Except for the food, it was pretty good, actually." His fingers teasingly glided over the slots. "Still, I think you deserve your twelve hours."

Hooch groaned. "If I begged on my knees, would that sway you?"

"No," Matt told him, his tone cheerful. "How about I let you do whatever you like to me, as soon as the twelve hours are over…" trailing off temptingly as he propped himself up, hand under chin, looking straight at Hooch.

"Anything?"

"Absolutely anything." Trust and mischief warred in Matt's eyes while his grin grew. "And now back to silence. I need my sleep." He stretched out next to Hooch, head on pillow, and closed his eyes.

"Lucky bastard." Hooch murmured, before he shut up and succumbed to his body's suffering—and his mind's peace.

* * *

Hooch had finally fallen asleep towards morning, lying prone, arms and legs spread out. He did not move as Matt slid out of bed to throw on shorts and T-shirt in preparation for letting Rex out. The dog was not happy at being woken up and persuaded into the main part of the gym with access to the small grassed area in the back, and even unhappier when Matt filled up the food and water bowls in the reception area as the early morning cleaner could be seen pulling into the parking lot.

Hooch was still asleep when Matt returned to the bedroom, stripped and straddled Hooch's hips, then unlocked the plate that kept the metal plug in place. Hooch stirred, awake from one second to the next, dark eyes focusing on Matt, who said nothing, just smiled at him.

Fumbling a little, Matt unfastened the plug and removed it, causing a moan to escape from Hooch. Matt nudged him onto all fours, grateful for the design of the device that allowed him to fuck Hooch with no difficulty, while Hooch remained caged and desperate. Entering him with only the a small amount of lube to ease the passage for himself, Matt soon picked up pace and thrust deeply into Hooch, holding his hips steady with both hands. He was getting to the edge too soon, the view of Hooch's tattooed back, with his own initials permanently inked into Hooch's skin, and the chrome encasing Hooch's hips and ass, except for where Matt was fucking him, were too many and new sensations. By the time he came, Hooch was pleading in mindless whimpers, but Matt hadn't planned on mercy—fully aware that not showing mercy was the greatest mercy of all.

He pulled out quickly, still hard, and immediately pushed the metal plug back inside Hooch, and locked it. Matt's own voice was breathless, as placed a kiss on Hooch's sweaty back. "Now get more sleep."

Hooch's answer was desperate groan, but he lay back down as ordered. He closed his eyes, breathing still rapid and his entire body flushed, as Matt left the bedroom to take a shower.

* * *

Matt fucked Hooch twice more within the twelve hour slot. First after breakfast, during which Hooch had struggled to find a position to sit at the table that didn't drive him insane. That time, he ordered Hooch to remain in position: bent over the dining table, legs spread, ass open and leaking, and took photos of the sight, before the plug returned.

Next after he'd been experimenting with weights and chains in Hooch's nipple rings. Which had proved such an exquisite torment for a man who had come before by merely torturing his over-stimulated nipples. Once again he told Hooch to stay still, bent over and gripping his ankles, as he took more pictures, cataloging the gleaming metal around the abused flesh, framed by dark ink on sweaty skin. Some of his black and white photos of H's body had made it into a gallery at the club, blown up large and displayed along the theatre, and he expected some of these to be added to them.

Matt never altered the pattern of fucking Hooch until he had come and Hooch was desperate, then locked the plug back in place, keeping his cum inside. By the time Matt fucked him for the fourth and last time, Hooch was slick and loose, his body accepting Matt's cock without resistance.

When the twelve hours were up, Matt simply jangled the keys in front of Hooch's face. He had rarely seen Hooch's eyes blown so wide and dark, a new expression caused by new sensations. "I guess it's payback time." He grinned.

"Anything?" One word was all Hooch asked, while Matt worked on the locks.

"Anything." Matt repeated. Taking off the device was much simpler and faster than could be guessed, even with the integration with Hooch's hardware. He laid it carefully on the table, together with the keys, before turning back to Hooch. "Absolutely anything."

Hooch lightly touched his abused cock, breathing deeply a few times, before a wide grin spread across his face. "I'm going to fuck you until you beg me to stop."

"I'm counting on it," Matt managed to say, before Hooch attacked.

* * *

Later that day, Hooch came out of the bathroom, freshly showered and cleaned inside and out. All piercings carefully treated, his smooth skin moisturized, especially the areas where the device had chafed. He stopped at the open doorway to the bedroom, smiling at Matt who lay spread eagled, snoring softly. Hooch padded to the kitchen area to make a couple of strong coffees, then brought them back to the bedroom and sat down on the bed. "Hey, sleeping beauty."

Matt blinked, bleary-eyed at the smell, as he groaned and sat up, stiff and sore in almost every muscle imaginable, but the tired grin on his face told that he didn't regret it one bit. He accepted the coffee gratefully. "Nothing like home," he yawned, then looked at Hooch, who was completely at peace and relaxed.

Hooch studied Matt's face for a while. "No, there really isn't."

Matt hummed thoughtfully, taking a few sips of his coffee. "Mom is knitting a winter hat for you for Christmas. She insisted you needed one that's not black, you know."

"Is she?" Hooch smiled.

"Uh-huh, and Emily sent you another drawing just last week, didn't she?"

"She did."

"Lucifer needs to get ready for the show next week, doesn't he?"

"He does."

"And the fall charity horse trail you're leading is next month, isn't it?"

"It is." Hooch's grin widened.

"Sofia is going to stay over for a couple of days at the end of the month, isn't she?"

"Yeah, she is."

"And we're going to have a BBQ for your birthday, aren't we?"

"We are."

"You realize, Hubert Bozic," Matt put the coffee onto the bedside table, out of potential harm's reach, "that your big bad Delta ass hasn't just been tamed, but that it has become positively suburban?" Matt's grin was splitting his face.

The next moment his yelps were muffled when Hooch smothered him with a pillow, laughing all the way.

ABOUT THE AUTHORS

MARQUESATE

Marquesate lives in Scotland and has been associated with the British Forces for many years. Specialising in brutally realistic contemporary gay military fiction, she uses the insider knowledge of the 'bowels' of the military machinery and the insight into the soldiers' minds and modes of functioning, to write about men who are strong, aggressive and tough.

Marquesate's stories are gritty, often full of pain and hatred, but also full of courage, loyalty and determination. Above all, there is always love. However impossible it may seem.

Visit Marquesate's website at www.marquesate.org

TA BROWN

Deliverance is TA Brown's first novel. She lives in Australia and finds that co-authoring from the other side of the world is not as difficult as she originally thought.